The Thrift Shop

SMALL BEGINNING...AMAZING JOURNEY

Ron Mileham

MELBOURNE, AUSTRALIA

Ron Mileham C/- Intertype
Unit 45, 125 Highbury Road
BURWOOD VIC 3125
www.intertype.com.au

Book Layout ©2020 Intertype Self-Publishing Support Services

Ordering Information:
Quantity sales. Special discounts are available on quantity purchases by corporations, associations, and others. For details, contact the "Special Sales Department" at the address above.

The Thrift Shop by Ron Mileham —1st ed.
ISBN 978-0-6450010-1-3

Dedicated to my wife and best friend Hilary for her never ending support and encouragement.

"Adversity brings out the best and worst in people. I prefer the former, but understand the latter"

—ANON…

CHAPTER 1

Sarah strolled by ALDI's Bulletin Board with a trolley full of shopping. She looked at the 'Board' every day to no avail. Today, an A4 Sheet with a fluoro purple border stands out and beckons her.

The words CHARITY SHOP ASSISTANTS NEEDED headlined, then, WELL PAID POSITIONS FOR HARD WORKING LIFE EXPERIENCED PERSONS. New Store opening soon in Angel, Islington (opp. The Angel tube station). Apply in own handwriting. Tell me why you would be suited to the position. B. Baines. The Thrift Shop, 20 High St, Angel, Islington. N1. 9LQ. then scan it and send to: bbaines@thethriftshopangel.co.uk. The tear strip section on the bottom, was already half empty, so she pulled the whole sheet down and pocketed it. She NEEDED this job. It would suit her down to the ground. She could envisage it now.

She knew about people too. After all she had worked her butt off in that retirement home. She made the residents laugh and sing every day and her antics had them all in stitches. She only got fired after one of the old girl's Grandson's told management that Sarah had to go, before his Grandmother died from a laughter induced stroke.

The first time wasn't even her fault. She was working the last part of a double shift, and after all the residents had been tucked up in bed for the night, she slipped into the lounge, laid down on the settee, draped a blanket over her legs and immediately fell asleep. How was she to know that 92 year old Fanny Jenkins needed a piss? Sarah had left her pager in the kitchen, and although the kitchen was connected to the lounge, the pager vibrated away unheard for the best part of an hour when suddenly it vibrated off the table and onto the tiled floor. Sarah woke up with a start and a cuss, as she realized what had happened. Shit! Shit! Shit! She cussed as she pulled the blanket off and groggily retrieved the pager, looked at it to find Fanny had called her five times. Sarah walked briskly into Fanny's room, to find her sitting with her legs dangling over the edge of the bed and a large yellow pool of pee on the floor.

"Where the bloody 'ell were ya. You're supposed to be e're when I call ya". Sarah cleaned her up, put on new undies, changed the bed sheet and tucked back into bed. Fanny delighted in telling the Manager about 'the incident' the next day. It was then that Sarah received her first written warning. Sarah protested that if she hadn't had to work a double shift, it wouldn't have happened. The Manager's reply was, "you're getting paid to work, not sleep".

The second occasion was when Miss Krenshaw decided to put her fat finger down the plug hole of the bath one Saturday evening. Sarah heard her cry out, "help! Help me! Sarah thought she must have slipped over, but there she was bum up in the air, and warm water flowing between her legs, draining into the plug hole. She was bent forwards with what Sarah found out was her index finger pushed down the into the centre piece of the bath plug outlet. "Why the hell did you do that Miss Krenshaw"? Ï was poking some soap down the hole and I fell forward. My finger went right down the hole and I can't get it out. Help me please", she cried.

Sarah could not get the picture of Miss Krenshaw with her bum up in the air. She excused herself, saying she would call for help. She ran from the bathroom at the rear of the building, to the broom cupboard near the kitchen, where she got in, then let out the biggest belly laugh she could ever recall. When she had settled, she pulled out her mobile phone and called 999. "Police, Fire or Ambulance"? "Well I think Fire brigade and ambulance thanks. One of my clients has her finger well and truly stuck down the bath plug hole. She's elderly and in the nude, so she's not going to be best pleased if a couple of fire fighters walks in, but what else can we do"? Sarah gave all the relevant details and before she was out of the broom cupboard, she heard the wail of a fire engine siren. She decided to give Miss Krenshaw another quick look in, then draped a large towel over her, before going down to open the front door.

Well. Miss Krenshaw turned red all over as the two firefighters walked in. Little did she know that Sarah had deliberately left her butt crack showing, as retribution for all the times she had been treated like a slave by the bossy woman. Well, after this, Sarah would be holding an Ace - to play at any time she pleased - as she surreptitiously took a photo.

"Hello love. My name is Kevin and this is Rusty. Don't be embarrassed, we've seen this many times before. We'll have your finger out soon enough, but we have to put ice around your finger first as the hot water has swollen it. Sarah went off to get some ice flakes and placed them in a plastic bag with a zip top. Rusty gave Sarah a look which she interpreted as, 'you're a bit of alright, and this won't take long. We'll have a chat afterwards', or so she guessed. Maybe even willed.

As the firies were doing their thing the doorbell rang, so Sarah let in the ambulance crew of two, who were directed to the rear. Kevin came out and, "Hello, my name's Jenny" went in. Sarah meantime was telling the male 'clients' that if they went quietly past the bathroom one by one, and peeked in, they would be rewarded with a sight to bring tears to their eyes, and one by one they did, and one by one, they came down with grins that not even a Bingo win could top.

Between Rusty and Jenny, the finger came out. "It'll be swollen for a while love", Jenny informed the now seated on the stool Miss Krenshaw. "I'll put some Comfrey on it and bandage it up for now", said Jenny. Sarah thanked them all for coming and let them out. She went back up to help dry Miss Krenshaw, but found the door locked.

She knocked and asked if she needed help in there. 'I'm reporting you for embarrassing me", Miss Krenshaw replied. "You got your finger stuck down the plug hole. I just went for help. If it weren't for me, you'd still be in the bath with your skinny arse up in the air", Sara retorted. "It's not that. It's the fact that you told all the male inmates to come upstairs to look at my backside". Sarah didn't think Miss Krenshaw had noticed, but obviously she was wrong. "Look love. You made those old geezer's day today. Think of all the joy they got out of looking at your butt stuck up in the air". Miss Kershaw told Sarah to F---k Off. That was the first time Sarah had heard her swear. Next morning, Sarah received her second written warning.

One more warning and she was toast. She liked the job for the most part, but it was hard, and she was no spring chicken. She also thought that getting another job at her age was probably not easy to do, so she promised herself that she would try to behave.

The third and last warning came months later. On one of the rare occasions where many of the more jolly residents were in the lounge and where old Sophie was jangling on the upright in the corner, they all joined in with Sophie to sing – if you could call it that – many of the old favourite songs that they all seemed to know by heart – even the oldies with Alzheimers.

Sarah was flitting in and out, serving tea and biscuits, when the piano suddenly stopped, and Sophie called for Sarah to come over. Sophie whispered to her, then Sarah turned round and faced her audience with, "you all know this one. It's, 'Any Old Iron'. She led them into it and sang along too. Then Sophie asked her to recite one or more of her famous stories. Sarah feigned disinterest, but everyone knew she would capitulate, it would just take some cajoling and clapping. Sarah put on her reluctant act and swaggered slowly over to the fireplace. She turned and immediately came out with. "Krenshaw had a middle finger, she pushed it down a plug hole. Rusty pulled it out for her, but Krenshaw didn't linger". After the applause died down, she went on.

Her mood changed to a slow Scottish drawl. "A man was walking his dog one night on a winter's day in Scotland. The dog sniffed the hedgerow and started to dig the hard ground in a panic. The Scot looked down and saw a finger sticking out of the ground. On it was a gold ring. He thought about the situation long and hard, and after two minutes, bent down and removed the gold wedding band from the finger of what could only have been a man due to its size. He walked on until he got to the street lamp, then looked at the inside of the ring for an inscription. It said, 'Marty and Joanne'. Now that was strange, because he was married for the past two years to a Joanne, and their house was just a few streets away. He remembered some whisperings when he and Joanne first announced in the pub, that were to be wed, but no one said anything bad or sad to his face. He did later find out that her last husband had simply left one day, never to return. That was four years back. Joanne told the man that she was actually not married, but everyone thereabouts assumed they were. Had the man's dog found Joanne's ex-partner? and if so, why the inscription that suggested they were indeed a loving couple?

The man confronted his wife, and told her he was going to telephone the Police who were in the next town, to tell them of his find. Joanne took the phone and the ring from him, then produced from the back of the kitchen cabinet an old Colt six shooter pistol. She told the man to turn around and walk back out of the house. "Walk down to the pond at the end of the lane", she directed. The man did as he was told, but asked her the question", "why, and was that your ex-lover that we found the ring on? Joanne replied, "He was going to leave me for a man. I couldn't let it happen, so one night I followed him in the car, and bowled him over and into the ditch. I'm surprised that he hadn't been found before now. But you my husband, cannot be allowed to go to the Police, you see I am a Russian spy and I cannot afford to be caught. I only married you as a cover for my work". The man turned around quickly. She saw an automatic pistol in his hand. I married you, knowing you were a spy. I have been sending information to my superiors for the longest time now". They both fired at the same time. They both lay bleeding out, when the dog ran up to them and started licking their faces.

The moral of the story is, that animals don't give a toss if you're good or bad, so if you're thinking of getting wed, don't! Buy a dog instead!

Next morning, Sarah was again summoned to receive her third and final warning and told to leave immediately. When asked why, she was told that Sophies Grandson who was now her guardian, had complained about her, as he had walked into the building but had stayed in the hall whilst Sarah was delivering her show pieces. The Grandson felt it was wrong to elevate their collective blood pressures.

Sarah thought about fighting for her job, but she was also ready for a change, so she told them where to stick the job. "This is who I am, you silly cow. These people need to laugh, not be drugged up and sitting by the fire every day". She stormed out, walked into the lounge room to tell the folks what had happened. They all were shocked and surprised that she was going. With many of the wrinklies still giving her a sitting or stooped ovation, as she bowed her way out backwards, with a V sign to the supervisor who was now standing in the doorway. This gesture increased the clapping and whooping considerably.

She was home alone and hadn't worked for a few months, and funds were low, which is why she shopped at Aldi, and just as well, or she might not have seen the ad. After leaving Aldi then visiting the chemist, she scurried off as fast as her skinny legs and four bulging bags would allow, to her flat a few blocks away. After a cuppa, she slipped out again to take a look at this Thrift Shop. It wasn't far, and she'd be there and back in no time. She also needed to see if she did get the job, would she be working in a dive or on a rough street.

When she got back home she settled down, and mulled over what to write and what to leave out. "What would B. Baines want to hear", she asked herself out loud. Stuff it, I'll just lay it on the line, and if he doesn't like it, well, I'll find something else – I hope". She then muttered to herself, "Get your shit together girl. If you were good enough to look after old folk in a home, you'll be good enough to look after old folk looking for a bargain".

She thought about the hand written and scanned part of the ads instructions, and realized that this B bloke may be a smart B. First, he gets to see that the applicant can actually string some cohesive sentences together, then he finds out if the writing is legible, then he's testing whether we can use a computer. B will do, she thought – and, she now knew that B was Barry, but the other applicants didn't know if B was male or female – another test maybe? The Application read:

Dear B. Baines,

I was not sure if you were male or female, so I popped around to your new store, and spoke with the decorators. I hope that was ok.

Barry, I am looking for a position where I can use my skills as an Interpersonal Sales Consultant – some might call me a shop assistant – but with the skill of making people feel welcome and above all, happy to be in your store.

I also see from your location and the upbeat look of the walls and the new shop front, that The Thrift Shop will be appealing to the middle to upper classes. I think the location would be perfect for such an endeavor.

You can't tell from this letter - and that's why you need to interview me, but I have a clear middle class English speaking voice, with just a hint of Cornwall that I am told is lilting and fragrant (wish I'd thought of that phrase). Not that I've been to Cornwall, but that's what THEY say.

I presume you will require staff who are experienced in making your clientele (thinks: big word, Barry will appreciate that) feel comfortable, and how with simple and well-rehearsed explanations, they can be made to see the benefits of owning pre-loved items.

If I were looking for good, reliable, honest staff, then I would pick me. I have listed separately my previous positions. Feel free to contact anyone, They will all give me a good reference - although if you contact Gwendoline Short at the Good Times Retirement Village – my last job, she will tell you that I am a potential killer, because I made the 'clients' laugh until they peed themselves, and might even have led to heart attacks.

Looking forward to meeting with you face to face soon.
Sarah Walling. Unit 2, 14 Upper St. Highbury. N1.
Tel: 041 030 2033   sarahw@btuk.co.uk

On Monday morning, Barry's brassy secretary threw away the written letters that had been dropped through the letter box, along with the posted applications as per Barry's instructions (if they don't understand a simple request, then they are not the right person). She then opened the e-mailed applications and put them into a file she named Thrift Shop Staff (Angel). She culled quite a few more, as she believed she was doing Barry a favour. Many of them were obviously losers – especially the one that said her computer keyboard had tears of joy over it, because The Lord had posted the job on Aldi's Bulletin Board – a sign from God, as she just happened to be there that day. Another one couldn't even spell Thrift. It came in as Frift.

She e-mailed Barry on Tuesday, that there were several potential candidates, and she had marked the ones she thought worthy with an asterisk. Barry actually trusted her instincts, so he replied asking if she would set up interviews, and that she should see them first, then recommend a short list which he would then second interview.

Wednesday had been and gone, and Sarah presumed that the job had been given to someone else, until she opened up her laptop, to find a message from The Thrift Shop, advising her that interviews were being conducted for the successful applicants, and if they pass the next round of questioning, then they could assume that a position will be made available for them. Could she please tick the box allocated to her for Thursday at 10 am, if she was able to attend. She hurriedly ticked the box and sent the email back to the sender.

Thursday morning, Sarah got up bright and early, then fussed over what she should wear. She was who she was, so she put on her red and white striped leggings, a short blue dress, and cashmere jumper with red tassels (to match the leggings). Her hair had been arranged with one bun at 45 degrees to the side of her head. The other side braided into corn stacks with rubber bands.

At 9.30 she walked boldly to the Angel tube station, crossed the road, and in to The Thrift Shop. Barry's secretary came round from behind a desk at the rear of the shop. "You must be Sarah. I'd recognize you by your letter of application any day". "Not too over the top is it"? "Nah", said the secretary, "you're like a breath of fresh air. Love your outfit by the way. Want a cuppa?" The secretary told her that she was one of the last to go through the interview process, and that ten had been short listed from forty three applicants. They needed around five, she said. Sarah waited in the short hallway on a grey cloth upholstered bench, with a cuppa and biscuit, getting more nervous by the minute. Twelve minutes passed – but who was counting – when the door marked B. Baines Director, opened, and a tall brunette with long black flowing tresses down close to her waist and a painted burgundy smile, looked passed Sarah and strutted off on very high heels. Sarah thought that her competition had probably cost her a place, even before she had gotten through the door.

Barry popped his head out and invited Sarah in. "Sorry for keeping you waiting, but I had a couple of phone calls that have made me late. Take a seat". "I'm Sarah", she blurted out, thrusting her hand out at the same time. "Well I'm Barry", he replied, and the interview got under way.

Sarah knew before the interview had finished, that she would be working there, and by what Barry had told her of his plans, the look of the place, with its modern decor and facilities, it would be a pleasure to receive their weekly donation of 200 Pounds for five days, with one Saturday morning every second week.

Sarah sailed through the interview with Barry. "I just wanted to say hello, and to meet you in person. I trust my secretary's judgement completely. She tells me that you are just what we need as a meet and greet, and to make sure the customer looks at all of our merchandise. As you can imagine, we will be getting a huge variety of clothing especially, and I'm thinking that with your dress sense, we could make up a corner for the more Avant garde of our clientele. Do you think you can manage that"?

Another test thought Sarah. I'm not sure if he thinks I'm dumb, stupid or both, so she replied, "Avant garde seems too radical a concept for this area, I'm thinking modern rough chic. That's what all the younger set are wearing today. We can graduate down from the way out to the more traditional for the older clients". I can set up mannequins and change the clothes daily, so the clothing area always looks fresh.

Barry let out a hearty roar. "You'll do me". He picked up the phone and spoke to Audrey. We are starting Sarah next Monday week at 7.30 am". Please come in and escort her out.

CHAPTER 2

Monday week soon came around, with Sarah in the meantime getting ideas from the more well-frequented op shops in the area. The good ones were always full. She took many notes. Notes that would come in handy down the track. Once she was well established.

Between 7.30 to 8 am, Sarah met with the other new hires, whilst Audrey flitted from person to person, introducing each of them in turn to Barb who was their new Supervisor, and who placed each of them at their work station and told them what was required of them. If they didn't know, they were to come to her.

At 8.30, they were invited to help themselves to tea. Barry came out from the back office after he was satisfied that his secretary had been through all the preliminaries, such as where the toilets, the tea making facilities were, and how the till worked.

Audrey handed each of them a card with their names on, and explained that the personalized card allowed them to touch a panel as they came and went from the store. This would log their start and finish times and calculate the number of hours worked. The same card needed to be touched on the till black pad every time a purchase was made. This way, all purchases would be recorded. Any person making a sale and not recording it using their card would be instantly dismissed. Cards were to be held securely, and must be brought to work every time, or they would have to go home to get it, and they would lose time doing so.

The stock was amazing. There was a dedicated furniture department. A book department. A clothing section. Bric a Brac and jewelry. All had prices on, that Barry or his secretary had placed there, and were not to be deviated from. Barry told them. "If a customer complains or wants it cheaper, your standard reply is, remember sir or madam, that after we take out the running expenses for the store, much of what is left goes to various charities, so if I give it away, then we are not helping anyone", said Barry.

"If you find out that any of the items are worth more than we have priced them, please let either Barb or myself", said the secretary.

Barb Charming was asked to say a few words. After introducing herself, she said. "I am the Store Manager and your Supervisor, and as such, I control the roster. I run the day to day operations, so any problems, come to me and I will either fix it, or square it away with the boss. I have run several operations similar to this, and can tell you that there can be times when you are tempted to either take cash and not record it, or find an object that you believe can be sold for a profit elsewhere. Now I can't stop you from recruiting the services of a friend to come in and buy items, but you cannot make a profit by buying goods from the store directly. You are prohibited from offering any monies to any person bringing goods into the store. This is a charity, so we girls can only take donations. Only Barry has a second hand dealer's license, so only Barry can buy. So, goods offered for sale to the shop must go through myself or Audrey first, then Barry. If Barry is away, we can describe the items to him, and he may authorize us to purchase on his behalf".

An uttering under the breath from behind Sarah, said, "I didn't go through Afghanistan only to be bossed around by another Sergeant Major". Barb piped up, "Sorry Reggie, I didn't hear you". Reggie replied, "I was saying, you need to speak louder, I'm a little hard of hearing". "This is Reggie Green everyone, he will be bringing stock in for you, and taking it out for clients. He also drives the delivery van at times, but he also has two helpers to look after any heavy lifting and shifting. If someone comes in and wants to talk about a deceased estate or buying up job lots, then you need to tell me, and I will advise Barry or his secretary. If none of us are here, make sure you record all of the person's details along with contact numbers. These people can make a BIG difference to how much money goes through the store, so we don't want to lose them".

Barb turned to Sarah. Everyone, this is Sarah. She is predominately here to make sure the clothing department is well advertised and promoted using mannequins. She can also advise clients regarding fashion and suitability of clothing choices. But like us all, we must all get to know every department, so that we are all interchangeable, should any of us leave or are away sick. Talking of sickness, I need a Doctors Certificate if you are away, or you don't get paid. So, if your particular section is quiet, move over to any department that is busy, and learn what you can when you can.

Hilary and Jean are all round assistants. Hilary has a nose for tidiness and general layout systems and procedures. She has extensive knowledge of retailing, so if she advises that certain things look better in certain ways, then I want you to stick to her advice. She will also advise on mood and colour changes, along with music and scents, as it has been proven that subtle changes in these areas can mean a big difference to sales outcomes. Remember what Barry says, "We are not a charity, but we give to charity".

"Jean will be looking after the more expensive items and the watches and jewelry sections. She held a senior rank in the Police force before retiring. She knows security very well, and will be advising Barry on how to keep the store and us safe. So, over the next few months, expect to be a part of certain drills and procedures, so that we all know our obligations, and how to comply with the law at all times. About security. The doors are alarmed, and there are sensors and cameras installed. These are to protect the store and the staff. So, if you have any dishonest notions, then you will probably end up on camera and in court. I will open and lock up every day. I will nominate others to do that job if I am away. Only management and I hold the keys. If a break in occurs, a silent alarm will advise the local police, who will then call someone in management first, and if they know nothing about anyone working at that time, the police will send a patrol car to inspect the premises. In the event of a robbery, armed or otherwise, you will accede to the perpetrators wishes. You will not put yourself in harm's way, but you will be expected to memorize everything you can about the suspects, and any loiterings or vehicles associated with that time outside the store. Do you have anything to add to what I've said Jean". "Only that there have been reports of smash and grabs at jewelry stores across the city, which is why our jewelry section is situated at the rear of the store. We won't have the price tags that jewelry stores have, but then some wise boy might think our place would be easier to rob. If it happens, don't get in their way. The cameras will pick out their faces or features, just observe and remember what you can".

At 9 am, Barb wound up proceedings then opened the front door, inviting the waiting crowd with a wave and "thank you for supporting your local Thrift Shop, please come on in". The advertising had done its stuff. "Bargains Galore at the Angel THRIFT SHOP – Opposite the station. Grand Opening Monday 12th at 9 am. Free drinks and snacks whilst you browse. 10% off, first week of trading only.

CHAPTER 3

Barb manned the tea and coffee table. One old man walked
through the door, sampled the cake, and sipped the tea then left.
"Lovely caff you got 'ere," he said, as he walked out.

'Ello, I'm Millie from down the road. I'm so glad you lot have
opened up 'ere. I 'ave to walk a long way to get my clothes from Vinnies up at the market". Sarah asked Millie what sort of clothes she had
in mind, Millie browsed, then browsed again, to declare, "I don't want
anything yet, but I'll be back, then picked another piece of cake from
the tray on the way out. "I might be back later today - if you've still
got tea and cake".

Jean manned the jewelry cabinet and made sure that no more than
two items were out on top of the glass top on two velvet pads at any
one time. Takings from this area were brisk, as the locals seemed to
know a bargain when they saw it. Jean also used her new found
knowledge of gold and silver hallmarks to educate the buyers, as to
why they were getting the real deal at less than wholesale in most
cases.

As details from all the departments were scanned from the tickets
into the till, it was evident, that the opening day of The Thrift Shop
was going to be a huge success.

Lunchtime saw Jean and Hilary walk out together to get a sandwich and coffee from Greggs, whilst Reggie and Sarah went out back
and devoured sandwiches they had brought in, along with a company
cuppa. Barb went out to lunch after the others had finished their
breaks. Barry and the secretary popped in a few times during the day,
to see if everything was ok. Barb advised them that the ship was,
"sailing well".

Sarah had kept them in stitches all day long, and no time more so than when a couple of teenagers made a bee line for the section of clothing reserved for its outrageousness. "Cor blimey, Synth, look at that 'at wiv the big purple fevver in it, thas right dahn your street that is". The girl dressed almost as outrageously as Sarah, tried it on. She whispered, "iss ony a pahnd, an iss bleedin gawjus". She wandered over to the till and paid. "Oi Mikey, look a these". Mikey moved alongside her and felt the corduroy trousers, along with the designer slashes in the knees. "Two quid for these, bloody ell, we betta getem". Sarah pulled in behind Mikey, and in a loud voice announced. "Hey, mate, if you wanna drop your trousers, you can try these on". She looked around at her audience, and added, "In the dressing room you silly sod", and pointed to the room where Mikey sheepishly went. He came out beaming and with the trousers still on. He lifted up his smelly, stained and torn jeans. "Ja wanna gimme somefin for these", he enquired of Sarah. "Yeah, I've got a dustbin here. Now come and pay, then sod off. I mean come again soon". The shoppers and staff applauded the couple as they paid then left. Sarah gave them a flourishing bow as she held the door open.

Barb was the experienced one. She flitted between departments, giving the staff hints and tips on how to upsell and cross sell. She explained how the last customer had bought a ring from Jean, but Jean could have made much more if she had asked the woman what her preferences were in the way of jewelry, or did she want a free ring cleaning voucher, so she would come back again, or did she know that the store offered to inspect her jewelry at any time, want to see if the clasps holding the gems in her rings have been compromised, or that the links in chains had become worn. Jean was getting an object lesson in sales, and although she appreciated that working in a store was different to pounding a beat or working in the detectives office, you still had to interact with the public, but now, the public needed to be persuaded to part with some of their cash, "and that is what sales is all about, along with the knowledge of how to make the most of every sales opportunity", advised Barb. "And by the way, you have a lovely smile, but you don't use it often enough. A smile is welcoming. A scowl – even though you don't know you are doing it - says back off, I don't want to talk to you".

Jean went on to appraise another batch of jewelry for a pensioner, asking Barry to come over to the shop quickly, as she thought that one of the rings had a nice cluster of what she presumed were rubies, set around a central small diamond. "The hallmarks, suggest 21 carat, and the diamond looks to be almost flawless", she told him. Barry was puffing, but took a couple of deep breaths as he approached the two women. "Hello, I'm Barry. Jean tells me that I should be looking at some of your jewelry to see if there is anything of significance here, is that ok"? The woman nodded, so Barry took out his jeweler's loupe to examine the ring. "Where did you get it, may I ask"? "It was my grandmothers. It has been passed down. I can't wear it, my arthritis you know, and I don't have any kids or grandkids. If it's worth a few bob that would be nice".

Barry checked the hallmarks. 21 carat. Moles of London. The stones were indeed fine rubies and the diamond was of a very high grade. Barry felt like he should do the right thing by this woman, and offered her the princely sum of 400 Pounds, knowing that he could wholesale it for five and get seven retail and still be underpriced against any modern ring set with similar stones.

The old woman was shown an armchair and was given a glass of water. "Thank you so much Barry. I popped into the jewelers a little further down the High Street the other day (Barry knew the thieving bastard in there, but kept schtum). He told me that the stones were probably fake, and that he would give me 40 quid for it. I knew it had to be worth more than that". "Tell, you what, all the other stuff comes to another 75 Pounds so I'll give you 500 quid all up, how does that suit you? The old lady, with tears in her eyes, could only nod her thanks, whilst Barry removed a wad from his pocket and counted 5, 100 Pound notes into her hand. "Now I'm going to get Jean to get you to sign a receipt for the goods and the money, then she will organize a taxi to take you either to your bank or home, and I'll pay the fare, what do you say"? "Oh thank you, thank you, I can't tell you how much this money means to me. My friend Toby died a week ago, and I have to pay for his plot in the pet cemetery, then I'm going to the shelter to get a new kitten". "Gawd, for a minute there, I thought you meant a human friend had died, and you were having to bury him. I was thinking that 500 quid wasn't going to go that far". They all had a chuckle as the old lady was led out to the waiting taxi.

Hilary also got a visit from Barb, after Barb had been watching her for some time. "Hilary, I love the way that you keep the counter spotless, and that the antiseptic wipes come out after every sale, but bric a brac has a certain charm of its own, when people look at things with a patina that suggests age, not Brasso'd up until you can see your face in it".

Hilary knew that she had a fetish about cleanliness and that bric a brac was not an area that she was comfortable with, but that was all that was on offer, so she took it on, hoping that another spot would open up later. In fact people in general also turned her off, especially if one of them offered to shake her hand. If she couldn't get out of it, she would surreptitiously turn around, whip one of her antiseptic mini bottles out, flip the lid, apply and rub in to her hands with such speed, that no-one ever suspected, as she turned back again in a few seconds.

Hilary also had a winning smile that no one except Sarah, when she chose, could emulate. Customers were drawn to her. She epitomized good old-fashioned values, with an ease that allowed customers to feel very much at home with her. She would tell them things like, "that jug has a crack in it, which is why it's priced so low. If you buy it and it breaks, we can't give you your money back. I just wanted to let you know". Or. "I just wanted to say, that the fire iron set you are looking at has been priced too low. It is actually hand made from around the 1800s – I know because my grandfather was a blacksmith – and you could get more than you paid for them back, if ever you wanted to sell them again".

The staff all knew that there was no fooling Hilary, and that she was as straight a shooter as ever they were going to find. She also didn't tattle, as most of the others did. She never spoke ill of anyone. An all-round good egg.

CHAPTER 4

Barb had found her niche. It was definitely in her nature to help and nurture. She also found time to make some sales as well, especially when one of the staff was becoming overwhelmed. Her back up role proved invaluable time after time. She showed the novices how it should be done, and when they weren't too busy they would take mental notes. At one time she walked out the back and brought Reggie Green in with her. "Right Reggie, John here needs to get this wardrobe back to his place. I'll leave you to it". Reggie didn't have time to argue, as Barb had walked away with another customer. Reggie was heard to say, "Well mate, looks like you and me, but first I'll bring in the piano trolley and we can wheel it out to the back". Reggie made sure that his struggle was exaggerated and his moans amplified, as the two men the wardrobe and the trolley, slowly made their way through the furniture to the loading bay at the back. The van was already backed up to the dock, so the wardrobe entered the van ready to be encased in a felt cloth, then tied down. What Reggie didn't know, and John wasn't about to tell him, was that the flat was on the third floor and there was no lift – but they would worry about that when they got there. John gave Reggie the address. When Reggie met a smiling John outside the block, Reggie knew instantly that he had been set up.

John said, "Don't worry, I've arranged some help". He whistled at the block, and three doors opened up. Each fronting a linebacker type with huge muscles showing through T shirt sleeves. In fact they took over the whole job. Reggie did not lift a finger and that's exactly how he liked it. John handed Reggie a 5 pound note before they took off with the wardrobe, then Reggie took off. The lads and John manipulated the wardrobe up the stairs and around the landings like pros.

Reggie was busy all day, taking goods in at the back door, consulting Barb and the secretary regarding pricing stickers, and taking new stock into the store whilst helping folks out the front and into their cars, with stock the ladies had expertly sold them, or they had convinced themselves that they had bought a bargain.

When he arrived back at the store, he noticed a 20 Pound note on the floor by the till. Jean was keeping an eye on the note also, by glancing in a wall mirror as she worked away in the jewelry section close to the back door. The note had been dropped by Sarah, out of her back pocket. Jean was about to alert Sarah to it when Reggie walked in. Her coppers instinct kicked in. This was a perfect opportunity to test a couple of people. Reggie had told Jean when they had first met, that he was a paid informer for the Tax Office. Later when he found out she was ex Old Bill, he told her that he was only testing her, but Reggie was on Reggie's side first, last and always, and rarely missed an opportunity to better himself – even at the expense of others.

His eyes darted around the shop, and seeing only Jean's back, decided that the time was right. He bent over, picked up the 20 quid note, and slid it into his pocket – at that moment he heard a loud voice. Jean said, "I've been watching that 20 Pound note, ever since Sarah dropped it out of her back pocket 10 minutes ago. I suggest you go and tell Sarah to check her back pocket, NOW! And by the way, I've got your measure. You step out of line again and I'll have you". Scared, Reggie gave her a death stare, then as he approached Sarah, changed his face to a sickly smile and announced to the rest of the store that Sarah had dropped 20 quid from her back pocket, and that he had found it. Sarah gave Reggie a peck on the cheek, thanking him, and announcing that that was her fare money home, plus money for groceries.

CHAPTER 5

After a long, exhausting and hectic day, and after Barb and the girls had each chosen a settee or chair whilst Barry brought around a tray full of cups of tea and a pile of biscuits, the store was closed up by the secretary, who delighted in advising everyone that, "they had all done a bloody good job, and looked forward to seeing them on Tuesday".

The takings were a revelation, more than 1100 pounds. Even Barry couldn't believe it. He counted out ten one pound notes. "One for charity and nine for Barry. I like those odds". The cash was placed into the safe - in his office at the rear. The wall panel hiding the safe, looked to all intents and purposes to be a fireplace, but was in fact a steel door with heavy duty bolts that when slid along, locked the door to the heavy steel frame embedded in the wall. Only Barry knew that the lever to open the panel was under the tip backwards grate, and only Barry knew the safe combination.

He had planned to tell his secretary the combination, once he had fully committed to her, but that now seemed very unlikely, as Barry had sought the services of a detective agency to check her out – just in case. They reported back that her brother had served time in jail for larceny, and was seen frequently with her – after hours mostly, and in different pubs each time. The detective explained that with his directional mike, he had taped many conversations that Barry did not like to hear. Most of it was about Barry and their interest in his business affairs.

After listening to the tapes and looking at the pictures, he decided to keep her as happy as she made him, but that a commitment was never going to be. He trusted his accounting system to be foolproof, but nevertheless, he also instructed his accountant to employ the services of specialist to check the books now and then, looking for any 'leakage'. He would also feed her dis-information from time to time to see where it led – with the detective in on the moves. Sooner or later she would show her hand, but not before he had had his fun.

One by one the ladies went home to their lone lives – none of them had a significant other, and each of them congratulated themselves on firstly securing a job, and secondly that they had done good. Unbeknown to them all, they were all raising a glass at the same time in a toast to a successful first day. Sarah slumped in the old leather armchair, and didn't wake up until ten pm. Barb went about her home chores whilst snacking, until she collapsed exhausted on the bed made for two but now for only one. Hilary ate dinner, washed then put away the dishes, then cleaned the kitchen before deciding that she could now rest contented.

Jean later called in at the local coppers pub The Hunters' Hound, for a round or two before consulting her forensic accountant friend Ronnie, who told her how to attach a dongle to the work computer, when it had been turned on but left attended. She was to type in a code comprising her birthdate, and the dongle would allow him to take over the machine remotely. The dongle could be removed after 10 seconds when his machine would have logged on. Ronnie reminded Jean that this was all highly illegal, but she would at least be able to track if the secretary and her rough looking brother was able to divert or remove funds that weren't theirs. Ronnie explained that he would put an algorithm in place on the start-up sequence that wouldn't be traceable, and it would alert him any time the accounts were accessed. "I could if I were a villain, actually manipulate the accounts myself – but of course I'd never do so". Jean finally got to bed around midnight, tired but happy that she had some ability to help keep Barry's business safe.

That evening, Reggie drove the van around to pick up a couple of mates, then headed to the address where two kids had abandoned their old folks to the nursing home. Here they met Barry, who had by this time stickered everything, and had placed many small items into cartons, of which each had been marked with 'store' or 'warehouse' and securely taped up. After the van was loaded and many unwanted items had been unceremoniously dumped outside in a large pile - awaiting Reggie and the lad's morning visit to the tip - Barry shouted them all dinner at the nearest pub.

The first day at The Thrift Shop was over.

Day two, and everyone was buzzing. Barb called them all together before opening time. "What a great start eh. I thought you all shone like stars yesterday, considering none of us had a clue about where things were or how things worked, but you worked it all out, and I couldn't be more proud.

Remember, every day that passes, we need to learn something from it and adapt. That's the only way to survive. Today, I'm going to swap you all around and throw you in the deep end. You're not expected to know anything about the other persons experience or the products, but as I said yesterday, we need to be nimble, because if one of us is not here, then someone else can jump in quickly. Normally that would be me, but if two are out, then we need to cover more ground".

Hilary suggested that they in fact take a new station every hour. The idea was adopted, and the merry go round began.

"I know a lot about schmutter, but naff all about jewelry", said Sarah. "I reckon, by the time next weeks over, I'll be able to take on any store sales job anywhere. In fact, I've half a mind to go down to Bonds Jewelers tomorrow. They probably pay double". Barb piped up, "so you want me to make up your two days' pay then"? Sarah relented with a 'nah let's see how it pans out' face, and dunked another shortbread biscuit in her tea.

They all knew that it was working out and everyone was getting along well.

Barb and Sarah, who had become pally, agreed to go down to the pub together after work. What they didn't expect to see was Barrie's secretary Audrey, deep in conversation with a rough looking male in a booth at the rear of the old fashioned themed pub, with faux beams and wooden alcoves along the back wall. The girls took a side wall booth, which enabled Barb to take furtive looks around the dividing panel occasionally at Audrey and her man.

The secretary did not see them and left after half an hour. The individual was seen to pull out his phone, so Barb agreed to sit in the booth next to him, hoping to earwig. What she hears changes her perception of the secretary. She would let Barry know the next day. In the meantime, over another shandy, she discussed the conversation with Sarah, who immediately suggested that she dressed up in one of those jibab thingys, "so I can walk around incogwhatsit, and then get close behind him, then pull out my sharpened bicycle spoke and shove it in his spine. I saw a documentary. The bloke said that's wat they do in Souf Africa. The robbers you see are on a train, and the trains coming in to the station. They stick the spoke in, then the victim falls forward and the robber hangs on to the handbag or briefcase, as the one who got stabbed falls over and the robber walks out the door. The bloke talking on the video said that the victim can't call out, because they're dead straight away. So that's my plan. Have we got a jibab in the shop"?

Barb loved to be with Sarah. She'd only known her for a very short time, but she was always good for a laugh. Barb told her that she would sort it out tomorrow.

Barb thinks about the conversation she overheard in the bar, between the secretary and the rough looking man, after she heard this phrase from the bloke, "one day, you and me, we'll take this lot over. Just feed me all the financials and I'll find a way to siphon it off, so they won't know it's even gone. Then it'll collapse and I'll buy it in a fire sale from the liquidators".

Next morning before the store opened for the day, Barb confided in Jean. 'Her being security and all'. Jean said, "Leave it all to me. I'll talk with Barry discreetly and your name won't be connected. If things get nasty, they'll come after me not you. Barb was relieved that at least someone who knew more about these things, was taking it on. Jean told her that her intel was invaluable, but that she and Barry would be on the case, so she could forget what she knew, but asked her to keep her eyes and ears open for any new information. Barb was pleased that someone was doing something.

Around lunchtime after Audrey had told them all she was just going out to get some lunch, Barb wandered in to Audrey's office, hoping to catch a glimpse of some incriminating evidence. She knows instinctively that Audrey is probably too clever by half, but she feels helpless, and besides she's just either too stealth-less or the Secretary is too wary. She sees nothing incriminating and wanders out again.

Jean decides that she needs to do the same, so as Barb comes out, and with a wink, she goes in. The computer was on and Jean manipulated the mouse to bring up 'Financials'. The records showed a healthy stream of cash going through the business, but Jean didn't have the training to read the figures, so she pushed the dongle into a spare port and set the wheels in motion for her forensic accountant friend to capture the screen at any time. 25 seconds later and she was out of there. She ambled over to where Barb was folding clothes, to tell her that from now on, she had this and That Barb was not to go in the office alone again, and to talk with no-one but her about it.

CHAPTER 6

Business builds quickly. At the end of the first full month, Barry announces that staff pay will increase due to a shared bonus scheme, and encourages them all to continue the good work.

Jean is getting her eye in for the good stuff in the jewelry department, and Barry is chuffed with her 'put asides' – the ones that are underpriced or need his appraisal. He shows her how to spot a fake Rolex; how to test for real gold; how to tell the difference between real and fake diamonds using the diamond grading machine; the 4 Cs and some types of older style faceting and settings; where on the computer to find stolen goods; serial numbers, and much more.

The local paper is singing The Thrift Shop's praises, as Barry announces many donations to local charities. Of course, they are a miniscule amount, compared to the store's turnover. No one questions the amount of profit going the charities until the local Member for Hackney, asks *the* question during an interview on local radio. Barry quickly shuts the question down with an impressive answer.

Barry starts with, "The Thrift Shop is a legitimate business, started to create local jobs; to help a charitable trust that I have set up; with some of the profits going to local charities that are helping the local poor and needy, but as importantly my trust will help make current and ex-servicemen and women's lives more comfortable, and to help struggling service families; for those suffering the effects of PTSD and other mental illnesses sustained during and after active service. I didn't mention it at first to my staff, because I didn't want to be seen as anything but a local employer, and as everyone knows, we need employment in this area, especially for single mums, but now that it's in the open, I want to make the trust into a well-respected organization, that all service personnel can call on for mental, physical and financial assistance when they need it. I know the armed services run their own, but many of these brave men and women are falling through the cracks, as red tape prevents them from getting immediate help. This is where we step in and step up. So I ask everyone thinking of buying goods, to think of our pre loved items at the Thrift Shop first, and how your purchases and indeed donations help us to help others.

The politician was the first to congratulate Barry, as everyone else in the studio broke out in spontaneous applause. The crack in the announcer's voice when he told his audience on air, that, "this day has made me so proud to be a Londoner. Get behind Barry and the Thrift Shop folks", radiated through the ether to the listeners, most of whom were reaching for a hanky by that time.

Later that day before closing up, Barry held a store meeting, to explain to one and all what the Thrift Shop and Estates R Us are all about and where they are headed, just in case they heard the radio news second hand. Applause, "well done Barry", and, "that's so nice", were just a couple of the favourable comments. Barry told them that, "together we can make this place a lot of money for the trust and local causes, and if anyone hears about a genuine case of hardship, they should make the details known to him or Audrey.

Over the next few weeks, Barry had the secretary target all the local rest homes, undertakers and other op shops with a flyer announcing that Estates R Us was now operating in their area. It specialized in valuing property and estates, with a view to expertly appraising all manner of furniture, jewelry, art, clothing, and personal items, to allow the owner or their appointed guardian, the highest possible cash return, as Mr. B. Baines was pre-eminent in Personal Property Evaluations.

Immediately, there was a strong response, with Reggie and the two lads – now full time offsiders, and with one of them also being a driver, the inputs to the shop and into Barry's re-working warehouse were going gangbusters. The strip down and rebuild team were working overtime every night, and Barry had problems trying to find suitably skilled woodworkers to keep up with demand, especially from European buyers.

The store gets a call that is passed directly to Barry. Barry negotiates to visit a deceased estate where he meets up with two forty somethings. The older children - whose parents have become infirmed and have been shipped off to a nursing home, and whom the children believe are not long for this world - believe it is their right to have their parents chattels evaluated and the home sold off, as they now have power of attorney, "and our parents are never coming home anyway".

The woman, whom Barry internally names dumbbell, after Barry checks out the house and contents, ask Barry why the estate is only worth a small amount. Barry knows from the Estate Agent, whom he spoke to before leaving the office, that the property needs to be sold quickly to pay down debt – even though he has seen enough 'good stuff' in the house to pay off all debts and leave a lot left over, if only dumbbell and her brother stupidass knew anything at all.

Pulling out a bundle of high denomination pound notes, Barry watches their faces as he peels a couple of thousand worth and lays them on the table. The kids look at each other. The female says "I know this stuff is worth way more than you're offering us. We'll get another appraisal. Barry, starts to move the two lines of currency together slowly, all the time watching their crestfallen faces. "Look, you understand that it takes four men, and two truckloads to get all this stuff out of here. Most of the furniture would be hard to sell as it's just prewar. It's neither antique nor modern. I can make a few bob on two items only, but hey feel free to get in someone else. Most of my competitors not only offer less than I do, they also charge you to take it away. You see, I have restoration facilities, they don't. I have vehicles and man-power, they don't. So, last offer, and I'll add another 100 quid just to seal the deal. Put your hand there, or I walk away now". Barry is on the way out, praying the duo will call him back. His prayers are answered as he reaches his car door. "Right, sign here. I'll have my men come around this afternoon. You'll get paid when I see everything that is on this inventory signed off, and in my warehouse".

The men are instructed to deliver the goods to his warehouse after 7pm when the day shift workers are out of the way. After 7 the truck rolls up and Barry greets them at the warehouse double sliding door, where the truck drives straight in, and the doors are pushed closed.

Barry walks into the warehouse via a side door and inspects the furniture. He places red stickers on some, yellow on others and green on the rest. Only the red stickered furniture is offloaded and directed to the rear warehouse, through a roller shutter door.

One of the cartons marked 'special' is also offloaded and directed to be placed on a nearby table, whilst from inside the rear section, four men come out to help move the furniture into that factory, where artisans set about inspecting the pieces, before deciding how to change the looks of the artifacts to another period piece. All the original work is left intact where possible, but now a sketch of what it will look like is sticky taped to the piece, so that they can all start working on transforming it into a new piece in a new old piece. The rear section is where all the transformation work is done, the front section is the warehouse for the finished items.

Jean has made it her business to make sure that she works for an ethical business, besides she can't help herself, so she's sussing out the operation by spying on the truck arriving that night at the warehouse. Earlier on she found a New York style pull down ladder that led to another vertical ladder that reached the roof. The pull down section was out of her reach, but she found an old broom handle in one of the dump bins in the back alley, then wound a sturdy coat hanger round the top, bending it over to form a hook, which she snagged the last step with. It creaked and groaned but did the job. She guessed it was a way to service the air conditioners. From a skylight she sees the lads using a trolley to cart some boxes and bundles to the side table, and the large furniture to the rear. She couldn't see what was happening down the back, but feels someone, somehow is being cheated. Why else all the secrecy and at night.

Jean in her role of security advisor already has all of the girl's numbers in her phone. She calls them one by one and asks them to

meet at a café close to the Thrift Shop half an hour earlier than opening time next morning. Jean tells them it's important. Most are very
reluctant to get up and out earlier than usual, but they all agree when
she tells them she has concerns which may be important.

Next morning, she tells them that they ought to know what she
found out the night before. They all listen wide eyed, as Jean tells
them that she is going to front Barry when he gets in, and she will let
them all know what his response was later in the day. "In the meantime, keep your eyes and ears open for anything that might be
knocked off or any strange goings on – especially where Reggie
Green comes in".

Jean waylays Barry five minutes after he gets in and closes the
door to his office behind her. He listens intently, then laughs. He tells
her that he is surprised to find out that she knows so much about his
business, because she only just started in the job. "Although I
shouldn't be surprised I suppose, given your background. That's why
you are going to be so valuable to me. You are certainly on the ball".
He tells her about how his business - Estates R Us, transforms furniture into new old pieces and sells them into Europe mainly, whilst the
cheaper furniture and smaller estate items actually get donated to The
Thrift Shop. As far as the items in the cartons are concerned, he personally gets them appraised by his trade mates, and again some of the
items end up in the store, whilst others get sold in order to finance his
operations.

At the first tea break Jean explains the situation to the staff, and
everything settles down again, although Sara pipes up, I still don't
trust bloody Reggie Green", even though red faced Reggie was sitting
opposite her. "Bloody hippy", uttered Reggie as he stormed out with
his tea and biscuit, spilling it as he went. The girls laughed at Sara's
temerity and Reggie's stupidity at taking the bait.

The work dynamic changes, with the workers bringing up more
and more ideas that Barry hadn't even begun to think about, so business is booming. Barry reminds them often that, "The Thrift Shop is
not a charity, but we do donate to charity".

Jean puts her ex—cop hat on again. She thinks that she needs to prove Barry's stated honest intentions, so a few nights later she stakes out the factory again. It is the unloading late at night that concerns her. Surely no legitimate business works into the night. She watches as many large wardrobes are unloaded by hand on trolleys, down a large ramp at the rear of the rigid truck. She sneaks down from her hiding place on top of a neighbouring wall, and in through the back door, to hide in one of the wardrobes now stashed in the rear warehouse. After a while she opens the cupboard door slightly to find out what is going on, only to come face to face with two burly men who call Barry in from the front factory. Barry asks her what she thinks she's doing. She explains that no business operates after hours unless it's dodgy. Barry tells her to meet him in his office first thing next morning, as he's rather busy getting on with business right now. The two men grab an arm each ready to escort her out, when Barry tells them that it's all ok. Jean walks out in a huff.

The next day Barry reads Jean the riot act, then explains that his operation in the two factories is perfectly legal. He buys and owns the furniture. He just can't sell it as it is, as it's not that old and besides a family member might recognize it, after seeing it had been cleaned up and was functional and restored. They might want to claim it back for the price he paid for it, so his team of artisans changes the look and sometimes the use of the pieces, and he ships most of them overseas for private buyers, or they may go into auction rooms.

He also explains to her that most of his Estates R Us business is done after hours and weekends, as that's when most people have time to be there to oversee the cataloging, to ask questions and to haggle about prices. It also helps Reggie and the lads as its all paid overtime for them

Barry switches the subject around to the accounts. He tells Jean that a problem he has, is that his secretary knows all about the business, the banking and the accounts, and that he is having a fling with her. He tells Jean that Audrey has told him that he will one day she expects him to marry her. It is not his expectation however. It is just a little distraction – as his wife is ready to walk away – any day now.

Jean apologized for the undercover work – even though she got caught coming out of a cupboard. Thanked him for his explanations and agreed that Audrey might be a problem, then proceeded to tell Barry what she knew about her. Barry was neither shocked nor surprised. I have someone looking at the accounts for anything out of order, and from now on will be extra vigilant. I will start to make moves away from Audrey, then we will go separate ways.

Barry got another call prompted by the message on the flyer that had been left at one of the nursing homes in the area. "Ello. My name's Arnold. I've been lumbered with me grandmuvver's stuff. She died and left her stuff to me. I need someone to look at it all".

"How do I know if you've got a legal right to sell the goods"? asked Barry. "Well, she wrote it all dahn on paper like. Ang on an, I'll read it to ya". Barry was satisfied that Arnold was telling the truth. He asked for the address and told Arnold that someone would be round about 5 pm if that suited. Arnold replied that he'd be there. Barry asked if they wanted a valuation first, or should he give them cash after it had all been cleared out. "I do like cash, mate", said Arnold.

Reggie drove the van around to pick up his two offsiders, then headed to the address given to him. Here they met Barry, who had by this time stickered everything, and had placed many small items into cartons, of which each had been marked with 'store - bench' and securely taped up. After the van had been loaded up, as much again had been placed in a pile at the curbside - to await Reggie and the lads pick to the tip the next day.

Barry gave the young guy a list of all the items taken from the house, and advised him that his valuation of the job lot was 435 Pounds, less the fee to take the stuff out on the pavement to the tip, so he handed Arnold 400 Pounds. Arnold was well pleased. "Pity she didn't own the house. That would a bin a nice windfall", said Arnold.

After seeing the van doors closed and padlocked, and after placing two small cartons in the boot of his car, Barry suggested he shout Reggie and his two workers dinner at the nearest pub, provided one of them was a designated driver. He told them that two good hauls within a few days, hopefully meant that business was picking up. Barry knew he was on to a winner, and the lads all agreed that the extra money in their pay packets had come in very handy.

German traders were especially keen to get hold of the re-works, as the economy was doing well and they were in the middle of a renaissance in furnishing expensive homes. The nouveau riche wanted the old pre-war look but were reluctant to pay antique prices, so the clever furnishers cottoned on to Barry's re-works, offering originals but without a provenance. The beauty of the scheme, was that the re-worked furniture looked great, more modern and still authentic, but it cost Barrie very little apart from his team's time. Using modern tools and materials, they could strip, restore and re-polish a piece in no time at all, and command amazing prices, because the timber was solid and sometimes exotic, sometimes inlaid, sometimes with mortise and tenon and dovetail joints or even wooden dowels, so they could not be matched by modern furniture, and there was a lot of it out there. Simply by adding a set of turned finials or filigree, a dresser could be turned into an armoire. The pieces all had exotic names, even though they were not original, they sounded close enough to be spoken of in the same light, and anyway originals could only be bought by the uber rich and that was not his target market.

Soon, word of Barry's high quality relatively low cost 'antiquated furniture' range spread throughout Europe. Income from Estates R US soon overtook the proceeds from The Thrift Shop. Re-sellers in Prague and Basle were particularly keen to buy in bulk, so Barry accommodated them, not with his better quality range, which he kept back for his direct sales to his London based clients, but the dealers were still happy to have a range of furniture that no-one else could provide, and in 40'container lots. They marked the goods up by 100% and the clients were still clamouring for all that they could get a hold of. Barry was reminded constantly by his secretary that not only were his first two dealers looking for more stock – just days after the first container had arrived, but now there were more potential new Dealers from right across Europe, wanting furniture.

Barry understood the supply / demand dichotomy. He knew that the more he kept them dangling, the more appreciative they would be, and would not complain if he edged his prices up too. He also did not want two Dealers close to each other. He knew that each selected Dealer would need to have shown a deal of get up and go in the past, and to reach kpi's (key performance indicators) every month, if they were to continue to be able to deal with him.

The UK was starting to go into recession, but far from being a concern, business was booming, as residents started to look for ways to get more money in, and one way was to sell surplus furniture. Barry always got the best deal, and the punters got a few quid to keep them moving along until the next squeeze. He didn't care if it was an estate, a house lot or even a single piece, provided it returned at least 200% on cost. Usually he aimed for around 500% on average. When he sold direct, he could look forward to an 800% mark up.

Business was so brisk, he had to move the re-furbishing operation to a new factory close by, but now having three times the space, he could expand rapidly. He also invested in a lot of woodworking machinery, and as he needed only a fraction of the items that he could produce economically in a run, he decided that he would add a side business called Furniture Fashion, where all types of turned, sawn, moulded and shaped pieces were presented inside display cabinets in an office out front of the factory. Julian Morrow from the Furniture Mart in Edgeware was lured into the sales job by Barry, and he took advantage of the fact that Julian a very colourful character also knew his stuff relating to antiques, so he now often accompanied Barry on his estate valuations to the older and larger estates. His job was to select the pieces that Barry might have rejected as past their prime, when Julian might tell him why he should re-think his decision to leave it. On one occasion, Julian pointed out to Barry that the pile of sticks in the corner was in fact a Louis 14th chaise longue. Barry was learning fast. He also could explain to the buyers how and why adding a fleur-de-lis to each side of their cabinet would really enhance the piece, and increase its sale price considerably.

As word got around, Julian had to hire another assistant who looked after the public mainly, whilst Julian looked after the trade, who were quickly cottoning on to Barry's ideas, even though entry to the factory was banned to all except the workers, and Barry had read them all the riot act about blabbing to their mates, but sooner or later they probably would – if enough drink was poured down them or enough money changed hands. Barry was a little concerned about getting hold of enough stock, but fortunately he had also amassed enough pre-worked stock to almost fill the new warehouse already It was just big enough to allow him to accumulate a couple of container loads, whilst still having room to work.

Barry asked Julian to consult with his many antique dealer friends about what they could sell quickly. He came back with a list that Barrie discussed with his artisans, who quickly came up with designs, then produced some very tasty items that were quickly snatched up by the local dealers, who were now on board fully with Julian, Barry and the made to order faux antiques, which also commanded good prices.

CHAPTER 7

Barry asked Audrey to get an appointment to see the Principal of the Borough Polytechnic Art and Design School. He explained his idea to her. The Principle was all excited, as the competition prize for the best looking authentic restoration would be 500 Pounds.

When back in the office, Barry called the Editor of Furniture Magazine. He told him about the competition. The Editor couldn't wait to get his daughter Kirsty - a reporter – and a photographer / videographer, down to the design school where they interviewed Barry, the Principal22 and several of the young students, who all agreed it was a chance to not only test their design skills, but maybe get a chance at the prize money. Kirsty advised Barry that tomorrow was the deadline for the magazine, if the article and photos was going to appear next month, so Barry and many students were quickly interviewed. Even though Barry's business was mainly local, the magazine was a national one. He envisaged Furniture Fashion going the franchise route, and took the opportunity to tell Kirsty that. After all the UK and the continent were all about refurbishing at the moment, and adding value to houses rather than the costly exercise of selling then buying another house.

Barry was quick to point out to the reporter, how a few hundred Pounds spent on beautifying furniture could add thousands to the sale price of the home – sometimes because the new buyers liked the furniture so much that they were willing to pay a premium price for pieces that were perfect for their location, and they couldn't envisage any other piece working.

Barry purchased some serious German machinery, where, once the design had been fed into the computer, the CNC machine could automatically feed timber through whilst simultaneously cutting it to length then shaping it. It was capable of spitting out hundreds, of pieces per hour, and that was what was going to make him ultra-rich when the other Furniture Fashion stores were up and running. He had a model workshop. He had skilled Artisans, Designers and computer nerds. He had the right machinery and he had Julian Morrow.

The Thrift Shop was a different animal. It was all cash. It would be hard to franchise. Vinnies and the Salvos managed theirs well because they had armies of volunteers to do the work, and so what if they lost some money through leakage or petty theft, there was still plenty left to go around, and the main thing was that it helped the local economy and laid the foundation for his philanthropic endeavors.

Barry had organized for two of his woodworkers to make up six high class display stands for the showroom. Julian arranged for them to be taken to the design school to be used as a backdrop and a talking point. Julian packed them full of the current designs that Furniture Fashion offered the discerning DIY-er and the movers and shaker designer types who frequented the art and design school looking for talent, and who Barry had invited along for the presentation, mainly so that they too could see what Barry was producing and to get them to name drop during interviews with the reporter, and to push them in front of the camera whenever the opportunity arose. Julian was up for it. He dressed up in his finery, and sported a name tag that trumpeted JULIAN MORROW – Design Studio Manager – FURNITURE FASHION. He flitted from celebrity to celebrity, passing out leaflets depicting various furniture transformations using Furniture Fashion accessories, colour and mood changes, with occasional glass panels of differing hues – even leadlights. The transformations were dramatic, and everyone commented on the brilliant ideas, and of the Furniture Fashion concept.

Students co-mingled with their heroes, many of whom were graduates of the fashion design school, and a few who had gone on to make a name for themselves on the telly. Mike Bradford-Jones was the remodelling guru on Channel 10's 'Houses into Homes Show'. Mike never missed an opportunity to show his fashionable lace cuffs outside of his purple corduroy jacket and black leather tight fitting trousers, designed especially with a side affected cod piece that left the viewer with no doubt that Mike was sporting some serious tackle under that pop fastened patch, and many had wondered aloud how easy it would be to just peel it downward to reveal Mike's treasures. Others had spoken of the space behind being a nook for Mike's socks, but that was mean, as everyone knew that Mike didn't wear socks.

Barry and Mike were now centre stage in front of the camera. Kirsty Evans the reporter was cueing up with the videographer, and after completing a sound check, turned to Mike, and said, "We are here today at the Islington Art and Design Centre, and with me are the infamous Mike Bradford-Jones and local businessman Barry Baines, the owner of The Thrift Shop and Furniture Fashion. Barry, please explain why we are all here today". "Furniture Fashion is a company that manufactures a range of accessories that can simply and quickly transform your furniture, from mundane to marvelous. We are offering the chance for any one of the current crop of design students, to come up with a new and innovative accessory that will enhance any piece by simple application. We have six display stands featuring our own range, and we will add to that range after one lucky student is selected. That piece will also be named after the student".

"Thank you Barry. Mike Bradford-Jones the star of the popular Houses Into Homes Show is also with us. What do you think of this opportunity"? "Well as you know, I am not one for gimmicks. I look for a palette of colours that suit the home we are re-modelling, but when I see an item of furniture that is God awful plain, it makes a lot of sense to me that the piece could be enhanced by adding finials, lace or a moulded piece to it, without detracting from its design brief or function, so in that respect I applaud Barry Baines for having the foresight to invest in some incredible machinery that can not only re-create those design accoutrements from a bygone era, but can also 3D track and repeat any design conceived by computer. I wish all the participants well in this competition, and look forward to judging the entries, then awarding the prize".

"We will now show you around the exhibition, and talk with some of the students, including the Morris Weitzman Trophy winner from last year and other famous designers who have passed through these halls before now". The segment went on for close to ten minutes, Ten minutes of fame that Barry could never have afforded, and certainly his 500 Pounds reward money would be well spent, plus he had made a friend of Mike Bradford-Jones, whose idea it was, that he hand out the prize. "A win - win old boy".

Many more people attended the exhibition due to the early coverage. The local newspapers picked up on it, as did other designer mags, so Barry and Mike Bradford-Jones were kept busy into the late afternoon when Julian Morrow moved close to say, "Barry, it's time for the prize giving, but first, will you talk with last year's Morris Weitzman Trophy – Jenny Howes. I have briefed her. She will keep it short. You just lead by introducing her and asking her if she has enjoyed today's exhibition. After that, talk about the great success the day has been. Mention the good work the Thrift Shop is doing for local charities and our favourite returned services charity Mind Games, then introduce Mike Bradford – Jones, who has graciously agreed to present the winner with the 500 Pound prize for the most imaginative idea for re-purposing furniture, as judged by the expert panel of the Islington Art and Design Centre. Bradford – Jones has his own short script and is ready to come on after your intro". He then watched, as Julian rounded up Bradford-Jones, and handed him a script. He then talked with Kirsty Evans. Julian was then ready and holding up a cue card for Barry with the salient points on it – just in case – and outside the range of the camera

Kirsty Evans had called back in with the videographer for the presentations, and cued Barry in with a three finger countdown. Barry was now relishing his part.

His intro went well, then Mike Bradford-Jones took over with amazing panache. The camera seemed to raise him to another level of showmanship. He rarely glanced at his notes. He waved his hand to the contestants, who all filed on stage next to him. He introduced the three winning contestants to the crowd. He thanked them all for their amazing ideas, and said, "How difficult it would have been for the panel to have chosen a winner, so due to the extremely diverse and high quality answers, all three will receive the 500 Pound prize, and all three are pronounced the winner. Ladies and Gentlemen – it's a three way tie". To thunderous applause and a look of bemusement on Barry's face, all students were asked to turn around to watch on a giant screen, their before and after videos, where each piece of furniture was transformed using time lapse photography from ordinary to sublime, with Mike Bradford-Jones referring to his notes as to what had been used from Barry's new accoutrement line up, along with the skills of each student to make each piece un-recognizable. One by one, the new pieces were wheeled on to the stage behind each student. Then each student produced their new piece and showed Mike and Barry before it was passed around to the general public. Mike Bradford-Jones reminded the students that they needed to hand their pieces in, as the technicians will scan them and have them produced by the CNC machine the very next day, to form part of the collection.

Mike Bradford-Jones handed each student a large format cheque, so that the cameraman could easily pick up the recipient's name, the sum involved and of course the sponsor Furniture Fashion. With a winning grin, Mike Bradford-Jones thanked everyone for coming, and reminded them, "that a new season of Houses Into Homes is starting on Sunday at the prime time of 8pm. See you all there".

Barry thanked Kirsty and the camera man for their work and asked if they wanted to stay on for drinks and finger food, which they gratefully accepted. Kirsty asked Barrie and Mike if they would be willing to be interviewed on TV if she could swing it. Both agreed to be available.

Julian Morrow, looked as pristine as when the gig started. He looked at Barrie, and said, "Mike and I cooked up the additional prizes idea along with the large format cheques, so that you could get maximum exposure, and Mike kindly donated the other prize monies, as the exposure for him and his programme was well worth it". Barry gleamed and realized what a treasure he now had in Julian Morrow. "I'm just so surprised that you could pull all that off in a very short space of time. The videos. The showcases full of product behind us on stage. The three winners. The large cheques. The exposure and the party organization. You are one clever publicist". Julian blushed, and with a wave of his hand over his shoulder as he turned away, said, "boss, you aint seen nuthin yet".

CHAPTER 8

True to Kirsty's word, she lined up Barry and Mike for three different TV network interviews the following week. The cameras loved Mike Bradford-Jones, and paid lip service to Barry, until a smart arsed presenter asked Barry, "just how much his business had donated to charity, and could he please tell us who they are". Barry was prepared for this, and reeled off who had received what, then dropped his bombshell. "Furniture Fashion is another of the lead sponsors of the inaugural Mind Games, dedicated to helping past and present members of our armed services, and their families who are suffering mental anguish. The finals are scheduled to be held in fourteen months' time and Islington Arena will host it. It is not your Invictus Games. They cover those who are physically able to participate in sport.

Mind Games is for those who cannot handle sports as such, so we will hold team darts, cards, chess, bowls, and many other events all around the country. Many games will be via video broadcast, so the contestants will not have to travel – unless they reach the final. Even the showcase night at the Arena, will be beaming heat winners live from around the country. If you are not overly physical, and you are or have been a services member, you can participate. There will be prizes for every category. We want to keep services men and women's minds active. If they go to our website at www.mindgames.co.uk, they can register their interest. There are no fees to pay. The site also holds information relating to service personnel grants; aid; interest groups; catch ups; and much more. The presenter caught a breath, then said, "folks, you heard it here first on The Morning Show', back with you after the break".

Barry was getting a hold on this publicity lark, especially after he and Julian had spent many hours together, role playing for his TV part, and to consider how Barry could keep this juggernaut rolling along, so the Mind Games theme from Barry was the ideal, 'drop it in their lap and run', idea. This was also certain to generate another round of interviews from the other networks, so he asked Julian to flesh out the Mind Games idea into a working model, and most importantly to try to get some well-known sponsors on board, because although the format would be low cost, there would be prize money, the hire of the arena, and much more, that would suck up funds. Barry also liked the idea that not just super fit persons could be involved, after all service personnel are most affected mentally than physically, but this was not widely recognized in the community, so here was a chance to showcase the plights of hundreds of thousands of people who could not or would not, collectively speak.

The publicity generated over recent months, was beyond Barry's wildest dreams. He even took advertising space on many popular radio programmes, with his, "Hi, Barry Baines from Furniture Fashion here. Come down to our Islington Store at 22 Marquis Lane, and we'll show you how you can transform your own furniture from ordinary to fantastic, or you can take home one of our magnificently re-modelled pieces. 20% off until March 31st. See you there". He also had another ad running. "Hi, Barry Baines from The Thrift Shop here. Come visit our store opposite the Angel tube station for amazing bargains in fashion, toys, clothing, homewares and much more. Only the best quality products. Oh, did I mention we fully support the Mind Games charity, where your help, helps many others. See you there".

Barry now had another problem. The Thrift Shop was bursting at the seams, and some customers were becoming disgruntled because they couldn't get served in time, or they looked glum, as they had to wait for the changing rooms to become empty, so Barry decided to visit his neighbours on each side, starting with Martha at Soft Toys R Us. "Hey Martha, how you doing"? Martha looked glum. "I've just looked at our sales for the last quarter and we are losing money. You know the soft toy business is not what it used to be Barry. I'm seriously considering giving it away. Look at me. I'm 72 and I need a rest". Barry asked her if she would sign over her lease to him, AND he would buy all of her stock at cost price, AND he would continue to sell a reduced inventory through his store, and she would just supply him as required. "You could do that from home you know, said Barry". Martha's eyes lit up, and said, I will talk to the shop owner to-day. I don't think there will be any problems. I will let you know later". Barrie put off talking to the other store, because Martha's store was bigger and better – than all three of them.

CHAPTER 9

"Hi, is that Barry Baines, this is Wally Walker, the freehold owner of the Soft Toys R Us store. I understand that you may be interested in taking over Martha's lease". After Barrie stopped laughing inwardly at the name, he calmed down sufficiently to say, "Hi Wally, that's right. Can you tell me if that's possible, and what the lease terms are"? "Well if you take a sub-lease through Martha, you have 3 years to go before it must be renewed and rent reviewed, which will be an increase of 5% above the current rental of $20,000.00 per annum, or, I can release Martha and sign you up to a 3 year + 3 year option at a slightly increased rate from today at $20,500.00 per annum, with a 2% per annum increase for the life of the first three years, along with a review at the three year mark. If the economy hasn't changed much, then you continue on to the second three year lease at the same rate increase per annum". A quick mental calculation comparing what he already had, to what Wally was offering, and Barry said, "Ok that's fair, I'll take on a new lease today, and Martha can then rest easy. There's only one proviso, I need to put a hole in the wall so that customers can go through from one store to another". Wally said, "If you can get permission from the other owner, and you put in writing that you will make good the wall if or when you leave, then I have no objection". Barry agreed. Wally had the paperwork ready, and Barry had all the paperwork he needed to complete the transaction later that day. Next morning Barry broke the news to Martha. "You can sell off as much stock as you like for the next two weeks, so you will get retail for it. In the meantime, my team will be knocking a hole in the wall and make a few alterations. In two weeks' time, I will pay you for the stock that's left, and you can take that retirement holiday in Greece that you've been telling me about, so start organizing your tickets girl". Martha cried openly. Barry handed her a tissue from a nearby box. "You know Barry, this is the perfect end to my shop-keeping career. Thank you, thank you".

Barry called a staff meeting after the store had closed for the day. "Thanks for staying on. I won't keep you long. I am taking on Martha's store next door in two weeks' time. We will be knocking a hole in the wall and expanding to more than double our present space. We will have a new section selling soft toys, which Martha will supply, after she comes back from her holiday. Our building team will try to keep the disruptions down to a minimum. Each of you will get more display space, plus, any other changes you think would help, come and see me, as now is the time to make them.

The ladies were impressed with Barry's go to attitude. They were up for a challenge, so the brassy secretary asked the ones that had ideas to put them on paper, so that she would have a record, and she would make sure they reached Barry and the ears of the builders – if their ideas were any good!

"That bloody cow", hissed Sarah, after Barry and his secretary had departed. "Who does she think she is? Tuesday night, I saw her and a tattooed lover boy behind the pub after closing time. Going like the clappers they were. Her with her pelmet over his curtain rod, and blimey she was certainly shaking the dust off those curtains". Her cackle ignited the whole crew, who always appreciated Sarah's stories. The brassy secretary looked even brassier after that. "By the way, do any of you lot know her name"? Of course they knew. It was Audrey, but they went quiet, knowing that Sarah also knew. Sarah played to her audience. "Well then, I'm going to call her Amazon – coz she's always open for business, and ready to deliver at any time day or night". The adoring crowd cheered, then dispersed as Audrey – I mean Amazon, re-appeared ready to take their written notes.

Sarah wanted to start a new division. She knew a dress designer, who was always looking for a place to sell her returns. New stock that hadn't sold and had been returned for credit, and Sarah could get them for a quarter of the original price and sell them for half of the original retail price.

Barb wanted Barry to spend money on including better change rooms with mood lighting and piped music.

Jean suggested two more display cases were in order, so that her jewelry could be better shown. With spot lighting and sophisticated price tags that were changeable using the computer. Plus all expensive products and clothes to be fitted with an RFD tag, just in case someone wants to walk out without paying. The ex-cop in her was coming out again!

Hilary wanted a cleaner line to the store, as it was getting cluttered – and better signage – and the one till to be placed near the door in each store, rather than towards the back. She also wanted an illuminated sign above the till saying 'PLEASE PAY HERE', along with a dedicated cashier manning the de-gaussing / pay stations rather than each assistant attending each sale. "If all the items are price tagged, and we all get to share any bonuses equally, then there's no need for us to log on with our card any more. More efficient, cheaper to run and lets the sales people get on with their jobs of selling", asserted Hilary.

Lonely, the black part timer was in the store when Barry made his announcement, so she was invited to also put in her two-pennuth, but in conjunction with Hilary, as she was training her – as the part time replacement body for anyone needing a break. Lonely asked Hilary if she thought Barry would mind her also taking an interest in the soft toys. Hilary thought that would be good idea, as Lonely could make it her own, so she asked for a designated corner, and suggested Lonely run it, with the corner being called 'Lonely? You need a cuddly friend'!

Lonely had just walked in one day, and asked Amazon, "is there anything going"? Amazon asked what she meant. "I'm looking for work. Full or part time, I don't care". Amazon almost mentioned that she was black – but didn't. Almost mentioned that she sounded just like any other east ender – but didn't. Almost asked her what experience she had - but didn't. Instead, she asked her what her name was. When she replied, "Lonely", Amazon said, "Oh I'm so sorry. I can talk to Barry the boss, and see if we can get you in for a couple of hours each week, then you won't be so lonely. "No, you don't understand, my name is Lonely, Lonely Carruthers – no middle name. It comes from my great Grandmother who was Jamaican. My Mums been in England since 1939, and we have never been to Jamaica, so I'm basically a black east ender, probably went to the same school as you". Lonely smiled with a knowing smile that said, "I'm just like you dear, only a different colour". Amazon was drawn to the woman because she had such a warm and friendly way with her, and knew she would fit in well. "Leave it with me Lonely. I'll see what Barry says. Either way, I'll get back to you soon". "Thanks miss", replied Lonely. She turned, and left with a smile on her face. With the new extension, Lonely knew that they needed more workers, so she thought she was in with a chance. When lonely had gone, she approached Audrey. "You know Lonely's made amazing strides since she started part time a few days before. She's very quick, and has a degree in psychology. I think we should give her a full time position straight away, as I think she'll move on soon if she doesn't get more pay – at least that what she was hinting at. Amazon talked to Barry and reported back to Hilary, that it made sense to bring her in full time, and that she would telephone her that night to tell her.

It took Barry's team just ten days to turn a single front into a double fronted super thrift store, the like of which had never been seen before in Britain, and Barry needed to tell the world, or at least Islington and surrounds, so again he enlisted the help of Julian Morrow from his other business, who set the promotional wheels in motion. Julian contacted Kirsty Evans. He liked how she had organized the Furniture Fashion videotaping and promotion of the prize giveaways during the recent competition to find the best young designer using Barry's furniture bling.

CHAPTER 10

Kirsty told Julian that it was hard to get enthusiastic about a larger Thrift Shop, and that he needed another angle, preferably one with significant human interest, before any editor would even think of running with it. Julian told Kirsty that Barry had already started the publicity machine for Mind Games under the Furniture Fashion banner, and that The Thrift Shop was donating all the Polo Shirts with Mind Games logos embroidered on, to every contestant who gets through to the semi-finals, in any part of the country. The Thrift Shop was also independently donating 20,000 Pounds to the charity, and encouraging other businesses to do the same, and so far 120,000 Pounds had been pledged. "Is that enough of a feel good story for you, because if it isn't, I can certainly ask around, to see if any other news hound wants it". "Smart arse", replied Kirsty. "I'll get things moving. Firstly, I'll get the camera crew around to the re-vamped Thrift Shop on Thursday. Get some of your girls primed to say a few words about the new layout and how it's all going to help Mind Games".

Julian went round to see the new Thrift Shop for himself on Tuesday and was very impressed. He met Barry and Amazon inside. Barry gave Julian carte blanche to run the promotion however he saw fit. Julian asked Sarah to sit in Amazons office and seat to be interviewed, whilst Amazon was sent out to get lunch for the office staff and Julian. Amazon was not amused, and vowed to spit in Julian's sandwiches before she got back.

"Sarah, Barry has put me in charge of publicizing Mind Games. If you don't know what they are, I'll explain". After a few minutes Sarah was up to speed. "I need to interview very briefly, some of the staff, and you always come across as likeable, so if you don't object, can you please tell me in your own words, why helping returned service personnel is a good thing to do". Sarah thought for a few seconds. "Those poor bastards are keeping us safe, aren't they? Some live in shit conditions, and many of them are likely to either get blown up or be badly wounded. I know they get paid well, but all the money in the world can't replace your legs or your eff'd up mind, so I'm glad Barry is supporting them, and I know all the girls in The Thrift Shop will do their bit to make it happen. Is that what you want to hear"? Julian wiped his eyes, and replied, "I couldn't have said it better. Can you please say something similar when Kirsty comes along on Thursday with a camera crew"?

Julian asked Sarah if there was anyone else she could think of that might want to make a verbal contribution. "You mean speak, like me? I know this sounds strange, but the part timer, who's just gonna be made a full timer – Lonely, would be good. Don't forget, many of these service people are black, and her name sounds good too". He asked for and received a little of Lonely's background, then asked Sarah to ask her to come in.

Lonely refused the offer on the grounds that she had never spoken into a camera before, and that she could never remember lines even for the Christmas nativity play when she was asked to play baby Jesus. "But baby Jesus didn't speak, surely", asked Julian. "It was all those baby noises. I never could get the hang of 'goo goo' and 'dada', so I just laid there schtum, although my arm waving was worth an Oscar". Julian loved the way Lonely looked and spoke, and asked her what she thought of Mind Games that Barry was organizing. Lonely admitted that she knew nothing of it, and thought the on camera talk was to do with The Thrift Store's new image. Lonely, then volunteered the fact that her brother Billy had served in Afghanistan and had been killed. She told Julian his story, and Julian for the second time, reached for the paper hankies. "Course I'll tell the people all about Billy. Especially how he told me on many occasions that his mind was full of images that no-one should ever see, and that he was going to see a counsellor when he got back from his final tour. Unfortunately, he never made it. So although I didn't know about the Mind

Games project before I started here, I think fate must have directed me to The Thrift Shop, as I think there can be no greater good than to help someone less fortunate than yourself".

CHAPTER 11

Another 'blow in' walked in to the store during the week. She saw Hilary beavering away, and slowly walked up behind her then coughed discreetly, Hilary turned around and asked what she could do for the woman. "I look for work. I can find no work round here, Can you help me please"? The Asian lady wearing the gold and green silk dress, with a light shawl around her shoulders immediately impressed Hilary. Not because she was fine boned, beautiful and tall, but because she spoke so courteously. "What is your name"? "Ming Su, and yours"? "Oh, mine is Hilary. What sort of work are you looking for"? "Well, I have been standing over at the station for some time every day, watching the people who go into your shop. Did you know that most Asians, especially Chinese, look in the window but do not go in. I asked some of them why, and they say, "There are no Asian looking staff in there", and they have bad or little English, so they feel embarrassed to go in. I speak Mandarin and Cantonese and I understand a few other Asian languages, so I think I can increase your numbers. All I need is a chance".

Hilary took Ming Su in to see Barry – Amazon was away. Hilary explained the situation and advised Barry to give Ming Su a chance by starting her part time a couple of days a week, and if her theory holds good, then they would not only be seen to be multi-cultural, they would also capture more passers-by. Barry agreed to the plan on the spot, but made Hilary her boss as far as teaching her the ropes were concerned. Amazon was to be advised first thing next day, and Ming Su was to come in Tuesday and Thursday to start with. Ming Su was ecstatic, and thanked Hilary many times before leaving. Hilary was now teacher to two part timers, but she loved helping them – to help themselves. Hilary asked Amazon to make up a poster that would be placed on the window close to the door. 'We speak Mandarin, Cantonese and Cockney'!

CHAPTER 12

Barb was eying up a particularly shady looking character, whom she observed furtively ducking down behind one of the display cabinets to try the lock holding the sliding door fast. Barb knew that only the assistants had keys, but this fellow seemed to have a lock pick set. Barb approached all of the assistants. Told them what she had seen and hatched a plan. The man got up and walked around, then slowly made his way back to the rear of the glass cabinet. The one that held the war medals and war memorabilia. He bent down and looked as though he was tying his shoelace, but whilst trying to pick the lock at the same time. The lock popped open. He slid one door along and grabbed two medals and a gold coin. The whole floor staff quietly formed a half circle around the man. Reggie held the man down by pushing down hard on his shoulder. Barb said, "That's a neat trick. We now know that the locks aren't foolproof, so we'll change them tomorrow. Meanwhile the law is on its way, and you are on Candid Camera - sucker. We might be a bunch of old ladies, but you need to get up earlier in the morning if you want to pull a fast one on us". The man struggled to get to his feet, but Reggie's firm downward pressure, along with that of several other arms, pinned the man against the display case as the two beat constables strolled in. "Well done ladies and gentleman. You have just upset Wally Reaper's day. There's a small reward for information leading to his conviction in another case. He's a burglar, thief and fence, and specializes in antiquities. He glanced at the coin and the medals now on top of the glass case. From my limited knowledge, you may need to have that coin valued properly. The 25 Pound price tag is about right for a standard issue, but this coin has an anomaly. See the M over the crown. That means it was minted in Maidenthorpe, and there were only a few hundred minted there before the die was sent to the Royal Mint where the M was removed, so it could be worth several thousands. Matey boy here has just helped your cash flow considerably". The constable's zip tied Wally's hands behind his back and started to lead him away.

Barb asked the constable, "What's your name, and how come you know so much about coins"? "Sorry, I'm Jim Knowles and this Jodie Siskin". I just happen to be an amateur numismatist, so this is your lucky day. If I had been off duty, I might have strolled in one day and picked that beauty up for a song. As it is, arresting Wally Reaper is a good result too. By the way, I would also get those medals checked out. Wally doesn't pinch anything that doesn't have some value".

Barb could see that Jean was distressed so she let it go for about an hour before she invited her for a cuppa. "I know what you are going to say", said Jean. "I should have noticed the anomaly by doing more research, but frankly, I thought it must be a run of the mill gold coin, because the chances of us getting anything better would be remote, but now I know that I need to make sure, so you can tell Barry if you like, and I will own up to it". Barb said, "as far as I'm concerned you've learnt a good lesson here. Never to take anything at face value, and I'm sure you'll be more diligent next time. All in all, it was a bit of excitement. We all bagged a blagger. We all share in any reward. We can advertise that even the best crooks think our stuff is worth stealing, and Barry will get some publicity out of it. So, all in all, not a bad day". The women laughed and Jean proposed a toast to Wally Reaper. "You also need to check up on those medals girl. We might have another treasure trove on our hands".

Barry joined the girls as they were leaving the tea room. "Nice work ladies. I have a coin dealer friend who will take that beauty off our hands. I'll also take the medals and he can tell us what he knows".

CHAPTER 13

The double fronted store looked amazing and people were already commenting on how much more stock was on show. Lonely's corner was an instant hit, and sales from her section alone, made Barry take notice. After just two weeks, Lonely was promoted to Section Head, and hardly found time to get around to see the other girl's displays, as she was always busy either selling or re-arranging the stock into themes, like Easter bunnies, gnomes or elves. Martha, the original owner of Soft Toys R Us, was well pleased with the displays and with Lonely's efforts. She confided that if Lonely had walked into her store before she had to close it down, and had performed the way she had done with Barry, then she might still be in business. Lonely suggested that as they only had one corner now and fewer overheads, this might still be the best option. Martha agreed and took her next stock order from Lonely, each of which was growing larger every week. Barry had also created more sales, by bringing the prices down to where everyday Thrift Shop visitors could afford to buy the cuddly toys, plus the displays and stock rotations kept everything looking fresh and new – this effort was not lost on Barb, who suggested to Barry, that the other girls might learn something from Lonely. Barry agreed, so Barb organized each Section Head to visit Lonely's corner, whilst she explained what she was doing, and how they might take her experiences back to their own departments.

Sales were still rising as the girls became more proficient in promotion and display. Barb asked them all to contribute a story about their customer's experiences, and these were passed on to Julian Morrow for use in his advertising.

Jean was the first to submit a story. She told the juicy story about Wally Reaper's attempt to steal a gold coin that had now been valued at 1500 Pounds, and two war medals, one of which was returned to the family of an ex airman, because it had been the proceeds of a theft from the family home, and the other, that because there were only a few ever awarded, and because there were no longer any living family members, Barry asked the local war museum if they would like to display it, as the awardee displayed gallantry above and beyond, and the story surrounding the award was so amazing, that Barry and his team agreed never to sell it, even though it was valued at 800 Pounds. Julian loved this one. He also found out more about the museum and what it meant to the locals. The story was heart rending and did not harm The Thrift Shop's reputation in any way.

CHAPTER 14

Sara was next. She told a story about Lucille West who wanted a big wedding but could not even afford a wedding dress after her Mum's house was fire gutted and her fiancé had just lost his job. Lucille didn't want to put her wedding off, but as there was no permanent home to go back to – the council house was being restored, and wouldn't be ready for another three months – her and her Mum were living with her Mum's sister a few blocks away. Lucille had gone into The Thrift Store just to get some everyday clothes as theirs had all been lost. Sarah took her under her wing, and whilst she was looking for clothes for her and her Mum, Sarah went to see Barry, to ask if he could allow the clothes to be donated to Lucille. When Barry heard of the girl's tale, he recalled how the fire had been reported in the local paper, so he knew that her story was true. When the girl had selected enough clothing to get her and her Mum through, and now in front of Barry who had popped out to see her, Sarah asked when the wedding was going to be. Lucille replied that it looks like another six months from now we could probably manage it, provided her fiancé could get a job by then.

When Lucille offered up payment, Sarah looked at Barry, who nodded slightly. "Barry has asked - if it is ok by you, can we donate these clothes to you and you're Mum as a gesture of good will from The Thrift Shop"? Lucille looked amazed, and thanked them both profusely. Barry chimed in. "We also would like to donate a wedding dress when the time comes". Lucille couldn't contain her excitement, and threw her arms around Barry, then Sarah. "Oh I can't thank you enough. Not only did the fire ruin all our clothes but we also lost our dog Terry, as he was old and couldn't get out fast enough, so when we are back in, we are going to get Terry 2. Barry went into Lonely's corner, picked out a fluffy terrier and handed it to Lucille. "Maybe this one will help until then". Lucille burst into tears. "I will tell everyone I meet how kind you have all been". At that juncture Sarah asked if Lucille would mind if her story appeared in the local newspaper as a follow up story to the fire. Lucille agreed and Julian Morrow followed it up. He also asked for donations which poured in. The money helped the family get on its feet, and the fiancé found a job too, so everyone was happy.

CHAPTER 15

Next, surprisingly, Ming Su was asked by Julian, if he could feature her, as he had been observing a trend over the past few months of how she not only attracted a large Asian group to the store, but how many Chinese men had been coming in on the pretext of looking for men's clothing, then rejecting the advances of Sarah, for the attention of Ming Su and how she had been seen shooing them out of the shop, telling them, "she was not for sale – at any price"! Apparently Ming Su, had been getting up to three marriage proposals a month.

Barry was asked to comment on why sales of Chinese dresses, saris and loose fitting lightweight Asian women's fashions had suddenly taken off. "Since Ming Su has been here, she has shown us just what an ethnically diverse place London town is. She is catering to a demand that frankly the High Street shops are simply not doing. We at The Thrift Shop have hundreds of styles suited to the preferences of Asian women, and she has taken that on board and run with it. Half the stock is new. They are called returns. New stock that has not sold in traditional Asian and Indian clothing stores – and which are sent back to the importers. Well we buy the best of them at cost and add a small margin. The other half is inspected and cleaned pre-loved clothing that is a fraction of the cost of new clothes, so I thank Ming Su for bringing this niche to our attention, and wish at this time to advise that we have staff that speak many languages – including Cockney, so come on down to our new store opposite The Angel tube station. You may be surprised that although we are a thrift shop, our quality and value for money cannot be surpassed, and always remember that we support an amazing charity in Mind Games, so your donations and your patronage help many people in more ways than you can imagine".

Julian continued to collect stories from the others, and was fast building a story book that he could re-visit and add to as time went on. Needless to say, the local and surrounding papers always had time for his advertorials as they always contained a human interest element, plus he made sure to always include a paid ad for The Thrift Shop in one of the papers in rotation.

CHAPTER 16

When Barry received the call at 2 am, that the new – ish restoration factory was flooding due to a burst main, he called up Reggie, who in turn called up his two henchmen, who then called up any friends and volunteers they could on the way in. The first thing they saw when they opened up the roller door was an antique chest of drawers, bobbling along on a foot high wall of water. It swept past them ending up on the middle of the road, whilst the rest of the water poured down the road and into the drains. Following the chest of drawers was an eighteenth century chaise longue with no covering as it was being restored. A hefty wardrobe followed, along with myriad other objects. The fire brigade had just arrived and had turned off the stop cock up the road. The Fire Marshall accompanied Barry - who thoughtfully had shoved his wellies in the car boot before leaving – into the building to find the leak, which was quite evident, as it was still gushing from the base of the rusted out fire hose reel pipe. The Fire Marshall announced that the water main would remain shut off until Barry got an emergency plumber in to replace the old pipe. The plumber promptly announced that the job would cost 2500 Pounds, as he and his apprentice needed to cut out the concrete, follow the pipe along to its last connection, then fit a new pipe, and then connect it to the hose reel. "It'll take the best part of a day – maybe two, Find another plumber if you wish – SIR"! Barry knew when his knackers were in the vice, so he agreed to the terms and the likely lads set to work. By late in the next day, Barry was informed that the Fire Marshall had approved the plumbing and that he was back in business.

Meantime, Barry had to move six truckloads of damaged furniture to a nearby warehouse he managed to get a short term rent on, whilst the original factory was being cleaned then dried out with massive portable bottled gas heaters.

The wet furniture was also undergoing heat treatment. Barry had several steel frames made up, with sheet steel coverings and a hinged top opening. Each one housed a piece of furniture. Each one had a tunnel going to an electric fan heater. This was the only way he could remove the moisture in the furniture without destroying it. Each piece would take two weeks to dry out, but controlled drying was his only option.

The supercilious insurance adjuster stood in the door of the factory, with his clipboard at 45 degrees, surveying the scene and tut tutting. "Hello, my name is Peter Tomkins, your Able Insurance claims assessor". Barry shook his clammy hand and introduced himself. "My, my, Mr. Baines". He tutted once more for effect. Tomkins then took pains to make sure Barry understood the terms of his insurance contract, one of which each was now holding. He pointed to Page 3, para 4, sub section 5. "It clearly states Mr. Baines, that you are not covered for flood damage, as the flooding was not caused by natural water flow – and of course there have been no storms in the past week. This was caused by a burst mains pipe, so unfortunately, we must reject your claim. Good day sir"! He turned to walk away, when Barry shouted, "Hey you little prat, come back here". The man stopped abruptly then swung around. "Are you talking to me sir"? Barry walked towards him, brandishing the contract. If you care to read the last page, you will note that we have taken out separate insurance that over-rides storm damage. We are claiming water damage from any source. I have had the stock, the building, the plumber's bill and the warehouse clean up independently valued at 30,000 Pounds. I expect your cheque to arrive within seven days from now, or I take this case to the Insurance Ombudsman. Now you can piss off, you jumped up piece of shit – sorry, I mean, SIR"!

Barry made sure that Julian Morrow had his story in the papers the next week. Barry did not ask for sympathy or donations, instead he was announcing that as he had to move to another warehouse that was twice the size of the old one, and he was now looking for artisans, apprentices and labourers. He also made sure that Julian had re-told the story of Lucille, and that her fiancé was the first to be offered a job at the new site.

CHAPTER 17

Jean knew that Barry was on the surface, playing a straight bat, because she had her man monitoring the accounts surreptitiously, but underneath she suspected that there was more to this operation. She decided to do some sleuthing after she overheard Barry talking to a 'Jim' on his mobile phone, about a shipment that was due in that night. The thought that furniture would be delivered at night seemed far-fetched, so her cop's instinct kicked in. She arranged to be at the new bigger warehouse by 11 pm, the time Barry said he was expecting Jim – and she presumed Jim's mates.

Jean kept out of site, eating her ham, cheese and Branston Pickle sandwich and sipping coffee, whilst seated on a folding camp chair. The powerful binoculars gave her a distance advantage. Away from the scene, but with enough magnification to jot down number plates and to check out the shipment. Around 10.30 Barry and Reggie arrived in separate vehicles. Reggie drove the company van. He was accompanied by his two wranglers. The roller door moved up automatically.

The double length semi arrived with two containers at 11.20. By this time Reggie had organized a fork lift and a loading ramp, which the driver managed to back up to after the doors had been swung back and fastened on the last container. A forklift driver from the factory started unloading what were obviously pallets – not furniture at all. They were all stretch wrapped and every one was an identical size. They were placed one on top of the other. Two pallets high. It only took the forkie half an hour to unload all 24 pallets from the first (last) container. The driver pulled away, unhitched the two trailers, left the last one on one side of the yard, unlocked, swung and hooked the doors of the second container, then reversed against the container ramp ready for the fork lift driver to unload it.

Meantime, Barry, Reggie and his cohorts were busy unwrapping the first of the pallets which were all just inside the roller door. To Jean's surprise, the most exquisite pieces of pottery, vases, large ornaments, garden pieces, wall hangings emerged from the now several crates that had been opened up. Jean knew that this was no covert operation. It simply was a late delivery from the continent, and all hands were needed to unload the containers before they attracted storage charges if kept overnight at the docks.

Obviously, Barrie had now branched out into something new. Whether he intended any of it to go through The Thrift Shop she doubted, as it was in a class of its own. The next day, she would find out. For now, she needed sleep. Her cop's curiosity had been sated. She told herself that she wouldn't have fallen asleep until two in the morning anyway, so she might as well have been in on the action here.

True to form, Barry next morning called the troops to order to announce his latest venture.

"It is called House & Garden Accessories, to continue the theme of Furniture Accessories. There may be other accessory themed stores to come, meantime House & Garden Accessories will be opening up in the previously named Angels Garden Centre. There will be no plants, manure, etc., only classy indoor and outdoor accessories, such as waterfalls, genie vases, fake (but lifelike) flowers and shrubs, glass ornaments, and much more. The household items will be undercover, whilst the garden ornaments will be displayed in a natural outdoor setting. There is also a shipment of outdoor rattan furniture due soon, along with outdoor kitchens and barbecues, so we are taking this space by storm. I fully expect to have at least three more outlets open before the end of the year".

The girls and boys all clapped politely. "I know none of this seemingly affects any of you or the store, buuut I tell you all this, because there will be many smaller items in the shipments that I want to donate to The Thrift Shop. They will not be expensive, but they will be exclusive to you, and it's a good chance for us to fill up some of the smaller spaces in the containers. So there's yet another reason for visiting The Thrift Shop over our competitors". They all clapped more enthusiastically this time around.

CHAPTER 18

Jean approached Barry after the speech. "Can we talk"? Barrie invited her into his office. She shut the door behind her. "I can't tell you how I know this, but I hope you will thank me for telling you, rather than sack me". "Go on", Barrie said, looking sideways at her. Jean looked him squarely in the face, and said, "You are being robbed. You don't know it, but your secretary Audrey – whom we all call Amazon, is systematically siphoning off profits through her scumbag boyfriend". Barrie looked nonplussed, and waved a hand to indicate Jean needed to carry on with her tale.

"I have recordings of them discussing the scheme. Here's how it works. You send cash to the bank via Reggie Green, backed up by his boys twice a week. The money is held in the safe between bank runs. The cash money is counted by Amazon, and you sign off on it. She produces till slips to equal the amount to be sent to the bank. What you don't know is that many of those slips get mislaid between the till and her counting the cash, so she siphons off the difference. For the past two months since I noticed the discrepancies, I have totaled up 2400 Pounds. The two months prior to that I had suspicions but was not sure, so I got the label makers to supply sequentially numbered till slips. All the girls and boys are clean, except for Amazon and by association her scumbag boyfriend, who calls in a couple of times a week to see her, and that's when she hands over an envelope full of cash. The last time he came in, I got the handover on video. I have the case notes here, with times, dates, amounts, etc. I also have a copy of Amazons boyfriend's bank pay-ins – illegal, but solid proof as the totals match. Sorry I haven't been able to stop this sooner, but I had to build a rock solid case. What do you want to do about it"?

Barry had been listening quietly and intently. "I'm absolutely flabbergasted. I had no idea this was going on behind my back. All this time, you have been monitoring things and looking after my interests. Well done and thank you. What do you think is the best course of action? You are after all ex Police".

Jean looked concerned "If you take this to the Police, there will be a lot of paperwork and a few questions like how did I come across certain documents, and who authorized surveillance on a private citizen, so my suggestion is that when Amazons boyfriend comes in next – that's tomorrow, and we see an envelope passed to him, we confront them both, take back the envelope in exchange for not prosecuting – unless we have to - based upon their future actions. Show them a whole heap of documents incriminating them both, along with the old video feeds. I can threaten them with a Police involvement option. That should convince them never to set foot in the shop, and when you sack her on the spot for theft – which you are legally able to do, don't offer her a reference, but make sure she has all of her pay and leave entitlement monies in another envelope. I can get that sorted for you if you wish. I can also recommend a bookkeeper who can come in two days a week to sort out the books and pay – if you wish".

Barry was bowled over. "Blimey Jean, I never thought you had it in you. You can be a bulldog when you need to. Thanks again for all the work and the suggestions. I'll leave it to you to gather the evidence for a showdown, when the scumbag comes in tomorrow to collect his ill-gotten gains, I'd like to see Amazon's face when she knows she's been caught red handed. Can we get a hidden camera installed before then to capture this wonderful moment? We can then offer to send them – and the Police - a copy, should we ever hear from them again".

The camera was installed and connected to a spare computer in Barry's office. It was triggered by a switch under Barry's desk. When the scumbag came in next day, he was invited to come into Barry's office along with Amazon. Barry thought he would cut up rough, but after he had heard all the evidence, he looked at Amazon, who just shrugged. Jean made sure that she had their confession on camera before advising them that they had been videoed and that they would be holding the copy in the safe. Amazon spoke. "You know Barry, I hated this job from day one. I took the money, but you never paid me enough to put up with all your shit, and by the way, I only let you jump me in order to keep you sweet, my man Loz here would make two of you".

Barry looked at Jean, who imperceptibly shook her head. He kept his cool and called in Reggie and the lads. "Reggie, could you and the lads please escort these two people from the shop, and make sure they don't pinch anything on the way out. Oh, and make sure you escort them to the gentleman's car so that we have a license plate number and make of the car, just in case our video surveillance picks it up loitering around the premises in the future". They left with the word "arsehole" trailing behind Audrey as they walked heads low to their car, dutifully followed by the three men.

Barry gave Jean a hug, and thanked her again, before she turned and left with a smile on her face, but not before saying, "For the record, I'll delete the last word uttered by Amazon". Barry took it personally for all of three seconds.

CHAPTER 19

Six months had passed since the shop opened, and Barry could not have been more pleased. Not only were the takings increasing by an average of 50% each month, the donations to Mind Games were also going up as they accounted for 10% of the net profit – before tax.

After a series about charity shops on Channel 4, where many of them had been openly accused of siphoning off profits to enrich the directors – showing expensive houses and cars but no contributions, two charity shops closed in one week. The story showed many did not support charity in any meaningful way – or they would not reveal donation figures or to whom they gave money, or they simply dried up in the face of Barry's progressive attitude, range of stock and amazing staff. Barry was featured in the programme as one of the shining lights in this arena, because he had allowed the director and a team of accountants in to check out the books. He was given the opportunity to tell the viewers exactly how much had gone to local charities and Mind Games and what that money had achieved so far.

House & Garden Accessories started out with a bang, as Barry took over the only garden centre in Islington, immediately turning it into a profit centre. The old clientele found there were no plants or potting mix, but they were still happy to look around for their garden accessories, then wander inside to see the amazing carvings, pots and glassware that were all new to the area. Barry also gave out 20 Pound vouchers to Silvers Nursery up the road, to those customers who bought 50 Pounds or more of items. Barry had made a deal with Silvers, who not only gained an immediate influx of customers but agreed that by selling the vouchers to Barry for 5 pounds, the exercise was a win - win for both parties.

Barry had asked the girls at The Thrift Shop, if they knew anyone capable of running or serving in his new venture. Barb immediately put her hand up. I can manage the place for you, and it will only cost you a 10% raise", she brazenly offered. "Deal", said Barry. He knew Barb's worth, and also knew that it was just around the corner from where she lived. He called Barb and Jean in for a chat before telling Barb what he expected of her. He asked Jean if she would set up the same bookkeeper to manage the new centre. Jean agreed, and told Barb that she would be over next week to get things moving and to advise on security. Barry offered Jean a rise also, as she had solved a theft problem, advised on security and kept an eye on things all round.

Barb was not replaced in The Thrift Shop, but the two part timers had now become full timers, with Ming Su becoming the surprise Barb alternative, as it turned out she had extensive training and retail experience in Hong Kong, and was able to impart her knowledge of medium pressure selling systems to the girls. Ming Su was indeed a dark horse, and the Chinese community came to rely on her to tell them what was fashionable in London, so that they looked more like locals than foreigners. When several of her clients expressed surprise that there were no silk dresses on display, she mentioned it to Barry, that it might be worth importing some from China in order to gauge the reaction. He told her that he had no clothing connections in China. Ming Su had all the connections he needed, as her background in fashion in Hong Kong meant that she had plenty of contacts, and could she make some calls. Barry agreed at once.

Ming Su asked Barry to pay for a first consignment of silk dresses. They took two weeks to arrive. After showing Barry the invoice for 40 dresses, he asked. "What do you think you can get for these dresses"? "I am thinking of a 500% mark up and they will still be cheap", she replied. Barry was impressed. He told her that he would pay the invoice by bank transfer straight away. Ming Su said, "Please pay the Invoice less 100 Pounds. I had to send a deposit with our Order, to get them to send the dresses – even though they know me". Barry was clearly impressed that she had used her own money to start this venture off. He invited her into his office, where he settled up with 250 Pounds. "That extra is for taking the initiative and using your own money. I'm more than impressed. Thank you".

Ming Su accepted the money gratefully then went back to work, and filled in Sarah about the transaction, and what was in the large carton that had just been delivered. They needed to make room for a new display. Sarah suggested some Chinese looking mannequins to show them off, then suggested that they find some oriental type wall-paper as a backdrop. Ming Su also started to teach Sarah some basic Chinese language phrases so that she could greet her new customers at least. If she encountered any real language problems, then Ming Su would always be around. Ming Su suggested single small spot lights be installed on a rail overhead, that could be directed to each dress, to highlight the sheen and colours of the silk to bring them alive. Barry approved all of the ideas, and had a tradie start on the projects. By the time the spot lights had been installed, everything else was in place. A sign in Chinese calligraphy – with English underneath - was posted in each window, announcing the arrival of authentic, handmade Chinese silk fashion wear, chosen personally from a top Hong Kong supplier by Ming Su, fashion expert now resident in London, and personally on hand to help with fitting, alterations and comments.

CHAPTER 20

Fashion Week had started and Ming Su had, off her own back, contacted the organizers, and offered to put on a runway show (during the intervals only) on behalf of The Thrift Shop, to demonstrate just what could be bought locally. Would they also ask in their advertising for their wealthy patrons to donate at least a gold coin that would be given to the Mind Games charity The Thrift Shop was organizing and sponsoring in order to help Britain's returned service men and women overcome mental issues. Each person on the day would be given a leaflet describing what Mind Games was all about, along with contact info, should they be able to help further.

The Fashion Week organizers initially turned down the request on the basis that Thrift Shop clothing should not be confused with expensive designer clothes. They changed their minds after Julian Morrow and Kirsty Evans turned up praising the organizer for such a wonderful idea of adopting The Thrift Shop and Mind Games, and how their efforts will undoubtedly make the fashion mags news, as their contacts were well established. They also had the temerity to bring along a stack of leaflets advertising the relationship and the expected gold coin donation on the night, to support a very worthwhile endeavor by The Thrift Shop, along with a special interval display of Chinese silk fashion dresses.

The shop displays were sensational, and shone on into the night as the spotlights in the store brought out the amazing colours accentuated by the dark background of the stores interior. The Fashion Week interval catwalk displays got more publicity than anything else. Julian Morrow and Ming Su commented on each dress as the local Chinese girl volunteers strutted their stuff once every night for seven days. Every magazine was being fed the same line, 'Fashion Week supports local talent and local charity'. The Fashion Week organizers had to admit that this had been their most successful week since inception 8 years ago, and thanked everyone involved with after show cocktails and canapes. Julian announced that Fashion Week had raised 1420 Pounds in donations during the week, and that a cheque had been made up showing Fashion Week as the sponsor and giver of the over-sized cheque to Mind Games. This too went into the publicity mill, and hurt no one at all.

Julian and Kirsty allowed no time to elapse before releasing a statement advising that Mind Games was only eight months away, and to date The Thrift Shop had collected from Furniture Fashions and House & Garden Accessories, the sum of 5200 Pounds. The Thrift Shop had donated 8100 Pounds. Fashion Week had topped up their donation to 2000 Pounds and local businesses and individuals had do-nated 1360 Pounds to date. A grand total of 16,660 Pounds, most of which would go to organizing events around the country, with an esti-mated 50,000 Pounds in prize monies plus funding to kick start the charity, by the time the Mind Games was due to kick off in Feb next year, and that now was the time to enter, volunteer or donate.

Julian was put in charge of organizing Mind Games, with the brief of making things as interesting as possible, but with little effort re-quired on the part of the participants, apart from attending a local pub or hall in order to participate. The first thing he did was to contact all the pubs through Pub News the magazine that every pub received once a month. The online version would be available from day one, so he could tell the story about how publicans could seize on this initial foray into helping Britain's service men and women serving and re-tired, who are suffering from any mental illness, or simply just want to indulge in any of the games on offer, not to win, but to participate for a worthwhile fund raising cause, as it takes money to help those who cannot help themselves, especially as they contracted the problem in the defence of their country, and how many of them had simply been forgotten.

Imagine being trained to kill, and being subjected to images that no person should be, then to be discharged in the expectation that you could forget and forgive, as you assimilate back into normal society. This is a monumental challenge. Our service men and women need help to be rid of their war demons. We know that psychiatric help is of enormous benefit, but many are too proud to seek it. Many will not admit they have a problem. Many do not want to see other ex-service personnel. Some need to speak with ex service personnel. The problems are complex. Funds from the Mind Games will help overcome this terrible burden. A burden that frankly we all should be sharing. How can you help? Respond with your ideas for games your pub can sponsor, that's how. Want some help organizing? Let us know.

There are approx. 48,000 pubs in the UK. They are closing at 500 per year. Let's make them relevant again. Let's show the public that you stand for more than just drinking, which as you know is being frowned upon outside of our own homes, due to drink and drive laws. We can sponsor Mind Games and give the local community a reason to once again visit our pubs, but this time for a higher purpose. You have the room. You have standing in the community. You have the opportunity to give something back. It might also be a chance for you to show off your new restaurant or refurbished accommodation'!

Next on the list were the church groups; the scouts and guides, and any other group that used a hall as a meeting place. The publicity machine was in full swing, with TV, radio and magazines being alerted about the types, numbers of games and where they were being held, all promoting the big event. "The main aim of Mind Games being to raise funds for better mental health facilities, specialists, outreach workers and carers for service personnel, as there have been far too many suicides, family, marriage and personal breakdowns for us to turn a blind eye to. We expect our service men and women to guard our freedom, and sometimes to lay their life on the line, but we forget about those who have been traumatized by events that you and I will never see", said Barry in one radio interview.

CHAPTER 21

Furniture Fashions meantime had spread into most of Europe with Milly the bookkeeper running the show, until Barry asked the door knocking person to come in. Milly looked tired and worn out. "What's up Milly, am I working you too hard"? "Frankly, Barry, that's exactly what's been happening. I just took on too much, and now I'm stuffed". She flopped down on the armchair and told Barry that she alone had been sorting out all the paperwork, and financials – and was personally looking after 11 franchises throughout Europe, as well as looking after the books for The Thrift Shop, his own Furniture Fashions store, the Mind Games paperwork and his latest venture House & Garden Accessories. "I need help", she exclaimed, and threw her arms in the air.

"Bloody Hell, Milly, I had no idea, and I must say I didn't stop to think either, that you had been running the finances of the operation all on your own. Tell me what you need to make all this work well, and how you can get what you need". Milly handed Barry a sheet of paper listing everything she thought should happen from now on. First on the list was a CFO (Chief Financial Officer). Milly was not offering herself up. The CFO would take charge of the group's financial affairs including overseeing the accounts, and advise Barry not only on his day to day finances but on the best structure to minimize taxes and how to take the company forward financially. Barry perused the information, then peered over the top of the sheet. "You've put a lot of thought into this Milly. I have let things slide, and relied on you and the accountant to make sure the books were straight, but I've also overwhelmed you, and I'm sorry. How does Jack feel about things"? "Jack's been your accountant for 15 years, and he and I have been working closely together since I started here. I pretty much hand him the finished paperwork that he looks over, then adjusts for deductions and liabilities, then submits your return, but he is worried that now you are on the verge of making over 4 million pounds profit this year, you are going to need some heavyweight accounting firm to look after you going forward. That's why I'm here. You'll notice that my job description as bookkeeper would change to Accounts Executive. I would report to the CFO who would run the top level stuff, whilst I run the local business accounts – that I can do easily, but the CFO needs to handle the foreign investments, franchises, and upper level stuff. That also means that I will get a pay rise. So, what do make of all that Barry"?

Barry was actually lost for words for a few seconds, then a big grin brightened his face as he replied, "I'm going to shout you and your man Michael a big dinner at Marcello's on Saturday, as a thank you for all your hard work and for all the time you've spent away from him – looking after me. Please let me know what part I need to play in executing this Master plan of yours, and tell me how much all this is going to cost me"? Milly said, "Well to start with, my salary needs to increase by 20%. That brings me in line with other bookkeepers doing a similar job – I looked it up. A CFO with international business experience is around the 80,000 Pound mark". Before Barry could object, Milly held her hand up. "He or she should bring in a multiple of two to five times an increase in revenue over and above the current figures. If they don't, you look for another. Jack recommends Ogilvy and Standish as your future accountants, as they are just the right size for your operation. They will be able to select a CFO for you also. Jack will hand over the books to them and he will retire, but says he will always be available to consult – if you need him".

"A masterly coup Madam. By the way, can you arrange your own booking at Marcello's? I am happy to endorse it with the Maitre'd if he needs me to. Again, thanks for all your magnificent work. I'm sorry I've been blind to what's been going on in your department, but it just goes to show that you had everything in hand and it was one less thing for me to worry about. 4 million profit. Blimey. I think your salary should increase to 40%". Milly raised herself slowly from the deep padded, velour covered padded winged armchair and walked slowly over to Barry who had come around from his desk. They embraced. As she turned round to leave, two salty runnels trickled over her high cheekbones. Barry was not only a good boss, he was a good man.

CHAPTER 22

Barb had taken on the management of House & Garden Accesso-ries, and was surprised when Barry and a tall man walked in to the centre whilst she was busy arranging a group of new pots that had been delivered that morning. "Morning Barb, this is our new group CFO Michael Stanning. I'm taking him around to our various enter-prises to see how they stack up financially. Would you mind showing us round and telling us how things are going as we walk"? Barb pulled off her gloves and stood by the display. "Well Barry / Michael. This display tells a good story. Here you have a range of pots in different sizes, and in four colour types, predominantly red, green, blue or yel-low, with splashes of other colours in them so that they can also blend with other themes in both the house and the garden. These pots allow the customer to pretty much use one or more of them in just about any setting, and they are prepared to pay a premium as we also advertise them as fashion changers, meaning that they will rarely see their pot in someone else's home, as we bring in new and different stock all the time. The secret is to think like the customer. Bring in the stock to suit their needs, not buy stock just because it looks good – although that also helps.

Net, net margins are around 30%, which as a financial person, you will agree is very good, especially when compared to run of the mill garden centres who manage a mere 12% - if they are lucky. So, it's a combination of knowing what will sell, then selecting products that are either unusual or interesting – without going overboard". Michael was impressed. "You seem to know your figures Barb. Are you an ac-countant"? "No, but being in management for many years and looking after many stores, the questions always relate to the stock, the cus-tomer and the bottom line, so I make sure I have the answers every week and adjust as necessary, Barry allows me to converse with the suppliers, and I have sole discretion when it comes to selection and pricing, so I see the transactions from the buyer and the sellers side". Michael and Barry left after a while. As they walked out the gate together to the car park, Michael piped up. "Barry, I'm so impressed with every one of your staff. They have a very keen interest in your welfare and they are damn good at what they do". Barry beamed. "Yeah I've been very lucky". Michael asked if he would consider letting Barb take over buying for all the businesses. "That's what she was born to do you know. That and merchandizing are her strengths". Barry thought about it. "You know, I never stopped to consider how far Barb could go, but you saying that has opened up my eyes. Let's go back in".

"Deja Vu all over again", said Barb as they walked in, whilst Barry indicated that they should go into her office. Barb sat behind her desk, and Barry and Michael took up the fashionable outdoor cane chairs in front of it. "Barb, Michael here has suggested that you may not be using all of your talents to the full". Barb took hold of the wrong end of the stick and stood up. "Barry, I give my all every day, to make sure this place looks and performs in the best ways possible". Barry put up both hands. "Stop right there Barb, that's not what this is all about. Michael is suggesting that you have more talent than befits this place alone, and is suggesting – and I agree - that you might seriously consider becoming Head Buyer for the group. What do you think"? Barb for once in her life was lost for words, and sat down with a thump. No words were exchanged for ten seconds. She just sat there open mouthed and stared at them, then finally said. "Well I never expected that. Do you really think I could do it", as she looked first at Michael then at Barry. "It took Michael to open my eyes as to your talents. I always knew you had a flair for merchandizing and display, which was why you were promoted from the Thrift Shop to here. Now if you are willing, I am prepared to send you to business school as Michael tells me there is an International Buyers Diploma course that runs part time for a year – if you are interested. Meantime we can get someone in that you can train to take over your job here, what do you think"? "I think I'd like that very much. I'm getting on, but I still have passion enough to make this new job my dream job". "You and Michael can work together regarding the financial side. He will bring financial expertise, whilst you bring the artistic side to the equation". Barb thought that Michael, although younger than her, would happily be allowed near anything she owned, any time he wished. Unknown to Barb, Michael had the same thoughts about his personal possessions, but also thought it was great way to first get to know her through business.

CHAPTER 23

Unbeknown to Barry, but known to Jean, as that was part of her job description – was to snoop. She couldn't help herself. She had kept an eye on all of Barry's business affairs from day one, and had recently uncovered what was a highly illegal people smuggling ring involving Barry's furniture shipments from Europe. Barry had buyers all over Europe and now the business extended into the old Russian states and the USSR itself. As she was wont, she often took herself off to her various hidey holes where she was able to watch Barry's employees doing business, using her high powered binoculars and now with night vision – well what else was she to do? She didn't go out to pubs or had many friends to party with. They were all mostly ex cops, and most of them had lives, so a spot of surveillance from the rooftop of the garage across the way from one of the import warehouses on this occasion, was as good a time as she was going to get anyway. She had done a deal long ago with the owner, that she would keep an eye on his place – on a random basis for no pay - provided he let her use the rooftop any time. Besides, being a cop would always be in her blood. She had hot coffee and sandwiches in a carry bag, along with her headphones, which when connected to her phone, punched out her favourite bands. Life was pretty good, and besides it had been a hot summer's day, but the temperature on the roof was mild. She needed only bug spray to finish the job before settling down. She strolled over to the far corner and gave herself an all over burst of foul smelling spray, before returning to her seat.

At 8.20 pm the first van arrived at the Estates R Us warehouse. The doors were electrically raised, and the night crew came out to unload each piece separately by hand down a long wooden ramp that had been placed at the rear of the van after the two large and heavy swinging doors had been opened. Jean noticed that on four occasions - each involving a wardrobe, which the four men handling it were struggling with the heavy load. Also, those same wardrobes were placed just inside the warehouse by the roller door, whilst the other goods were moved inside and into different sections according to the type of furniture it was.

Two more vans arrived between 9.20 and 11 pm. As with the first, the second and third each had wardrobes, that were separated from the main load and each placed just inside the roller door. The workers went home after the last truck had been emptied and the roller door was wound down. Jean had a pretty good idea what was going on, and it was confirmed at 12 midnight when a large white van rolled up. She took the number plate and van details. She set the video recorder up and zoomed into the area behind the van where the side door was. Sure enough after ten minutes, 11 people came through the door and were bundled into the van. The foreman closed up the factory, then jumped into the passenger seat of the van, whilst the driver locked the vans rear door then climbed up into the van and took off.

Jean was conflicted. Should she call her contacts in the force, or wait until a more civilized time. It took two seconds for her to contact a Detective Inspector friend she had known for fourteen years before retiring. The response was hazy and muffled. "Jean Stone, is that really you after all this time, and me in my bed. I presume it's urgent or you wouldn't have bothered me. What can I do for you"? Sorry boss, I mean Harry, but I've been staking out my bosses warehouse in Edgeware, and I've just witnessed what I believe are 11 illegals just getting into a white van and headed west along Edgeware Rd. I was hoping your lads might be able to intercept it". "Quick, what's the make and number? I'll call you back". Jean was glad that Harry Parsons didn't brush her off, or want to ask any more questions about the event. He obviously still trusted her word and her judgement. That made her feel good.

Time went by slowly, until half an hour later Harry Parsons got back to her. "Hey Jean, that info was good. We just pulled the van and the driver up, although the passenger got away. The rest are all on their way to the nick as we speak. How come you were watching this lot? Jean explained that she now worked at The Thrift Shop and that she also acted as security for Barry Baines. This stake out was just a time passing exercise. She was able to tell Harry who the accomplice was and his home address. "Thanks Jean, I'll have someone call round there shortly to pick him up". Harry invited her to dinner before he rang off. A good night's work thought Jean.

Next morning Jean broke the news to Barry, and thought his Edge-ware Rd warehouse might not be opening up today, unless he gave her his spare keys so that she could pop down there to square things up with the workers, open up, and let them know there would be a change of Foreman, which she was able to confirm would be Peter Graves from now on. She handed Peter the keys after a short spiel on what was expected of him. His jet black face beamed. "Come on then you lazy bastards, let's get to work. You know what to do. Get those ward-robes shifted from the roller door down to the wardrobe department. Chop chop". Jean left her telephone number with him, in case he needed anything. He said he was good. Jean informed Milly of the change of personnel along with a brief rundown of the night's events at the warehouse. Jean would get the original warehouse keys back from the Police, when they had done with them. She told Barry how the warehouse was now sorted and that he could relax, as he had no part to play in the illegal smuggling, although his wardrobes might have some food – and other – 'left overs' in them.

CHAPTER 24

The day started at 7am for Reggie, who now commanded a small fleet of three vans – one enormous furniture type, and six trailers that fit onto prime movers – other peoples. By owning the trailers only, Barry is able to get them taken to any destination, dropped off for loading or unloading, then picked up later by another prime mover, so he remains flexible at all times; doesn't have the cost of owning prime movers, and can usually match his vehicles with his loads.

All this in conjunction with policing the day to day traffic in and out of the warehouses – with many loads going to and coming from the continent, the Thrift Shop and the House & Garden Accessories centre, plus movements around Estates R US, Reggie had grown into an ever expanding role. What he didn't know was that his manliness and integrity were about to be tested.

One Saturday evening when Reggie was sat at the bar of his local pub, a well-endowed female sat next to him. He hadn't noticed at first, then he did a double take at what surely must have been the best looking visitor to his local bar in a very long time. She ignored him then turned sideways on. Extracted her mobile phone and began to dial. He couldn't understand a word she was saying. It sounded Russian but it could have been any language. She put the phone down on the bar and sighed before swilling the small cocktail she had ordered, then quietly but lithely exiting the bar. Reggie was bewildered. He had just witnessed an Angel in female form and what form it was. She was also foreign. She was fleetingly there, before she was more than fleetingly gone – with not even a glance in his direction. Her perfume still lingered. Then he noticed her mobile phone on the bar. He quickly left his seat, grabbed the phone and got to the entrance when the woman walked briskly back in and collided with Reggie. Her breasts made contact first. Reggie reached out to steady himself and inadvertently stroked one of them. The woman looked surprised and said, "Is that how you greet all women"?

Reggie now red faced, started to apologize profusely, when the woman held his hand with the phone in it, and declared. "I presume you were coming out to give me back my phone, or else you are a thief, which is it"? Reggie's face went even redder. "I, I, I was running out to give you back your phone", he blustered. She laughed. The honey trap was set.

"My name is Petrushka. I work between Leningrad and London. I supervise shipments from Russia into various businesses based here in the capital". Reggie explained that he was Logistics Manager for a large company dealing in international trade – especially from Russia".

The woman said, "I can't believe my ears. Do you have transport available if I need products shipping from Russia"? "Of course", replied Reggie. "Do you have a card? Here's mine".

Petrushka drank a few more cocktails before bidding Reggie good night with a peck on one cheek. 'Just enough to keep him interested', she thought. "I'll be in touch".

Two days later, Reggie heard from her. She had a shipment of woodworking machinery from Leningrad to London, and would he be interested in making a deal with her. She would be happy to pay above the norm because her regular transport company would have no trucks available for another 3 weeks. Reggie knew the rules, but her husky voice, her perfume, her face, her kiss and her protrusions, had addled his brain. "I need to send you an invoice and you need to pay before we can pick up the goods. I can have a truck there in two days' time". "Ooh Reggie, I didn't want to make this formal. I thought you might just do me a favour, and I could pay you directly in cash after the goods arrive. I assure you that the paperwork is all in order. All your driver has to do, is to deliver the load to our yard. We will unload it, and your driver can be away in half an hour. I think 4000 Pounds should cover it". "Let me call you back", Reggie replied, with a smile on his face.

Reggie knew that a normal load would cost 2500 Pounds. If he kept it quiet, no one would know that he had contracted for a truck and trailer with driver from a labour hire company. It had nothing to do with his work or his boss. He was simply managing an extra-curricular activity. That's what he told himself. There would be no harm done. He would of course have to fund the 2500 Pounds from his own savings, but the deal he calculated, was a 60% return on his investment. If he did that a few times a year, he could go on those expensive cruises he had only read about. He made some calls and arranged for a driver and truck to be available in Leningrad for a short notice pick up. He paid a 10% deposit to secure the deal, after receiving an invoice on his computer.

He called Petrushka back. "I've thought about your offer, and decided I can do it, so send me the details of the pick up and the load, and I will arrange it all. I also need the delivery address in London". Petrushka sent the pick up details to his computer. Reggie forwarded them on to his contact, who promptly sent another invoice for the balance. He phoned Petrushka back. She told him that the minute he had organized the vehicle, along with the drivers name and the truck and trailer registration numbers, she would pass them on to the pick up address who would be waiting for the driver. She would also be glad to meet him back at his bar for a celebratory drink. "Who knows, if this works out well, we might become intimate friends". The word 'intimate' was the second hook. It always worked. Men were so stupid. Reggie's knees were shaking when he met Petrushka in the bar later that evening. He even sprung for their meals and drinks. After all this was going to be the start of a very lucrative arrangement – for them both. She proclaimed a toast. "To our lasting friendship". The third hook was in and the barb set.

The truck and trailer picked up the load without incident. It crossed several border check points on its way to London, to finally arrive four days after he had met up with Petrushka, with Reggie calling her, to advise her that the load was now in the destination warehouse, un-loaded, and that the driver had just left. They should meet up tonight to finalize the deal. That was the message he left anyway. Alarm bells should have been ringing, but his Petrushka who had toasted their 'lasting friendship' did not return his ever increasing calls. After three hours, Reggie decided to go to the address on the freight docket marked 'Receiver'. It took him two hours through rush hour traffic to get there.

At least the address was real. It was a logistics company. Stock would be delivered, then they would ship it around the country on re-ceipt of an order from the owner of the stock. It was getting near clos-ing time as he walked briskly to the office. He had this awful premonition that he had been taken for a sucker. The receptionist called the Transport Manager who confirmed that he had paperwork for that shipment that had arrived, and that another freight company, whose three smaller trucks had been waiting for different parts of the load as soon as they had unloaded the semi, had been and gone. No, they did not have the number plates of the smaller tray trucks, so he should contact the local carrier who arranged for the transfers. Reggie got their office number and called them. Unfortunately they had closed for the day. He knew what he had suspected from the first call to Petrushka earlier that day that he had been well and truly duped. His savings of 2500 Pounds had already been spent, and all he got out of this exercise was a giant life lesson. Petrushka got free freight all the way from Russia, and free food and drinks. He didn't even get her into bed. One day he would get his revenge, but today, he needed to get back to his pub and drink himself silly.

CHAPTER 25

The Thrift Shop was doing so well, that Barry was wondering how they could ever top what they were doing, when out of the blue Sarah walked into Barry's office and declared, "Oi Barry, I reckon I could run one of these places by myself. Why don't you think about setting up another store? Not too far away as I have to travel, but far enough so it's outside of a radius that people can't walk easily to from here. I'm thinking Kentish Town, as it's on the same tube line, so I can get there in reasonable time. The shop has to be close to the station like this one, or people from outside the area won't be able to get to it easily. See, I reckon that you could have a string of these all over London, and that each one is close to the tube, so you can name them The Thrift Shop and underneath in brackets Angel or Kentish Town or Barnet – wherever. What do you reckon? Naturally I would need a Store Managers wage, and as you already have plenty of stock, it wouldn't be hard to fill another shop up would it"? "Phew, that took it out of me. Mind if I sit down, I'm quite dizzy".

Barry was smiling all the way through Sarah's proposal, and now laughed out loud. "Sarah, from the day you walked in here, you have been a ray of sunshine. The way you brighten up everybody's day. The way you treat the customers. Your work ethic. Your amazing ideas. I don't think I can make you a Store Manager". He paused for effect. "I would like to make you London Stores Manager. You see, I've been thinking on the same lines as you, and talk about coincidence – unless you've been peeking at my computer, I already have a store option in Kentish Town, and your idea of keeping them just far enough apart but all close to the underground stations, well it's like you've been reading my mind. So if that's the way you think, then you deserve to be a part of my management team. You've seen how Barb has been promoted twice, well you have the opportunity to grow with the business as well. What do you say"?

It was Sarah's turn to laugh. "You mean I've spent all weekend thinking about this and you were already on the case. Blimey Barry, it would be a dream come true for me, but I'm worried about knowing enough to manage more than one store".

"Barb had the same concern, but she's half way through a buyer's course at the Poly, and she's loving it, and she's putting her new found information to good use already. I would be happy to pay for you to do a general managers course there too if you would like that". "Oh! Do you really think I could do it? I'm not sure". "The problem with you Sarah is that you have so much hidden depth but you are afraid to show it, so you mask everything with your crazy antics, but I've been observing you closely. You are nobody's fool, and your ability to learn quickly is amazing, so if you want it, here's your chance. Let me know by tomorrow". Sarah put out her hand to shake Barry's. "If you think I can do it, then my answer right now is, yes"! Sarah went out of Barry's office with mutterings of, "Yes! Yes! Yes"!

Barry called out to her as she was leaving. "Let me know who would best be put in charge of a new store at Kentish Town, will you". Sarah waved a hand in acknowledgement. This was indeed something she needed to give some thought to. She went to talk with Hilary to get her reaction to the news.

CHAPTER 26

Sarah walked into Hilary's general goods area and spilled the beans about the new store and her promotion. Hilary could not have been more pleased for her, although deep down she didn't want Sarah to go. There was nobody she knew that could replace her, and she would miss her terribly, but she congratulated her heartily and hoped that the disappointment she felt was in no way evident upon her visage. "We must go out for a drink later, to celebrate", declared Hilary. "The problem is", said Sarah, "that I can't tell anyone else at this stage. The reason I've come to you is to ask who you reckon would make a good store manager for Kentish Town. Naturally, I would start it up, then train someone else to run it while I'm at college. Is this something you think you could handle"? She knew Hilary's answer before she said it. "I like what I do here very much. I do not have as much ambition as you do, and I wish you every joy and luck in the world, but we are very different people. I like to cross the t's and dot the i's. I'm not one who looks for new opportunities, so thanks for thinking of me but I am very happy here. However, have you considered Lonely? She has come on wonderfully since starting up Lonely's Corner and she's also made it her mission to get to know each of our sections, so she's able to fill in for anyone".

"Mmm" mused Sarah. "Good thinking. I'll keep an eye on her. I wonder how a black faced manager will go down in Kentish Town". "Sarah, that's bordering on racism. You need to get with the times. Lonely may have a black skin, but she's as much a Londoner as you and I, and she's proven to be whip smart and stands no nonsense, which are traits managers need. Anything she doesn't know, you or the others can teach her".

"You do realize Hilary that you will probably take on more responsibility once Lonely and I go, so with your permission, I'd like to suggest to Barry, that you be made Store Manager. After all, you and Jean will be the only original ones left and Jean's getting a bit past it. What do you think"? I think that Jean might take umbrage at that remark. She might well make a better Store Manager than me, so keep an open mind at this time. I will be happy with any position here".

CHAPTER 27

The old lady with the green floppy hat walked into The Thrift Shop, and immediately headed for the brightly coloured Asian style clothes under Ming Su's care. Ming Su was having some lunch, so Sarah was looking after both her section and Ming's.

"Hello, I'm Sarah. How can I help you"? "I want to try on that dress there. The one with the large red peony right in the middle". Sarah looked at the old woman, then pulled the dress off the rack and held it against the woman's frame. Trying to be diplomatic, but not really knowing how, as she had never resorted to diplomacy before, she hunted for words. "Well madam, that dress certainly is stunning, but do you think something less vibrant might be better. Maybe we should look at these dresses over here", Taking the old woman by the elbow, Sarah attempted to divert her to the less flamboyant selection. The woman glowered then raised her shopping bag and clapped Sarah over the head with it. The newly purchased toaster was probably now dented, but she wasn't going to be told what to do and what to buy. "I want to try on that dress, and I want to do it now", she demanded in a shrill voice.

Ming Su had heard the ruckus and stepped out of the lunch room, just in time to see Sarah getting a bag belting. Sarah rubbed her head and was in the middle of telling the old lady that she could be done for assault, so she should calm down, when Ming took the old lady aside and asked her what the problem was. Sarah jumped in. "She wanted to try on that silk dress. I suggested that she try on something else instead and she got all narky".

"Let's start again shall we. There seems to have been a misunderstanding. My name is Ming Su, and I look after the imported silk dresses whilst Sarah looks after fashions generally. Can I ask your name"? "Mrs West. Emily West. My daughter in law lives in Vietnam with her husband – my son – Peter. She and I are exactly the same size, so I saw your amazing silk dresses through the window, and immediately thought of one for her for her upcoming Birthday. If that Sarah hadn't treated me so badly, I would already be trying it on for size. Can you help me dear"?

"I'm so sorry – may I call you Emily? – of course you can try it on". She reached up and removed the dress from the rack, and led Emily to the Changing Room. When the curtains parted after five minutes, Emily, 60 to a day if ever she was, had pushed her hair into a bob, and with her radiant white skin showing off the red large flowered centre piece with the royal blue and purple flashed background, made Emily stand out from all the others in the shop. Ming Su announced to all. "Look everybody, that's what I'm talking about. How to turn an everyday situation, into the most exquisite sight ever". Ming Su asked permission to take some photos of her – which Emily agreed to. They would be used as posters inside the shop, she told her.

Sarah came over to ogle. "I'm so sorry love, but I got my wires crossed. You look so elegant and beautiful in that dress. It has just transformed you". Emily stared at Sarah. "I know I'm old and not stylishly dressed, but you looked at the cover, without opening the book, and in retail that's a big mistake. I hope you have learnt from this, young lady". All Sarah could do was nod. She was right. Sarah turned and walked sheepishly back to her corner of the store. Lesson learned.

"Now", stated Emily. "I want the one I tried on, and three others in different colours. The prices are very reasonable for such good quality". She came closer to Ming. "One of those will be for me. After seeing myself in it, I think I would very much like to go up west to one of my old haunts, to see what a modern male looks like. Do you have shoes to match"? Sarah apologized again and helped Emily try on the range of new shoes that had recently come in from the same source in Asia, and were now stocked between Ming and Sarah's sections. With all the excitement generated by Emily, other potential

customers had drifted over to Ming Su's section and she was busy
showing dresses.

Emily strode towards the counter where the assistant working the
till was sitting. She got up and tallied the amount owing using the bar
codes on each price tag. "That will be 85 Pounds please madam".
Madam passed her credit card over. The girl inserted the card and
spun the reader around for the pin number, then removed the card.
"Thank you madam, have a nice day". Emily turned round to wave to
Ming Su, who just managed to wave back before being engulfed in
questions from her new customers.

The checkout girl – who doubled as the keeper of the cosmetics
displayed behind the counter, left her station and sauntered over to Sarah. "Well, it's not every day that you get a real life dame in here is it?
Dame Emily West. She's featured in an article in the Mirror today.
She's patroness – if that's how you say it - of The Vietnam Veterans
Care Society. Apparently they look after the soldier's families when a
soldier has been killed in action and the family's not coping well.

Sarah could not have had a worse day. She clocked out early, apol-
ogizing to everyone, but feigned a headache as the cause. During the
walk home and into the evening she could not get the event out of her
mind. Dame Emily West comes to her for help. Not only does she
have a son who is married to a Vietnamese girl. She is patron of a Society. The Vietnam Veterans Care Society that helps families that
have been traumatized by the Vietnam War. Could it have gone any
worse? What would Emily think of her and the shop? She hoped the
fact that she had bought so much gear, that there wasn't that much
damage, but still that didn't stop her from feeling awful.

The next morning Sarah awoke with a start. She hadn't joined the
dots, but now a new day had been born and new thinking had wiped
the old slate clean. She could make amends to the shop and her next
action – if it worked out – could help Mind Games become even better
than it already was shaping up to be.

She looked up the Vietnam Veterans Care Society. Found an e-
mail address and sent off an e-mail addressed to Dame Emily West.

Sarah apologized for the misunderstanding at the shop, and told her that she had learnt her lesson, and it wouldn't happen again. She then explained that the Thrift Shop and the other businesses in the group were hosting and sponsoring Mind Games. She went on to explain what it was all about. She was sure that her Society had received a flyer, and she would also know that Mind Games was there to help all returned service personnel and their families, and would her Society care to donate to the cause or assist with planning, as they were both so closely aligned in bringing war ravaged families peace of mind. She pressed Send. No try – no hope. One of Sarah's mottos. She went to work feeling better about having tried. It wouldn't erase the previous day, but it might salve her conscience a little.

As the day went on, Sarah thought less and less of the previous day's tumultuous event. In fact, she had had a bumper day and sales were though the roof. She knocked off, then went around to a café serving all day breakfasts. She got back home after 6.30 p.m. She put the kettle on, closed the curtains, switched on the two reproduction Tiffany lamps on the mantel piece, and then settled down to a quiet evening. She rarely looked at the tele unless her favourite game show was on, or an unusual movie was featured. The news sucked, and she got more pleasure from trolling through the computer. After the screen had turned from black to password, to g-mail, she noticed that a reply from Emily West was in her inbox.

"My dear Sarah. Thank you for your e-mail. I realized after visiting The Thrift Shop that you were only trying to prevent an old lady from making a fool of herself. Everything worked out well, and I have no qualms about calling on you all again in the near future. BTW, I showed the Chinese silk dresses to some of my friends last night. I think your shop will be getting a visit from some of them. They were very impressed.

As to your request for help or sponsorship of Mind Games, you were correct in thinking that the Society is not directly involved – yet!, but also correctly you assumed that all families of ex and currently serving service personnel often have to bear the brunt of the consequences of war, so our emergency committee meeting last night approved a donation to your cause to the sum of 4000 Pounds. All we ask is recognition and a receipt, and for the funds to go directly to needy personnel and their dependents. Please let me have your Mind Games contact information.

I commend you on your willingness to turn a not so good situation into one for a mutual good cause".

Sarah sent a copy off to Barry's computer, with a note asking for him to get in touch with Dame West with all the donation information and how else they might help with the cause. Barry took no time in answering, and said that although he had no knowledge of the incident (even though he had - via the cosmetics / check out chick, who was always ready for a tattle tale), he praised her for making amends with Dame West, and how pleased he was with her efforts to help with the Mind Games sponsorship. He would take it from here. He then shot an e-mail off to Milly, who was handling the financial side of the Mind Games. Milly replied that he needed soon, to approve funds to pay for some of the events that had already started up, and for those to come. Barry suggested a meeting in his office in two days' time, and to send word to the organizing committee members to be there as well.

CHAPTER 28

The Organizing Committee welcomed the funds supplied by the Society and Milly reported to the CFO Michael Stanning and Barry that to date, there was close to 45,000 Pounds in the kitty. "I know that you Michael are not directly involved with the Mind Games project, but as Chief Financial Officer, it is right that you should be involved with the committee, just to make sure that all finances, donations and transactions are kosher and at arm's length to the business in general.

Michael acknowledged that his presence was purely as an overseer, and thanked Milly and Barry for keeping him in the loop. "As far as I can see, Milly is doing an amazing job with the finances, and no doubt, I'll find out what the committee is up to regarding the actual Games, after this session has ended".

The convener rolled out a chart showing the towns and cities that had either started some of the Games programmes or who would be coming on board soon. Barry reminded them all that in a few months' time the finals will have to be held, then the winners brought into London for the prize giving. He needed more sponsors if he was to get his target of 50,000 Pounds to give away, so they all put their heads together to come up with a plan for the last half of the contest.

"Ok, tell me what's been happening to date", asked Barry. Another member told how over 60 pubs had banded together to organize rounds of darts. All scores are circulated to all pubs, so there is fierce competition. The Deacon's Arms in Worcester is leading, but that will change. The top scorer will receive 600 Pounds, and there are fifteen runners up, with decreasing amounts as they go down the scale, with a total prize bag of 4 thousand Pounds. It's not much, but it is spread over quite a few players, and everyone knows that it is not about the prizes or winning, it's about promoting the Mind Games charity, and generating publicity for it.

Another member introduced herself as Jane, and told them her job was to promote cribbage competitions. Currently the Old Cheese in Cheshire was the leader. Prize monies were the same as the darts.

Yet another game being played was chess, and Romeo's Juliet in Earls Court was winning at this stage.

Texas Holdem Poker was another favourite, and the leader was The Oaks in Dartford.

What we have done is to charge each Landlord the sum of fifty Pounds, each time he holds a game. This money goes to the prize pool, so instead of us spending 4000 Pounds we end up spending 3000 Pounds as he is happy to donate 50 Pounds when his pub takings go through the roof each time.

Billiards is another game, and the Sailors Semaphore in Leeds is winning at this time.

Milly calculates that we should still have fifty thousand left to run the charity for those in need of urgent psychological help. If we had two hundred thousand Pounds, it would still be too little, so we need to step up and find new sources of income. If anyone has any suggestions, now is probably a good time to suggest it.

Things stayed quiet, and it looked as if the meeting was about to come to a close, when a large hand rose at the back. "Look, I reckon we could go hard on the big corporates. We haven't seen the big boys chippin' in yet, and they're the ones with the big money". "Hi err", – "Jim. Jim Styles – sorry". Barry asked, "What did you have in mind Jim? Remember we are just another charity to them. They usually need a damn good reason to get behind something and remember my saying, WIIFM – What's In It For Me! What is it that will make them think they are getting something beneficial out of this partnership? We need to be thinking and walking in their shoes – not ours. Think guys!"

Jim raised his hand again. Barry acknowledged him. "What about if we publish a list of the corporates that have helped the ongoing problem of our mentally wounded service personnel get re-integrated into civvy life. We could call them partners, with the biggest donor becoming a platinum sponsor, then gold sponsor, then silver and bronze, like the Olympics. If we tell them our target to become an effective force is 10 million, then we can't be accused of aiming too low, and you never know, some of them may just cough up for a worthy cause – and their name in lights.

Barry thanked Jim and all the rest for coming along. Barry asked Jim if he would mind staying behind for a brief chat. "Jim, I like your idea. It's bold but in my experience, unless we throw some weight behind it, no one will hear about it, so I wonder if you would mind becoming the owner of this idea. I was thinking of teaming you up with Julian Morrow my Furniture Fashions Manager and publicist and Kirsty Evans also a publicist and a reporter. What do you say Jim?"

"I'm not sure I'm up to the task, but I'm happy to have the meeting with them. Just let me know where and when". Barry agreed to set everything up through Milly, and that she would liaise with him in the future. "Again, Jim, I appreciate your commitment. Tell me, do you have a personal interest in the Mind Games?". "Apart from serving in Vietnam and knowing just what some of these poor bastards are going through, no".

CHAPTER 29

It came as a shock to everyone to find out that Ming Su had been run over on her way to work. Barry broke the news. He answered their questions as best he could, but he had only just received a call from the Police, advising him that Ming Su was in hospital with a broken collar bone, two broken ribs and spinal contusions, that meant she had to lay perfectly still whilst they sent her off for an MRI, and they would know more in a few hours, Ming Su's daughter How Su was with her, and it was she who told the Police to ring Barry.

"She's in a bad way, and we have to wait for more news. I will keep in touch with How Su to find out if there is anything we can do for her and her Mum. Ming also has a son who's a little younger than How, so they say they are coping at this time".

We in the meantime need to cover Ming's spot, and although Sarah is the obvious choice, she will need a hand, so I am giving Lonely more responsibility. She can help out generally, and still sell her soft toys.

Everyone went about their business with a downturned mouth. Ming Su was a quiet achiever, and her sales had climbed considerably over time. The trio got stuck in and managed to work all the positions between them.

Ming Su's results were now in and Barry at the close of play announced that Ming Su had effectively broken her back. The good news was that the nerves running through the central canal were not damaged, but she would need to have three vertebrae fused together, and what with the other broken bones, she would be in hospital for probably two months at least.

How Su was crying when Barry called her back later that evening. "I forgot to ask you, is Ming covered by health insurance?" "That's what I'm upset about. I just looked at our insurance paperwork and inside it is a letter of demand for nonpayment, so she either forgot to pay it, or couldn't afford to. She pays for our private education and English lessons, so I suspect it's the latter". "Well I called to tell you that every employee is covered by my business health plan, so whatever it costs to make your Mum better again, my insurance will pay for it, so don't fret, ok. I've passed on your Mums details along with your contact number. They will call you tomorrow to give you their contact details and claim number to quote. Don't worry. Your Mum is a fighter. All you need to do is be strong for her and let her see you are coping well. You can tell her about the insurance if you feel it will help put her mind at ease. If you need any financial or other assistance in the meantime, you have my number. Goodnight". How hugged her brother and told him everything was going to be all right, as she explained Barry's generous solution.

The ladies managed to just keep control of the situation in the shop for three months until Barry advised them that Ming Su was not coming back. "The Doc's say that her spinal condition means that she will never be able to lift any heavy objects, and full time work would be out of the question. Fortunately she was now of pensionable age, and she would receive an additional disability pension also. Barry received formal notification of Ming Su's resignation, along with a heartfelt letter to him and 'her family', that left them all in tears – including Barry. "This means ladies that we need another staff member, so I will be accepting any recommendations you might have, before I formally advertise the job".

CHAPTER 30

The Mind Games Ball was a roaring success. Dignitaries from every walk of life had turned up. A glass was being tapped. The crowd settled down. The talking stopped. The MC asked for silence for a word from the Mind Games organizer, Mr. Barry Baines. After the clapping had subsided, Barry rose. He had a speech prepared, but tore it up in a gesture of offering more heartfelt words. This was not a night for pre-selected, well thought through and thoroughly rehearsed words. Tonight was meant to be from the heart, and so it would be. Barry's speech - between meal courses, brought tears to even the most battle hardened. "Ladies and gentlemen, Lords and Ladies. The Mind Games will revolutionize the way Britons think about their military personnel. We, and I mean every one of us here tonight, recognize that many of our heroes are suffering. Some do it quietly, away from prying and sometimes condemning eyes. Some weep openly within their family unit, for the soul of the man or woman who went to war in such style and pathos, but was returned to them broken and mostly forgotten by the very service that asked them to fight for their country. Others we unfortunately hear about in the news, because the only way they could find release, was to harm themselves, many of them fatally. We have all pledged to stop this – NOW!

A big roar went up from the crowd with enthusiastic clapping. The front table stood. All the others followed suit. Barry acknowledged the applause and waved for them to resume their seats. "The Invictus Games is an idea of a similar nature, but it relies on hard physical participation, which is commendable but it is not for everyone. We wanted to include all serving and ex-servicemen and women, so Mind Games was devised. A series of games organized by The British Pubs Association, which enables any service personnel to take part. There is no pressure to perform. Simply show up and do your best. If you win – great. If you lose – great. Just by attending, you are furthering the cause. The cash prizes at the end of the games will help a few, but we – yes all of us here - and many more who couldn't be here but have pledged their time and money to the Mind Games, are already making a difference.

I am proud to announce that seven independent fully trained mental health counsellors have been employed on a part time basis, to become full time as funds allow. They will be on call to assist and independently assess, any services member and anyone in that service persons family with any mental health issue at all". All seven women walked on stage, with Barry stating their first names as they walked on. Their navy blue dresses and front frilled white blouses each sported the Union Jack lapel badge with Mind Games lettered underneath. The applause started up again.

"We have a full time liaison officer in Jody Marshall". She walked in in the same uniform with the same lapel badge, and joined the others.

"We have thirty volunteers, running Mind Games". They all walked on and formed a line behind the front eight.

"We have Milly, my accounts whiz, and Michael my CFO overseeing the financial side of the operation. And you have me, and I won't let this go until we make Mind Games the rip roaring success that it was always meant to be. Thank you".

As one, the crowd rose again, cheered, whistled and clapped, as the wait staff brought through the main course from six different entrances in large silver trolleys. The noise or re-seating, then chatter was deafening, as was the clatter of knives and forks, as the guests got stuck into a hearty meal.

As the stage cleared, Milly and Michael resumed their places at the front table. Around twenty minutes later, the MC rose from the front table and walked the stairs up to the stage. He stationed himself behind the lectern and adjusted the height of the microphone. He cleared his throat. The roar died down to a simmer. "Ladies and Gentlemen.

You will find in an envelope that accompanies your main course, that there is a Mind Games lapel badge for each of you. It is a reminder of our appreciation of your efforts. All contributors will receive one. Please take the opportunity to initiate a conversation using the lapel badge as a starter". Many of the crowd pinned their badge to their suit or dress at once, others placed their badge in a safe place.

Also on Barry's front table were Julian Morrow, Michael Stanning, Milly, Kirsty Evans and next to Barry, Denise Evans - Kirsty's Mum and Editor of Furniture Magazine. They had little time to chat up to that point, but once the main meal had been cleared they each had plenty of questions for the other. Barry had only ever spoken to Denise over the phone, and almost always to ask for favours surrounding advertising for his businesses. This was so nice, just to chat. They found out that neither of them had a significant other, so they arranged to meet for dinner in a week's time. As the taxi taking both Denise and Barry home, Barry asked the driver to wait whilst he saw Denise to her front door. Before the door had closed, they took the opportunity to kiss. "Looking forward to our next meeting", said Denise. "Me too". He waved and left, and started walking down the street, when the taxi sidled up beside him and the driver called out, "Sir, have you finished with me, if so, I'd like to be paid". Barry looked round. Jumped in the cab. Gave the driver his address which was miles away, and said, "Sorry my friend. I got carried away there for a moment". The cabbie replied, "I know what love does to you, don't worry about it".

CHAPTER 31

"Barry, I've got an idea. You know how the Islington Parade is coming up soon, well they also have stalls down Market Lane that are not your typical fruit and veg, but all manner of interesting stuff including arts and crafts. I was thinking that you might like to sponsor a stall with me and a couple of the girls who are willing to help out. We would be under The Thrift Shop banner, and we would sell the soft toys, the Chinese scarves, the wooden toys – that no one else would have. These would all make inexpensive but great Christmas presents, and the profits would go to Mind Games, what do you think?"

Barry was used to Sarah striding into his office with ideas, and because she was smart and good intentioned, he always sat back and listened, and after the tornado had erupted and was now spent, and she had flopped down in a chair, it was then his turn to speak.

"Sarah, you never cease to amaze me with your ideas and your good heart. Have you spoken to any of the others about this, as they may not want to volunteer?" "Oh yes, and they are all for it, so if you want to say yes, then my mate down at the council will save a stall for us".

Barry commended her on her enthusiasm and dedication to the cause. "The girls don't get a chance to contribute directly, as we don't have a lot of spare cash, so we thought this might be another way".

"I will only allow this, if you and your helpers take a day's pay for your efforts. You don't have to do this for free. Thank you for your good thoughts. Ask Milly if she can organize a table covering, a banner and a cash box for you, along with a stamp and duplicate receipt book. Remember to order in extra stock for the day. I understand it will be very busy. Get Reggie to organize a couple of lads to help you set up and carry the goods into the market. A long and wide table cloth will hide the gear under the table. Make sure they screw the cash box to the table, and nail the cloth to the table legs. That way no-one can lift the cloth and make off with the cartons".

"Blimey Barry, you've done this before, said Sarah". Barry's face lit up at the memory. "I used to have a stall down Petticoat Lane at one time. I know all the tricks those guys pull. The other one is while one bloke is asking you give him a hand with the trolley load he just overturned in the street, his mate is diving under the table and half inching your stuff. Another is that a bloke with a trader's apron on will start a conversation, and he will be biting into a sausage roll. He says he will mind your stall while you go and get some lunch. The offer is taken up. I've seen a stall stripped bare in two minutes by four blokes, each going off in a different direction. Very often, the gear is on another table round the corner in five minutes, being sold off as kosher".

The Islington Parade was a resounding success. Even though the day was crisp, the autumn sun was shining, and the crowds lined the streets then poured into the market lane, to see what was on offer. Sarah's stall was busy from start to finish, and not only had all the stock been sold by 2 pm, Sarah had arranged for more stock to be trollied in by Reggie's boys, so that they could work through to 6 pm. To everyone's surprise, Barry turned up at 5.30 to give them a hand to clear up. There was very little stock left for Reggie's men to move, and once the banner, the cash box and the cloth had been removed, they were clear to go. Barry invited the three women to dinner at Rizzo's Italian Restaurant around the corner. They all accepted. Before dinner was served, Sarah opened a cardboard box, to reveal the stamp, pad and receipt book and the cash box. "I've been keeping a tally, and we raised over 3800 Pounds today. If you take the cost of the goods out that leaves 3000 Pounds". Take out the cost of the banner, table cloth and Reggie's boys time, and we are left with 2400 Pounds. Barry reminded her that she now needs to take hers and the girl's wages out. "Me and the girls decided that we wanted to work for free, so that we could really contribute our time and money, so please hang on to the cash, and tell them it's from us girls". Barry was so moved that he added. "Well if you can do all that for a cause that none of you –as far as I know – are personally affected by, then the least I can do is to make all the costs disappear, and now you lovely ladies have just contributed the amazing sum of 3800 Pounds. Well done and thank you!"

When Barry told Enzio the boss of Rizzos Pizza what had happened that day, he immediately got out his mobile phone to call Rizzo. After a couple of minutes of animated hand waving, then finally "Bravo", Enzio told the gathering that the dinner was on Rizzo and he will also be donating 1000 Pounds to the charity. The four girls rose as one to surround and hug Enzio, who was weeping tears of joy. "My boss. E ad a boy, oo got urt in one of those war places, an ees ok now, but Rizzo knows ow bad it can be for the familee, so ee appy to elp". Barry got up and shook Enzio's hand. "Thank you my friend for organizing the donation and thanks for the meals. It's all very much appreciated, and your donation will certainly help. I'll get Millie to send a Certificate of Appreciation for your donation, which you can frame and hang on the wall".

Barry made sure that the amount was recorded as personal donations by the four women involved. Each of them received a lapel badge on the Monday, along with a Certificate of Appreciation. Each of them proudly talked about their involvement in the fund raising for the Mind Games with their customers, and so the word spread even further.

Monday morning saw Sarah rush into Barry's office. "I've just had another idea – that should have been done long ago. We need a donations box front and centre in the shop for the Mind Games. Any spare cash can go in it, especially if it's close to the till, and especially if that dozy Laura asks if the customers would like to donate their change to the charity".

The donations box and bolt down stand was made up quickly by one of Barry's artisans, with a large picture of the lapel badge underneath, and a sign on top saying, 'Mind Games. Helping Our Service Men & Women To Heal'. PLEASE CONTRIBUTE.

CHAPTER 32

From that first kiss, Barry knew where this was heading. He organized for his special table at Peligrini's to be free on Saturday. Auguste, the maître d', ensured Barry that his night for two, would be perfect, and yes he could arrange for the surprise to appear when Barry nodded in his direction. Barry then left a message on Denise's mobile that he had organized a date as they had agreed, the last time they had met.

Barry received a message in return, saying that she would be ready by 8, and would he pick her up from her place.

Barry hired a limo as he wasn't sure if he would be drinking. As it pulled into the drive, Denise walked through the front entranceway. Barry got out and walked around the rear of the vehicle and just stared at her. "I'm sorry, but I must have the wrong address. I wasn't told I was picking up an angel from here". She smiled and walked slowly to the car door that Barry was now holding open. When she was in, Barry leaned over and kissed her on the cheek. "Denise, you look radiant. I'm a lucky man". He nodded to the driver watching in the mirror. The limo purred forward, and on to the restaurant.

Barry had organized for his favourite four-piece string orchestra that specialized in slow to medium paced romantic melodies, to be playing. They were already into their first tune, 'You Raise Me Up', when they were shown to their seats in the bay window, looking out on to the lake where hundreds of floating lanterns of different colours, each illuminated by a single candle, swayed in the breeze, adding to the already exquisite setting.

The four course meal was the finest both of them had ever tasted, especially the main, where the thinly sliced veal was tossed onto a portable grill beside the table, before being placed into a silver dish, where a cream sauce was doused with cognac, then flamed, before the meat was added to the rosti potatoes, the florets of broccoli and cauliflower, with turned carrots resembling roses between them. During the meal they talked about their various families. He was 47, she was 45. He already knew her daughter Kirsty. She was surprised to hear that Barry had a son aged 25 – Trevor. His first wife had died of cancer five years ago.

She told him that her husband just upped and left one day, and eventually the divorce papers came through and she hadn't heard from him since. He and the other woman apparently now lived in the Bahamas. At least that's where he was three years ago. There was only her and Kirsty – aged 24 – at home.

After the main meal came the dessert, even though they had not discussed dessert, when Barry nodded to Auguste, the orchestra started to play The Anniversary Waltz, and Auguste wheeled in a trolley sporting a croquembouche with the words Happy Anniversary on it and a single lit candle on top of the cone. Denise knew immediately that it referred to their first face to face meeting just one week ago. Barry asked if Auguste would mind offering any of the cake that they did not eat to any of the other guests. Many accepted his offer and raised their glasses in a toast, as they savoured the delightful balls of crispy choux pastry filled with Crème Anglaise. The other patrons not realizing that their Anniversary was only one week old.

As the evening at the restaurant came to a close, Denise suggested coffee at her house. Barry accepted and called for the limo driver. At her house she suggested to Barry, that the limo driver might like to retire for the night as she could drive Barry home in the morning if he wished. That was exactly what he wished. He placed a fifty Pound note tip in the palm of the driver before thanking him for the great service. The smile on the driver's face matched that on Barry's.

There was no side and no secrets, as one drink led to another and as natural as it seemed to both, they retired to her bedroom and both wished that they had met sooner.

Next morning, Barry asked to be driven to his home on her way to work, so that he could change and get his briefcase.

The night had been exactly what he had hoped for. They made arrangements to meet again the following week when they would take a ride to Windsor Great Park to watch the horse racing, as it turned out they both were fans of. Barry would arrange for a picnic hamper to be supplied at the course. As the days were getting chilly, she needed to bring a heavy coat, but Barry would make sure they had a ground sheet and some rugs supplied also. "We could also go for a two hour pleasure cruise if you like".

CHAPTER 33

With Ming Su gone and Lonely Carruthers now Manager at the Kentish Town shop, it left Hilary, Jean and one relatively new girl holding the fort at the Angel, new faces were needed. Barry was on the phone to How Su, asking if she and her brother were managing ok. How Su told him that she had just lost her position at Marks & Spencer's, because she had had the temerity to tell her Supervisor that their displays were old fashioned, except that she then told management that, "I was continually being insubordinate and wouldn't obey orders".

"Well, if you were good enough to be selected for Marks & Spencer's, how would you feel about becoming one of the girls at the Thrift Shop. I know it's a step down for you, but you might have a more relaxed time here, and you can use your expertise to bring about changes, and it'll save you looking for another job, or you could work here whilst you look for another job".

How Su did not hesitate. "You know Barry, my Mum used to come home every night and tell us about the antics in The Thrift Shop. She loved working there. I would be proud to take her place. By the way, I also speak two Chinese dialects, along with German and passable French if that helps. When do I start?"

"How about Monday first thing. I'll let the others know to expect you. By the way it's full time, as we are very busy".

How went into the sitting room to tell her Mum and brother the good news. Ming was ecstatic for her, and started to pass on some tips, whilst also telling her that her pay would be less than she had been used to, but on the positive side Barry has a knack of promoting people who put forward good ideas and help the company grow. "Mum, I will have my own way of doing things after I have got the lie of the land, but thank you for your offer of help. Just tell me about the other people working there so I can have a heads up before I start".

CHAPTER 34

Lonely had built up the soft toys section, and it had been an amazing profit centre, before Lonely was despatched to Kentish Town, where she again was overrun with soft toy buyers, way before the builders had even started to work on the building, she had set up various departments all by herself. It was soon one of the most profitable sections of both shops. There was a soft toy for every occasion and the styles were always changing. One day a well-dressed man asked Lonely if the shop was able to customize a particular soft toy. "What did you have in mind, Sir"? "Well my company is the King Group, and I am looking for a mascot. A mascot we can use in our advertising, and one that we would like to give away to our clients, who would either leave them on their desk or cabinet, or give them to their kids or grand kids, so I have in mind a purple coloured bear, with a yellow face and a cheeky grin. He would be wearing a gold crown and have the words www.kingroup.co.uk embroidered on his chest. I would need to see a sample first, and if it is what I am looking for, then you can quote me for 30,000 units, then it will slow down to around 1000 units per month".

Lonely tried to hide her excitement as she took the man's business card. She wrote on a separate sheet of paper. Jonathon King. CEO. King Group. 041 030 2033. Soft Toy. Bear. Purple. Gold crown. Yellow face. Sample (price?), then 30, 000 units, then 1000 units / month.

"Thank you for the opportunity to quote Mr. King". I will be back to you with a quote within a week if that is ok with you?"

"Oh, there is one more thing. I need to give these soft toys away just before Christmas, so you only a little over two months to get the 30,000 units to me, so a speedy sample along with prices would be good ASAP. Another thing. If the 30, 000 units do not match the quality of the approved sample, then I will not accept them, is that understood?" "Perfectly Mr. King". "Ok then, from now on, please call me Jonathon".

Lonely could not wait for the man to leave the store before rushing in the see Barry. "Barry, this guy just left the store. Here's his card, and here are my notes as to what he wants. What do you think?"

"You get to work contacting Martha about this. Let her know also that we will be needing more stock for when Kentish Town kicks on, as we work towards opening day".

"You need to know Barry that Martha and I have been talking a lot this past week. She wants to retire, so I asked her about how we would be able to continue buying stock from China. She said that she had been treated very fairly by you, and no one had attempted to go behind her back or source product from other suppliers. I told her that's because she had been doing a great job, and had also looked after us very well too. I also told her that in fact I had gotten prices from other potential suppliers, but had found out that her margin is only 10%, so I thought it best to stick with her rather than buy direct, as she had all the contacts. Martha told me that she appreciated the business, but in the light of this potential order and the business growing, it was time to hand it over – everything - all the contacts, numbers, e-mails – everything - for free, to you. I asked her to put all that in writing. What I was wondering, could I have a stab at organizing the soft toy buying, and could you see your way to paying Martha something for the goodwill?"

Barry just gasped at the revelation. He picked up the phone and asked Milly to step into his office. Lonely was not sure what to expect, but presumed she had overstepped the mark and that Milly was about to make up her severance pay.

Milly greeted them both then sat down. Barry asked Lonely to repeat what she had just told him. Milly then looked at Barry and said, "What do you want to do Barry?" He replied with. "I think we have a future Group Manager on our hands. I am very happy to let Lonely run with this. What I need to know from you Milly, is can we fund the growth, and this special order without making too big a dent in our cash at hand or our cash flow". "There is no problem at all provided Lonely secures the contract with a 50% deposit, refundable if the goods are substantially – and the emphasis is on substantially – different from the approved in writing sample. Do you think you can handle that Lonely?"

"I can and will, if you give me a chance. I will need some guidance from you Milly to organize paperwork and contracts, etc."

Barry told Lonely, that he would consider her status after she had looked after this deal, and after she had taken over without a hitch from Martha, and, "yes, I will offer her an amount of money for the goodwill, after she has handed over all her contacts and pricing to Milly, who will work with you for the next six months to make sure you know how to handle the suppliers – especially in China. It's not what you might expect, believe me, and take a tip if you will, mine Martha for as much of her knowledge before she goes. Put as much in writing as possible, and share it with Milly".

Lonely knew that Barry was taking a big chance with her, as she had no formal business training, and was jumping into a potentially big business deal very early on, but she was determined to show him she could do it, and so she set about methodically researching the notes she had requested from Martha. She didn't tell Martha everything about the deal, as she wanted to do as much as possible for herself.

Her first task was to shoot an e-mail off to the company in China that produced this type of soft toy. They immediately responded with. "Very sorry, but unless you can guarantee an initial order of 50,000 units, and you supply the drawings in 3D, and pay US$420 for a prototype, we are not able to assist you. Lonely bit her lip. She had looked through Martha's contact list. She had trolled the internet, and was about to go back to Martha for guidance when she noticed a Chinese search engine called Alibaba. She typed in 'soft toys', and up came hundreds of possible suppliers. She scrolled down until she saw the type of toys she was looking for. In fact one was almost perfect, apart from having no embroidery on the back. It also had the word King on the bear's chest.

This company was more sympathetic, and could indeed supply the bear with the embroidered web address on the bear's back. The cost to courier a sample to her would be U$95.00. The company would guarantee the quality to be the same as the sample, or they would be happy for them to be returned at their cost with a full refund guaranteed. "Of course we could supply by November, provided the sample was approved quickly". Armed with that info, she dashed off an email, thanking them for their prompt reply, and could they send the sample immediately it was ready. She asked Millie to attend to the Telegraphic Transfer to their bank. Milly was impressed – so far.

The sample arrived three days later. Lonely telephoned the office of King Group and made an appointment to see Jonathan King. A 9 am appointment for the next day was arranged. Lonely took a taxi, and arrived in a black fitted skirt, red blouse and black bolero cape with a silver thread running through it. Jonathon King was already impressed – with her. 'A good start', she thought. And expressed under her breath, "All I have to find out now. Is this lion in the bag, the one he wants"?

Lonely showed him the sample and explained that they could meet the terms of his expectations and that the quality would be guaranteed or his money refunded in full, and The Thrift Shop would pick up the tab for shipping them back to China – "Which I am sure will not happen, but that's the guarantee that we are offering you".

The price for each 'King Bear' as we have named it, is U$3.40 or 2 Pounds 20 pence. I understood from our initial talk that you were proposing to post them to your clients. I have had a word with our supplier, and due to the quantities involved, they are also prepared to vacuum pack each bear in a sealed pack. This way, the bear will be flat packed and will fit through a standard letter box, so your postage will be only slightly more than regular post – due to the size of the envelope. Your client will get a pleasant surprise when they break open the clear bag, as the bear will slowly fill out the spun poly interior as it fills with air. This service is free of charge if you decide to go ahead. By the way, I called into an independent testing station on Friday and asked for an opinion as to the safety of this product. They declared in writing that it not only conforms to standard but is substantially better than most soft toys, and is suited to boys and girls of all ages as there are no loose parts. She showed him the letter. "I will give you a copy if we go ahead. The price includes shipping in cartons on pallets to your warehouse, the address of which I looked up on line. This relates to the 30,000 unit first order. We would then ship two lots of 6000 units twice a year instead of 1000 every month. Total order quantity over 14 months is 42,000 units. After this time, we reserve the right to re-negotiate everything".

"Our terms are 50% deposit along with your Irrevocable Order. The funds must be in our bank – our banking details are in the quote", she handed it to him, - "before we can order on the factory. When the goods are on the water, we expect the balance of the funds to be paid within 7 days. If the balance is not forthcoming, we will not release the goods, and after 30 days we will have the right to sell the goods or return them, and you will lose your deposit. These as you know are standard commercial terms".

Lonely had been soaking up Milly's and Martha's information in very short order. She sat back in the padded Chesterfield armchair and watched Jonathon again look at the bear, then look at the contract.

"Miss Carruthers, we have a deal". He held out his hand to shake hers. He then lifted the desk phone and asked his secretary to come in. "Please take Miss Carruthers to Accounts Payable and ask Ernie to start the ordering process and to pay the deposit requested, based on this quote" – that he handed to her. "I will take you up on the vacuum packing system Miss Carruthers. It will certainly save us postage, and in fact makes your offer one I cannot refuse. Well done. I look forward to meeting you again, for a progress report". Lonely turned and walked out after the secretary. She paused mid-way and turned back. "You may remember that my name is Lonely". He winked and said in a hushed tone. "I know. I will call you".

Lonely was keen to get back to work to report to both Milly and Barry about how well it had gone, and when she presented the deposit cheque to Milly, Barry and Milly exchanged smiles. "So lonely, run through the figures for me again". "Well you told me that the bottom line was the most important, and the order was only worth chasing if the margins were worth the effort. The total order is worth 92,400 Pounds. The margin is 45%, so net profit is 41,580 Pounds, and we already have his 50% deposit of 46,200 Pounds, so if it all falls in a heap, we will be better off by 4620 Pounds.

Oh, and there are two other things. "Milly, I was reading that we can lock in the price of US dollars that we pay the Chinese, so that we are covered by currency fluctuations. Is that correct?" Milly confirmed this and said she would take out a contract straight away. "Secondly, although the Chinese advertise their prices in US dollars, they have told me that they actually prefer Euros, and as the exchange rate favours the Euro against the US Dollar, we might get a better deal, and they would be happier". Milly made a note to check this out and looked to Barry. "This lady is fast becoming as big a wheeler dealer as you"

"I think this calls for a coming of age drink down at the pub later. Ask the others if they'd like to come along at 8pm. I'm buying", said Barry. "Now Lonely, is there anything else we should know before you take over the world"? "Well just one other thing. I made a separate deal with this supplier, to send us a shipment of a range of their other soft toys at the same time, so we do not have to pay for shipping. I got samples along with the 'King Bear' and have had Martha look them over. She says that the quality is excellent, and the margins are much better than many of her suppliers. I hope that was all right by you". Barry had nothing but admiration for her guts and business acumen.

The Chinese manufacturer was ahead of schedule, and had sent the back and front panels off to another company to get embroidered. When the samples came back through the email to Lonely for approval, she noticed that they had put www.kunggroup.co.uk on the rear panel. Lonely e-mailed back describing the mistake, and for them to tell her when the second sample was ready for approval. It took just one hour for that to happen, along with '1000 apologies'.

Lonely was keen to get more of this type of work, so she began to phone around other large corporations. On the rare occasions she was able to get through, she asked to talk with the person in charge of advertising and promotions. The reception was lukewarm and even though they had her contact details, no one was buying, until one day she hit on an idea. She contacted a magazine that specialized in company promotions and placed a quarter page ad in it, showing a cuddly bear with a company logo on the front. 'Free logo with every company bear', it screamed. 'Low cost, long lasting, cuddly, high quality bears to promote your company's cuddly image forever'. 'Free flat pack vacuum packing for orders over 5000 units'. The response was instantaneous. She fielded many calls from interested persons in just the first week, with one company accepting her quote on the Friday. By the following weeks end, she had another five quotes out there. Barry was impressed by her style and sense of urgency. He asked her to come into the office and close the door. She wondered if she had made a faux pas. When seated, he advised her that he and Millie had reviewed her work to date and the current efforts and ruled that it wouldn't be fair to wait until the New Year. She was therefore being given the title Import Manager – Toys, and her salary would increase by 40% immediately, and would that arrangement suit her. "That would be wonderful, thank you, but what about Sarah, didn't this new position collide with her job"? "No. She is overall buyer but because she has so much to look at, she is happy for you to look after toys. It helps her and allows you to concentrate on one area. After all, you have proven that this can be a profitable division, so it needs nurturing, and you are the right person for the job. Congratulations. By the way, how are your studies going"?

"I think I am learning much more out of school - with Milly's help - than I am in school, where most of it is about negotiating skills and determining profit margins, but it is all interesting stuff".

The end of November arrived, and the shipment of the commercial bears had been cleared and forwarded on to the King Group warehouse. Likewise, Lonely's new stock had also arrived just in time for the Christmas sales boom. All the new toys were an instant success, as they had never been seen anywhere before, and although the retail prices were actually cheaper, the margins were even higher, due to Lonely's buying power and price negotiations.

Jonathon King had not called Lonely since their meeting at his office. He emailed, mostly about this deal, but it didn't go any further. Lonely didn't think it had anything to do with her colour, but she had battled prejudice all her life and although things were much better these days, occasionally it reared its ugly head, so she didn't contact him, other than by e-mail.

CHAPTER 35

It was late November and the Kentish Town shop had just been finished. Lonely and the other girls had stocked and dressed the shop to match the first shop, and installed new staff all round after training them up at the Angel shop. The Thrift Shop style - which they had instructions to keep uniform to all future shops - was one reason why the new staff could integrate easily. It was almost a carbon copy of the Angel.

For the first week, each Angel girl took one day to go to Kentish Town to help out the new girls there. They were doing well even without help or supervision. The die was set. It was indeed possible to copy and paste, as Barry had seen for himself, when he and Milly visited after week one. He could duplicate this anywhere.

The beauty of this idea was that they didn't have to order in any other type of stock, just more of the same. The donated stock came in as always, and Barry was able to supplement the range with stock from his House & Garden Accessories imports and bric a brac and furniture from his Estates R Us businesses too. Each Thrift Shop was basically catering to the locals. They had neither the desire nor the need to travel further than necessary, so Barry asked Milly to determine just what number of people was right to enable each store to flourish without cannibalizing the others. Millie came up with a viability demographic of 10,000 people, so it would be possible to determine where next to open another store.

The same grand opening. The help from the local paper. The Mind Games association. This was a winning combination. Barry would be needing someone to head The Thrift Shop expansion up soon.

CHAPTER 36

Barry organized a bumper dinner for all the staff at a local restaurant, in fact he hired out the whole place for Christmas Eve so the staff could have Christmas Day with their families.

For the first time, Barry introduced Denise Evans to everyone. During the dinner he asked everyone for quiet as he made an announcement. "I wanted you all to be the first to know, that Denise and I are going to be married in the spring". A loud cheer went up and the drink flowed freely. "I also want you to mingle afterwards. Each of you has a name tag. It also shows where you work, so I would like you to introduce yourself to anyone you have not met yet. One day you may be working together. Remember that there are always opportunities to climb the corporate ladder – if you are that way inclined.

Since starting up the Angel Thrift Shop, we now have another Thrift Shop at Kentish Town. We have House & Garden Accessories and are looking for more sites. We have Furniture Fashions. We have Estates R Us. They all feed each other in some way. The more you can move around, the more you can be of use to your fellow workers, to yourself with more opportunities, and to us by making yourself indispensable. I encourage you all to maximize your opportunities here.

He called upon Barb to join him. "Barb has shown a willingness to not only take a Managers position from the start, she has gone on to become Manager of House & Garden Accessories. It has doubled in turnover in just under one year. It has been voted the most exciting retail experience in the gardening and home decorating space.

He then asked Sarah to come up. "Sarah started with us as the ferreter. The person who approaches customers to see what they are looking for. Her own fashion sense and her clothing displays brought many people young and old into the store. Sarah is whip smart. She volunteered to start up Kentish Town. She now has the title of Stores Manager, so she will oversee all the stores – and I have many more planned believe me.

Reggie was next. "Reggie has been a reluctant star from day one. He has been dragged kicking and screaming into managing our logistics, removals, trucking and storage systems that have grown exponentially. He now looks after all goods and freight that is ordered from around the world. It is his job to make sure you all get the things you ordered in time and in one piece".

Hilary was asked to join them. "Hilary was one of our founding members. She has a rock solid reputation for fairness. She settles things down when they overheat. Her temperament is very much suited to keeping the Thrift Shop on an even keel. We can all learn from her. She does not want to further her career. She is very content to do a mighty job every day.

Jean was asked to step up. "Jean is our security expert. An ex Inspector, she has saved our bacon on a number of occasions. She sees things that ordinary mortals miss. She is diligent and still serves all of us by keeping us safe".

"I want to personally thank all these people for embarking on a journey with me when the Thrift Shop opened. Each of them have contributed above and beyond any expectations I had at the time". The applause filled the room and only died down when Barry lifted his arms for silence.

"Later staffers include Lonely", who was asked to stand up. "Lonely has just cut her first deal on soft toys and is now Manager - Soft Toys, which threatens to be the most profitable section of the Thrift Shop. She is looking for more corporate deals, and she tells me she is now looking to wholesale toys to regular outlets. You can't keep a good woman down".

"Ming Su, who unfortunately cannot be here tonight is fondly remembered for her pioneering work with Asian fashions. Her daughter, please stand up, is How Su. She has stepped into the breach and is performing wonderfully well".

"Milly, please stand up, is next to me and is our financial whiz. Without her the businesses would be in a mess. She has been instrumental in mentoring anyone who has needed financial advice. She also stops me from spending unwisely. She works with Jack our external accountant employed by one of the big accounting firms".

"Michael Stanning is our Group CFO. He unfortunately cannot be here tonight. He is in Prague, overseeing a deal that Barb started, related to an amazing new range of artisanal sculptures. He is arranging the financing and shipping of dozens of crates that are ready to be shipped, so that our Homes & Gardens Centres will have this stock in by the spring".

"Julian Morrow is the Furniture Fashions Manager and publicist extraordinaire. He is mainly responsible for promoting Mind Games along with Kirsty Evans - Denise's daughter, and Jodie Marshall the full time coordinator".

"Martha is the previous owner of Soft Toys R Us. She sold her business to me, and has been instrumental in helping us to grow bigger and better in soft toys".

"Welcome to all the newer members of staff taking up positions vacated by the go getters, and staff manning the new Thrift Shop in Kentish Town. Remember if you want to better yourself, there is probably no finer group to be associated than this one. Never be afraid to come forward with ideas. We will listen to all of them. If they can't fly, we will tell you why. If they can, we will investigate them. If you feel capable enough, you can 'own' them too.

"In February we host The Mind Games. You all know about it. You all have been a major part in raising funds for it – even if you didn't know it, because a percentage of profits is donated to Mind Games each month.

"Next year is going to be huge, so hang on to your hats and come along for the ride. Thank you all".

As the evening wore on, Barry and Denise slipped away to enjoy each other's company back at his place. They didn't surface until Christmas Day lunchtime.

CHAPTER 37

A press release went to the front page of the Islington Times. It then spread to other London and regional newspapers.

CHARITY OPENS BOOKS. CHALLENGES ALL OTHERS TO DO THE SAME.

The copy read, 'Barry Baines, the entrepreneur behind Mind Games, the charity dedicated to looking after the mental welfare of active and returned soldiers and support for their families, is only one year old, but by publishing their first years accounts, it is turning the charity 'industry' on its head, as charities are protected by law from disclosing donation and expenses figures.

Barry's figures highlight just how much money has come in and from where. What expenses the charity has incurred. Where the charity is going, along with side notes about the charity 'industry' as a whole.

The side notes are also causing an uproar. Apart from some charities already lobbying the government to prevent Barry Baines from full disclosure, Barry cites: A. The 'industry' is worth 2.8 billion pounds. Larger than any corporation, yet they do not have to disclose anything at all, and they are tax exempt. B. As there is no disclosure, donors do not know how much of their hard earned money actually gets to the recipients. It is understood that as much as 75% of all donations is taken up running some charities.

Barry Baines has changed the rules. A good percentage of monies to run Mind Games comes from proceeds from The Thrift Shop, the first at the Angel, the second at Kentish Town. There are three more Thrift Shops to open next year. House & Garden Accessories, Furniture Fashions and Estates R Us - Barry's other businesses, all donate a proportion of their earnings to Mind Games. Donations boxes in the store also help gather up loose change. Functions, personal and corporate donations make up the rest. Donations this first year total 85,000 Pounds. Mind Games in conjunction with the British Pubs Association have been holding events up and down the country, and the Association alone has donated 12,000 Pounds.

Secondly Barry is breaking the mould again. Instead of persons in need, having to travel to see a specialist, Barry has approached every mental health facility around the country and asked them to supply a fully trained psychiatric nurse once a week. The Mind Games foundation will pay for the nurse. She will be given a list of persons or families to call on every week, until they no longer require her services. So Barry gets a fully trained person, and the client doesn't have to travel. Simple but brilliant. Mind Games has seven nurses under contract to date. This number will increase to 15 next year.

This is Simon Temple signing off, with a good news story that I personally believe should be emulated by the other charities. This is not a call to close ranks. This is putting you on notice that you need to change. Become more efficient. More open. Or become irrelevant'.

Then, a final plug. The Mind Games finals are being held in February at The Royal Theatre. All donations to www.mindgames.co.uk

The anticipation had been building up since Christmas. The press had been primed for two months that the February finals were going to be the highlight of the year, and that they had all been invited to attend the gala presentation at the Royal Theatre, where all the winners would be congregating.

Kirsty had even persuaded ITV 7 to video the proceedings, and that it could also screen live on the night. Julian Morrow organized all of the entertainment and prize givings. His coup was to bring back into the spotlight for the presentations, Mike Bradford-Jones from the hit ITV 7 show, Houses Into Homes. MBJ had a list of ideas that he wanted to put to Barry. The main thing that is was to be a slick fast moving show, with plenty of entertainment.

The TV rights would remain with Barry. He could use the footage however he wished. ITV 7 was willing to pay the charity 3500 Pounds for the right to show the proceedings on TV at any time, for any number of times, anywhere in the world. He asked MBJ about the deal. He went to the head of programming and got them 4750 Pounds and a 5% residual.

The day finally arrived. All their hard work was culminating in this one night, to display to the world what it was that they were trying to achieve.

'Ladies and Gentlemen, thank you for attending this one off, sold out, theatre production. All proceeds after theatre expenses will go to the Mind Games charity, which is why we are here". The MC was Billy Blogg, a local comedian. "Have you ever noticed how little kids always ask, "Why"? Every answer is always followed by another, "Why"? I told my little girl Emily when we went to the zoo, that Giraffes have long necks so that they can get to the leaves high up in the tree. "Why?" I should have remembered that that was going to be the next word out of her mouth, but I lost my cool when I heard it. I answered, "Because when little girls keep asking "Why"? All the time, giraffes will lean over the fence, pick the kid up by the neck and shove them up into the tree. Coincidentally, the giraffe started to lean over the fence. Emily ran screaming to her Mother. Mum. Mum. I promise never to say "Why" again. My wife looked at me as though I had belted Emily with a big stick".

"We have for you tonight a spectacular of song and dance and magic – ooooh! Your host is that popular presenter from Houses Into Homes, Mike Bradford Jones". Mike walked on to heavy applause. He reminded them that, "All the performers are donating their time tonight, for this very worthwhile cause - Mind Games. Your first act is Emily Jones with her new hit, befitting the occasion, "I don't want your charity". Next, an amazing magician Lu Fu, wowed the audience with his card and mind games. Billy Blogg came back on stage and guided the audience through an old fashioned sing along, with the aid of as big screen and words that brought back memories of London in war time. Then Billy Blogg introduced the audience to Barry, who gave them some background to the Mind Games charity. To a resounding applause, MBJ came on again - as Barry left the stage - to advise that the winners would be announced after the 30 minute interval. Half the audience left their seats to go to the loos or to get drinks at the bar – or both.

Just before the start of the second half, the lights dimmed and the orchestra tuned up, then the lights fully went down as the orchestra played the intro to a tune. MBJs voice over, introduced Emily Jones singing the new Mind Games signature tune written especially for the charity, called, "If you don't care – who will"? Emily walked on humming the first few bars, then slipped into the catchy song.

'I can pass you every day, you look just fine to me. But I don't see behind your eyes, to catch your misery. It's only when they say you've broken down, that I take notice and I frown. I wish I'd asked you before now – how're you doin' today'?

The stunned silence at the end of the song, told Emily that she had captured the hearts and minds of all those present. When the audience realized there was no more, they stood as one, whistling, yelling and cheering her off the stage.

MBJ walked on stage whilst the audience continued to clap. He put his hands up for quiet. "Emily wrote that song just for the Mind Games charity. She is donating all proceeds to the charity. The song will be used on every stage and commercial to remind us all that if only we would ask – "how're you doin' today"? We might prevent a mental overload by helping those in need, by at least sharing in their troubles. The men and women served and serving in our armed forces and their families need our help. We can help them through Mind Games. Please give your full support to Barry Baines and Mind Games as we bring Barry back on to announce the winners".

The new theme tune wafted through as 20 people filled the stage. Ladies and Gentlemen, I give you the winners, brought here tonight from all over the UK, of the Mind Games tournaments held in conjunction with the British Pubs Association who have kindly hosted the Mind Games up and down the country. The games included Chess, darts, cards, cribbage and many others. The aim was to get service personnel out of the house and to get them to mix with others. They didn't have to have any mental trauma, it was just a meet and greet exercise. Please welcome ex Lance Corporal Amanda Reeland.

"Thank you Barry. When I heard about Mind Games, I thought that meeting up with service personnel other than those I had served with, would be a great way to expand my circle of friends, after having had both my legs amputated after a tour of Afghanistan". The audience gasped. "As you can see, I can walk very well and don't need any sympathy, but what I always needed was to talk about it, especially with other service personnel that had been through the same as me. The Mind Games came at the right time.

I registered on line, then turned up one night at my local. I met up with Joe who had been battling with PTSD since he returned home. I told him my tale, he told me his. We only played darts for an hour then retired to drink and talk. He told me that his nightmares, stemming from the horrors of his particular war experiences, just wouldn't go away. I understood. I also understood that he couldn't possibly talk to anyone who hadn't been there.

Joe had talked with Veterans Affairs. They told him to come in – by appointment – as they were always busy. He told me that they listened, but dispassionately. They prescribed a number of drugs – mostly to dull his senses. Joe didn't make it to the next pub night. He took his life by walking into the sea. Another gasp from the audience.

I met his family. They are devastated. His wife had been expecting something like this for a long time, but still it came as an almighty shock.

I am hoping that Mind Games will help some of my current and ex-service mates and their families by filling in the gaps that government run programmes can't do or can't do well. That's why I support Mind Games. I won 50 Pounds in our local tournament. It was the most fun I'd had in a long time, and I now have not only many more friends to talk with, but I also have the support of a Mind Games counsellor, who not only visits once a week, but is also on call 24/7 if I need to talk. I am giving my 50 Pounds back to Barry as a gesture of my goodwill in return. Thank you".

There was not a single dry eye in the house. Even Mike Bradford-Jones came on with a handkerchief to his eyes. After composing himself and with a crack in his voice, he said, "Thank you Amanda. You have helped us all understand why Mind Games is so important. It may not affect us personally, but if we can help those that are suffering from war related sicknesses, then we are making a difference to those who are keeping us safe". It can also be seen that the prize monies are not what gets service personnel to the Games. That money may buy them a few groceries or a round at the pub. It says well done for participating and giving of your effort. For those who take it seriously, it is also recognition on our leader board that will inspire the others that come behind you.

The lights went down. A single spotlight highlighted a soldier drawing a bugle to his lips, who then played The Last Post. The audience clapped in appreciation. "Before I ask all of our winners and Barry to leave the stage, I have a surprise". A second spotlight shone on a soldier wearing a powder blue beret, saluted Barry. "Captain Trevor Baines of the United Nations Peace Keeping Force in Kabul – Barry's son, has been given special dispensation to attend this auspicious night, so that he can celebrate with his father and with us, the success of the Mind Games charity. Barry walked across the stage and embraced Trevor. Barry cried tears of joy. They left waving to the audience as the winners filed off too.

"Ladies and Gentlemen, we are going out this evening with a recital by the massed band of the Scots Dragoon Guards. The first tune is, "My Soldier Weep No More". The second is, 'Welcome Home'.

Thank you all for attending and for your support. Please spread the word whenever you get a chance. On your way out we have a gift of a Mind Games lapel badge for each of you. It will remind others that you support a very worthwhile cause, and it will be an icebreaker to lead you into conversation about the charity.

From Barry, Trevor, myself and all who participated in tonight's celebration. Thank you.

The auditorium filled with stirring music from the bagpipe led brass, wind and drums ensemble, dressed in tartan kilts and plumed caps.

CHAPTER 39

Barry was surprised to get a call from Reggie one cold January Monday morning. "Hi boss, we're here at 'Costyn Lodge' in Cambridge, the same place you came to a week ago. I've got your inventory and we are starting to clear things out, but this bloke called Pickering Remorse Costyn has arrived and told me to stop what I am doing as it's illegal. He says that his Mother bequeathed everything in the house to him in her will. He's shown me a copy and it seems to be legit. What do you want me to do?" "Put him on Reggie".

After a rustle, a deep voice said, "P R Costyn here. Are you the one who wants to steal my legally acquired goods from my Mother"?

"Hello Mr. Costyn. I also have a legally binding contract signed by Emily Grace Costyn who claimed that she had no kin, and that she had clear title to all of the goods in the house. She was in perfectly sound mind, and the signing was in front of and witnessed by, Mrs Grainger the housekeeper / cook. Her only staff member apparently. Mrs Costyn checked off each piece personally as we went through the house. I am sorry, but my signed affidavit dated one week ago, would appear to overrule your papers. Please put me back to my employee Mr. Green".

"You can't just dismiss me Sir. I have a legal claim and I am going to pursue it. You may not remove or sell any item in that house. It is my ancestral home, and you are desecrating it".

"Now I'm telling you – SIR", replied Barry irately. "You come back with a court order any time, and I will present it to my legal team for analysis and comment. Meantime, you have five minutes to vacate the premises, before I ask Mr. Green to call the Police. We have instructions to clear the premises of all the goods sold to us, and you are advised not to hinder my men. Now pass me back to Mr. Green".

Reggie took hold of the phone. "Reggie carry on business as usual. If that tosser interferes, call the Police and have him removed – unless he comes up with tangible evidence that, a. he is who he says he is, and b. that he has title to those goods. Bring them all back to Warehouse 2 and leave them in one corner, with a cordon around it and a notice that the items are not to be touched by anyone until I clear them. OK"? "Sure boss. Got it. Can I tell this bloke to piss off now"? "Do what you like, just get that gear out of there".

Barry called Emily Costyn. The person answering advised Barry that Mrs Costyn had had a major stroke, and was in Chelmsford Hospital. They were not sure if she would be able to speak or even move again. Barry asked if her next of kin had called in to see her. "She has no kin as far as we can tell. We looked at her hospital records, and the Police have notified us that she was on her own until her housekeeper found her two days later. Her housekeeper was in the hospital by Mrs Costyn's bedside. Would he like to speak with her?

Barry spoke with Mrs Grainger and offered his sincere hope that Mrs Costyn would fully recover. Mrs Grainger was so sorry that she had had a day off, otherwise she might have been able to save her. Barry told her that it was just bad luck. "Please tell me if Mrs Costyn had any kin, because I have had a P R Costyn tell me that he is Mrs Costyn's son, and he wants to take all of her chattels, as he says they were bequeathed to him some time ago".

"What does he look and sound like"? "Well I've only spoken to him, but he has a plum in his mouth and he wore a blue cravat according to my man at the house. He was there the moment we opened up to remove the goods".

"It sounds like a fellow that came around from a gallery last year. He was asked to call in by Mrs Costyn, as she had a painting by Gordon Fischer she wanted appraised. The ghastly fellow just pulled the painting off the wall with no reverence at all. He looked at it quickly through a rather large magnifying glass, and announced that it was unfortunately a worthless copy. He put it roughly and unevenly back on the wall, and muttered that Mrs Costyn really needed to get her facts straight, and to stop wasting the time of a professional valuer. Mrs Costyn had been told – she told me – that her father thought it could be worth a lot of money, but after that obnoxious fellow left, I presumed she felt that it was indeed worthless. Maybe it wasn't after all". Barry thanked her and advised her that he would let her know the results of his findings.

"By the way, did this fellow tell you which gallery he belonged to"? "Fortunately, I was in the kitchen – next to the drawing room, so I heard everything that was going on in there. I looked round the door to make sure Mrs Costyn was alright, as the man raised his voice several times. He asked me to call a taxi for him, and when it came, he asked the driver to take him to Pimlico. That's all I can tell you I'm afraid". Barry thanked her once more, then rang off.

Barry called his now fiancé Denise. "You know many gallery owners. Who is the best to value a painting for me"? "Who is the artist darling"? "It's by Gordon Fischer"? "Oh. You mean Gordio Fischer. There is only one person in London who has specialized in his art for the last twenty years. Give Max Walker at Loris Studio in Piccadilly a call, and tell him I sent you. He will be glad to appraise it". She looked up Max's number. "See you about eight. Love you".

"Max at Loris. How can I help"? "Hi Max, my name is Barry Baines, fiancé of Denise Evans. She suggested you were the only one to be able to look at a Gordio Fischer for me". "Well Mr. Baines". "Barry please". "Well Barry, can you bring it to me say tomorrow after 10. I can test it better in my studio lab". "What is the subject"? "Um, I don't know. I guess you and I will find out at the same time. Let me have your address and I'll see you tomorrow, and thank you for your prompt attention". "Barry, if this a real Gordio Fischer – and I tell you now that it is very unlikely – then it will be I who will be thanking you".

Barry called into Warehouse 2 and asked the Supervisor where the Costyn job was located. He showed him and Barry pulled the painting from a wooden crate, where it had been stowed with several others.

He asked the man to put the crate into the back of his Range Rover, then drove off to Pimlico.

Max Walker greeted Barry enthusiastically. Barry advised him that the painting was in a crate with several others in his car. Max summoned one of the workers and asked him to retrieve the crate from the Range Rover out front, and to place it next to his bench in the lab at the rear of the studio.

"Tea, coffee"? "Oh no thanks, I'm keen to find out what we have here". Max pulled out the first painting. They all had ornate gold frames and were of a similar size. He placed it onto a small easel on the bench, and went over it with a large magnifying glass, then a jeweler's loupe – especially in the corners. He looked at Max and declared that although it was not signed by the artist, it was in fact a copy of a Fischer original. The copy was documented as being by one of the artists apprentices work, a Manuelle Castilliano, who later went on to become a fine artist in his own right, but his works, especially the early copies, would only fetch a couple of hundred Pounds in today's market. "You can see the very small initials MC in this corner". Barry was naturally disappointed and was about to thank Max, when he reached down to look at the next painting. "Might as well see what else you have here".

The next here paintings were in fact brush strokes over printed copies of well-known old masters. They were rejected out of hand, and placed beside the crate along with the first one. The last painting brought a gasp from Max Walker. He scoured the surface with his magnifying glass and his loupe. He checked the frame and the rear covering panel. "This is obviously the painting that you need me to value. This painting is catalogued as a Gordio Fischer work, but it hasn't been seen for 60 years. Tell me where it came from. Barry told Max the story. "Now I know all about this work. I received a call from Mrs Costyn last year, and sent someone to look at it. He declared that the trip was a waste of his time. He was not only a charlatan I found out a month later, but he was also wanted by Interpol for fraud. Barry told him what he knew about the man, and both agreed that he was looking to get his hands on this painting because he knew what it was worth. "By the way, what is it worth"?

"You'd better sit down old boy", said Max. The last Fischer sold for 120,000 Pounds. This is considerably rarer and in much better condition, plus it now has a provenance that we can verify. If it doesn't go for between 200 and 250,000 Pounds then I'm no valuer. In fact it would be my utmost pleasure to represent you and this work to the world – if you wish".

Next day, the person passing himself off as Pickering Remorse Costyn called Barry's office, and demanded to speak to Barry immediately. "Mr. Costyn, hello. It seems I owe you an apology. It appears Mrs Costyn – your Mother passed away last night, and my legal adviser has suggested that rather than get into a legal battle with you, I should be prepared to let you have the goods from your Mothers estate for the same price as I paid for them. My receipt shows that we handed over 3400 Pounds for the whole house lot, plus we incurred moving expenses of 840 Pounds. The goods are in my #2 Warehouse at 17 Bletchley Lane, Islington. If you care to meet me there and bring cash, a truck and some labourers, you can take the goods and no harm done".

"Tell me Barry, are there paintings listed on the inventory". "Just a minute Mr. Costyn, I'll check. Yes there are five in total. That's all of the paintings in the house". "I will be there in two hours and I will do a deal with you Barry. I will just take the paintings and you can have the rest, how does that sound". I'm sorry, but I can't discount the price. I still have to shift the furniture around, store it then sell it". "That's no problem. I will be there with the full amount in cash in two hours' time".

Barry phoned Jean and told her the story. She immediately phoned her Inspector friend and apprised him of the situation. "If you've got an Interpol fugitive for me, then this could mean a better working relationship between us, so that will be terrific, thanks Jean. I will meet up with Barry in an hour. I will have a plain clothed constable with me".

Barry had a Bill of Sale made out to Mr. Pickering Remorse Costyn, for the sum of 4200 Pounds, to be paid in full, in cash. In return he would be buying all the furniture and movables as described below, from Mrs Emily Grace Costyn of Costyn Lodge. It is declared that Mr. P R Costyn is legally the rightful owner of such chattels.

Exactly two hours later Mr. Costyn turned up in a taxi and asked the driver to wait for him. Barry approached him and shook his hand. "Again Mr. Costyn, I didn't realize you had a better claim than me on your Mother's chattels. Please come into the office". He showed Pickering the paperwork. Pickering looked down the list to where the paintings were listed and noted that none of them showed who the artist was. He was satisfied that all was kosher. He handed over the cash and Barry counted it. "If you care to sign there, I will countersign there, as having received the funds". They both signed. "Follow me if you would". Barry led him to the corner of the factory. He had pushed the crate with the paintings in under a painter's sheet. Pickering pulled out the crate, sorted through the paintings and recognized the one he wanted instantly, but showed no emotion. He picked the crate up and walked out the door. His taxi had gone and in its place another station wagon with an UBER sign in the front window. The lady driver got out and opened up the hatchback. "Sorry sir, but the last cab driver had an emergency, so UBER replaced your ride. Hope that is fine with you".

"That's ok. Just let me put this crate in the back". When the tailgate had been closed and the passenger seated in the back, the door opened. The Inspector jumped into the seat beside him. Sir, I do not know your real name, as Interpol advise me that you have several aliases". He then read the passenger his rights in law, and advised him that he was being taken to Putney Police Station, "To await Her Majesty's and Interpol's pleasure".

With a nod to Barry, Barry walked over and lifted the tailgate. "You won't be needing these Pickering or whatever your name is, and by the way, thanks for the donation to the Mind Games charity. I knew there was some good in you. For your information the Fischer will be sold and the proceeds will go to Mrs Costyn's estate, most of which I believe will then pass to her longtime friend and housekeeper Mrs. Grainger, who by the way is looking after her as she recovers from a stroke. You will be pleased to learn that Mrs Costyn is expected to fully recover, and to give the Police a statement of your involvement in fraud". He closed the tailgate and walked off with the crate.

CHAPTER 40

Denise looked radiant in yellow and red. She had asked all the women attending, to go to The Thrift Shop and pick out an ensemble. She would pay. The money would help the shop and the charity. She had been in the week before the wedding, and How Su had found her a beautiful slim fitted dress, that she said, "Shone like the sun, and was definitely the most ideal dress for such an auspicious occasion". Denise ran a blue wide sash around her waist and allowed the uneven tails to flow almost to floor level. A single rose was placed over one ear and her hair pinned back to reveal it. The glittering gold shoes finished the job. She was ready!

As she walked down the stairs to the lobby, the bridesmaids stared then clapped. They were all dressed in powder blue with a purple long cape and a wide belt of gold and gold shoes. They all left the lobby to join the extended limo, whilst Denise waited until the car with her father in it, cruised up behind the parting limo. He got out to admire his beautiful daughter and told her how radiant she looked and that Barry was a lucky man. They had timed it at 20 minutes to get from the house to the church.

Barry, his mates and son Trevor, were all dressed in grey trouser and tails ensembles, with a gold cummerbund and frilly fronted white shirts and gold bow ties. They all piled into another stretch limo, in time to meet the first one with the girls now outside, as it was just about to sidle off.

The church was packed with every member of staff who could possibly be there, along with hundreds of friends, families and well-wishers. Two TV stations supplied crews and three newspaper reporters were also there to interview the happy couple, after they had made their vows, and at the reception held at the local pub annexe. This was

Barry's way of giving a little back to one of the pubs that had helped the Mind Games along.

Between courses Barry had arranged for a band to play both modern and traditional tunes. The singer being very versatile and who took requests also.

The crowd diminished somewhat after 10 pm, when Denise and Barry left to start their honeymoon in Monaco, using an old fire truck complete with firemen standing on the sides and the back, to make their initial getaway back to Barry's place, where they had their bags packed and would be at the airport for the 10 am flight next morning.

Barry could not have wished for a better 18 months. So many good things had happened to him and now this.

CHAPTER 41

Barb Charming was never one to sit still, and since becoming Manager of this division she had attended buyer's school, where she learnt the art of negotiation and international trading rules, along with finance instructions and banking from Milly. All this, whilst re-designing the flow, format and displays in the store.

Michael Stanning was an 'oh too often' caller. Barb liked the attention, and liked the fact that as Group CFO, she could tap his brain for more information, especially as he had international exposure that she didn't have to date, but she was desperate to change all that, as it was surely time to go meet some of the suppliers and also to find new and exciting ones. She mentioned this to Michael, who arranged for her to accompany him to Prague in two weeks' time, as he had to talk with Barry's furniture suppliers and retailers, explaining to her that Barry traded both ways – which barb found fascinating.

She looked up everything about Prague that she could. It was spring so she would not have to take heavy winter clothes.

The first day they spent in Republic Square. Barb talked to as many stall holders as possible. The ones that interested her she took business cards from, and left them with hers. There just wasn't time to do business with all of them, but she at least had some contact numbers now.

One stall holder displayed a range of brightly coloured bohemian glassware. Some were decorative, others were figurines. Barb thought that larger versions of these would make interesting talking pieces. The woman told her that at her factory only 30 kilometres away, they produced the types of larger glass ornaments that she was looking for, and could she visit there tomorrow. Barb looked at Michael who nodded. "We will be there at 10", she said.

Another stall displayed unusual wooden items such as bowls that were three cornered or included stands made from one piece of wood. The craftsmanship was outstanding. Barb and Michael agreed that most of the items would sell well at H&GA. The seller stated that he could supply a container lot every three months, as he belonged to a group of like-minded workers who had set up a co-operative. The prices seemed reasonable, but Michael advised her that a container lot by road would cost around 1200 Pounds for the transport alone, so they should bring their prices down by 10% to which the seller agreed. "That was my first negotiating lesson", said Barb. Michael laughed. They moved on to other stalls and finally ended up at the tourist information booth, where they found out about other artisanal factories around Prague.

Over dinner, they planned the next day's excursions. Barb commented that although H&GA could use the items they had selected, the Thrift Shop could also sell many of the smaller items they had seen, and wouldn't it be better if they had a container every month but filled with a range of products instead of just one type. Michael agreed, and told her that she was a quick study.

'The Factory' was in fact a converted barn. It was noticeable because of its double story steeply sloped roof. In the grounds were at least fifty objets d'art. From soaring eagles, flamingos, wombats, and much more, they were fascinated to find around fifteen artisans, each working on a separate project in various parts of the factory. Welding, cutting, grinding and beating sheet metal, until it started to form an object of beauty. At the end of the large building a section had been portioned off for spray painting. There was even a large bath used for zinc plating. Beyond the first building was yet another only slightly smaller. It housed the finished goods. When they got to this building, another ten people were busy wrapping and packing them into lightweight wooden framed structures, that eventually made their way into containers to fulfill orders that had come in up to one month prior.

Barb and Michael sat down with Agnetta, who explained that they had forward orders for at least a month, for most times of the year except January and February. If they liked the range, they could fill one or more containers fairly quickly for those months. She advised that they did not currently sell into the UK so they had the market to themselves. After checking the prices against the product pictures, and conferring on mark ups - which Agnetta assured them could go up to 300% easily - "as our re-seller in France does". They retired to the lunch room at Agnetta's invitation where a hot lunch of soup and dumplings was on offer if they wished. They accepted and spoke further. Agnetta invited a couple of artisans who spoke English to join them and to tell their stories.

Barb was much more interested in the 'sculptures' after she realized that with the artist's permission, she could also offer a story behind each 'piece', along with a general story about the co-operative itself.

Barb and Michael agreed on a quantity and price, but told Agnetta that if she wanted their business, she needed to include freight to the store. Agnetta put pen to napkin and said, "I will shake your hand for an additional four Pounds on top of each piece. That equates to both parties sharing the transport cost". They shook on it, and after lunch went back to her office to complete the paperwork.

Barb said. "Well that takes care of large indoor and outdoor artistic pieces. Do you know where else we should look for House & Garden Accessories pieces whilst we are here"'? Agnetta said that about 10 kms east there was an old mill that houses more artisans, but somewhat lesser skilled. They specialized in recovering old items from country estates and re-furbishing them. Things like farm gates, milking stools, counters, doors, tools, machinery, and much more.

Michael said that they were going to visit CzechSki's Export Emporium. Agnetta advised against it. "Let your competitors buy that rubbish. You will be glad they did". They thanked her and invited her to London as their guest. "Thank you for all your help, too".

REFURB was in an old castle – fittingly. The owner was surprised to see two English people just turn up, as, "they were off the beaten track". "Hi, I'm Michael and this is Barb. Agnetta from The Factory suggested you might be a fit for us. We buy for a centre in London called House & Garden Accessories, and we are looking for unusual items that home beautifiers might like to add as a talking point, or they might like to replace their non-descript front gate with something ornate and unusual. I understand you refurbish local items".

"Indeed we do. My name is Roger. Most of the people you will meet are related. That way we give employment to our own. We work hard and we are fair with our prices. The castle has been in the family for twelve generations. The work we do helps pay for its upkeep. Let me show you around".

Passing through a tall arch into a courtyard, thousands of items had been placed in more or less obvious piles or were leaning against walls. As they passed into what Roger described as the old barracks, through a mighty oak double door, of which just one side was enough to pass though easily, a number of men, women and children looked up. Apart from one corner where sand blasting was taking place, most worked on wooded benches. Some were sanding, some sawing, some upholstering, and some painting by hand. A most industrious place, and one where each piece took shape from beginning to end at that bench.

At the rear, close to the sand blasting area, the iron and steel items were being either sanded, scraped, forged or repaired. It was noisy and dirty. A spray booth finished the package.

Roger showed them some ornate gates of every shape and size. "As you see, we find many beautiful pieces and restore or mend them. We do not have a price list, and we never know what is coming through the gate at any time. We also have no idea as to quantities, so if we do business, you need to trust us to give you a fair price and to load a container when we have enough product to fill it".

Barb jumped right in. "Who do you sell to currently"? "Most of it goes to Russia, or I should say went to Russia. For the past two months the buyer there has stopped any shipments. Apparently the economy has tanked and they are holding plenty of stock still".

"Can you give me some idea of the prices you have been charging your Russian buyer to date"? "Sure, come with me". Roger's office comprised a rear room that had been modernized, and sported all the latest in office equipment along with several computers. An older lady looked up and Roger introduced Maria as his Mother and Secretary. "Mother, could you please show Barb and Michael the last invoice for goods to Russia". Maria showed them the original then copied the sheet for them to peruse. Michael knew instinctively that Barb would be excited by what she saw, so he went straight in. "We have many more places to visit before we go home in a few days' time, so with your permission we will revert to you before we go – if that's ok with you. We have certainly seen what you can do, and we thank you for showing us around. By the way, if we should decide to do business with you, what throughput could you manage per month"?

"I think one maybe two containers would be our max". Roger asked Maria if she would mind calling for a Taxi for them. After a cup of tea, Roger showed them out.

In the taxi. "I was champing at the bit to make a deal with Roger, what happened back there? Why did you pull out"? "I saw you were busting to do a deal, and the first rule of business is, never let the seller know you are keen. We just needed to insert a break before you committed yourself. We have a copy of the Russian company and the name of the buyer. I suggest we contact them to find out if there is anything else we should know about REFURB. At this point in time we have lost nothing".

Barb calmed right down. "You're right you know. I'm such a novice. I'm very glad you're here to teach me". "You're welcome. By the way, did you notice how I asked Maria directions to 'Old Mansions'? That would have gotten back to Roger quick smart, so next time we talk, he would have it in the back of his mind, that we have an option". "God, you're so smart". "No, just been doing this for a long time. I picked it up as I went along, just like you're doing".

They did in fact go to 'Old Mansions', but were neither impressed with the range – or lack of it – the finishes or the prices. The Manager could care less who they were, but they got his name as a bargaining chip if they needed it.

In the hotel, Michael called the Russian buyer. Boris Slotzic told Michael that there certainly was a dive in the economy, and that in fact, the business was shutting down for good. Another gem of information that Michael could use in his negotiations with Roger he advised Barb.

Michael in fact left it until the last day to contact Roger. With Barb listening in on the hotel's extension phone, he advised Roger that he had spoken to his Russian buyer, then offered the news that they were closing down for good. He told him that there were a few in his area that offered the same range of goods that he did, and that some prices were much lower than his. However, he would have to buy from a few of them then consolidate the goods into one container, whereas if he bought solely from Roger then he could load from one source only. Michael's proposal was; if he would like to send all of his refurbished products to London - to them, then he would have to lower his prices by 5%, and throw in the container shipping for free. He would in turn supply him with a contract to supply House & Garden Accessories exclusively. If Michael found out that there was a breach, the contract would be terminated immediately. They could take up to two containers a month, and would use the Russian prices as a benchmark.

Roger agreed, and asked if they would both come to dinner at the castle tonight, where they would sign and exchange paperwork.

On the way back to London, Barb thanked Michael for the lessons learned. "I think that time away was probably worth as much as a full year in school". "You'll find that you need both real life experiences and schooling to fill in the gaps, especially the fiscal and the export paperwork and regulatory sides, so keep going and learn as much as you can".

Barry asked them both to come into his office the first day back to report on the trip. Barb could not contain her excitement. "Barry, look at these photos. Aren't these things the most gorgeous you've ever seen"? "They look wonderful Barb, but can we make a profit"? Michael assured Barry, that not only is his centre going to stock the most eclectic range of goods, nobody else will have anything like it, so we can put a good mark up on them, and we've ensured supply using non-binding – on our part – contracts".

Barb looked at Michael. "You didn't tell me they were non-binding on our part". "I would only bring up the detail if one of the suppliers offered us poor stock or wanted to increase the prices to an unreasonable level, and we wanted to end the deal. If that day doesn't come – fine. If it does, we're covered".

"So Barb, have you learned a thing or two travelling with Michael"? "Oh Barry, that was so good. I saw them making stuff. I saw the way they live. I learnt heaps about negotiating. It was so worthwhile. I think I could handle it on my own if necessary next time".

"Ok, well done you two. I'll look forward to seeing the products when they arrive".

CHAPTER 42

One of the world's greatest guitarists heard the Mind Games theme song, 'If You Don't Care – Who Will', and began playing with the composition. Rocko contacted Barry by e-mail, asking if he minded him offering Barry a more popular version of the theme song. Barry was intrigued and asked when. Rocko invited him and anyone else that might be interested, to come along to his recording studios in Brick Lane on Sunday afternoon, to see what they thought of it, as he thought it might be able to go commercial with some popular treatment of the backing.

Barry put out a flyer in the shops, asking if any staff member interested in hearing a new rendition of the Mind Games theme tune wanted to come along, just rock up at the address below, this Sunday at 2 pm.

What Barry failed to realize, was that Studio 47 was Rocko's own mansion. It had been converted into several studios at the rear. When a crowd turned up – as everyone else but Barry knew who Rocko was, and employees, friends, relatives and hangers on, all wanted to see Rocko.

Rocko addressed the crowd, and told them that there was not a great deal of room in the studio, but if they cared to go through the side gate, they would see at the rear of the property, a giant covered patio, with removable side panels of glass. If they took a seat, they could witness proceedings inside the studio on the massive curved screen, and that they could help themselves to coffee and biscuits from the outdoor kitchen benches.

Barry, and the writer and singer of the theme song - Emily Jones, were escorted into the control booth. In the largest studio were assembled a drummer, bass guitarist, keyboard, percussionist, two other guitarists, all of whom were busy tuning their instruments or running through riffs as Rocko entered the room. It became hushed as he picked up his guitar.

He nodded to the technician in the booth. The red lights went on. All the 'Don't Disturb. Quiet – Recording' signs lit up, and an unfamiliar intro to the song took Emily, Barry and no doubt all the guests by surprise, as the powerful organ wove a catchy melody through to where Emily's voice was first heard. Behind the words – which were strong and heartfelt in their content – a slow but ever increasing in tempo, using the powerful strains of the catchy bass back beat, built in crescendo, then gave way to Rocko on lead electric guitar, with soaring riffs then lower soulful registers with evocative key changes, that then reverted to the bass guitar. Emily came in for the second verse, whilst the sotto lead hummed away behind her. The second break saw the piano organ jump in and mimic the lead guitar refrain from the first break.

Rocko and his band had transformed a good and memorable song and tune into what Barry felt could be a truly international hit song. He looked at Emily who had tears running down both cheeks. The song finished. The green light went on, and the band chatted among themselves whist Rocko placed his guitar in the holder, then strode into the booth.

"I'm not sure if they are tears of joy or madness. Did we ruin your song"? Emily wiped more tears away. "I thought we had done a pretty good job with this song, but your composition just blew us out of the water. Thank you for seeing in it, what I could never have imagined it could be".

Rocko replied. "I knew from the moment I heard it, that it had a magical quality, not least because the subject matter and your words are so breathtaking, but deep down, I felt the backing was not doing justice to you or the song. I was hoping you would like it".

Barry asked, "What happens next"? "Well with Emily's permission, I would like her to record live with the band, so that we can compare levels, and make any changes she might want, either to her vocals or our arrangement, then to make it into a single for sale both physically and digitally. The band has agreed that we are happy to perform Pro Bono, and that all profits are to go to Mind Games. We all believe Barry that Mind Games is just the best charity, and we are happy to discuss our part in re-vamping this song with any interested media, if you both agree". Emily flung her hands around Rocko's neck, whilst Barry was happy to shake his hand, once Emily had let go of him.

Four weeks later the song entered the pop charts at number six. Two weeks later it was number one. Emily, Barry, Rocko and Mind Games received unbelievable media interest, with all three appearing on various TV and radio shows. The song was being played on every radio station. It was feared by Barry, that people would turn it off, as it was now beyond popular.

Royalties began pouring into Mind Games. Appearance fees swelled the coffers. Merchandising started appearing with T shirts proclaiming, 'If you don't care – who will'? 'Mind Games is playing with my mind'. 'Service Personnel Are Human Too'. The rear of the T shirts sported the web address of Mind Games.

In order to maximize the efforts of the merchandizers, Lonely came up with the idea that a free soldier soft toy bear be given away with every physical record sold. That idea went down so well that Lonely had to ship thousands of bears by air urgently just to keep up with demand. With 'Mind Games' on the back of each one, the message was being spread to the kids also.

CHAPTER 43

As Barry walked through the shop, Hilary asked for a moment. "You know Barry, I'm getting feedback from many of our older female customers that we don't have any modern style dresses for them. We have the Asian influence and we have young trendy gear, but all the older women get are cast offs from another era. Some of this stock hasn't sold for over two years now. We need a re-think urgently".

"Do you have anything in mind"? Asked Barry. "Well, you know how some departments sell only new clothes or a mix of new and used – but modern. I propose we look at talking with some of the makers or importers of some popular brands that are available in the malls, and look at buying some of their last season's stock. The prices would be good, and we would have more modern clothes for sale. It's at least worth while trying, what do you think"?

Barry retorted. "The clothes we get are donated, so it doesn't cost us any money". Hilary was ready for that one. "It's true, but if they sit here and no one buys them, we eventually have to throw them out, so we might as well pay for product that people want, and we can still make a good margin on, but it also turns over your initial investment several times a year". Barry was impressed, but played it cool.

"If that's what you are experiencing, and that is your solution, then from this moment on, you own it. I will leave it to you make the contacts, then ask Milly to discuss financing the stock. If you need me or Michael to help at any stage, just give us a call. Well done. You know, that's just what we need, people who are on the ball and can adjust to change".

Hilary, although used to looking after the general merchandise, was now involved in turning around a staid segment of the shop. She had better get to work. Taking a lap top to her work counter, whenever

160

she had the chance, she would enter Google to find out just who supplied the various brands she knew catered to the older woman.

The first attempt failed. "You want what? To buy our old stock, so you can sell it in an op shop? Are you mad woman? We'd never sell another dress to our regular clients if we did that". The line went dead. "Well that went well. I may have to change my approach". She rang the same number again. She re-introduced herself.

"I thought I made it clear that I can't help you". "Just hear me out. What if we change the labels? That way, you could get rid of your last season's stock at a reasonable price, rather than having to discount to almost nothing in a sale, which by the way diminishes your brand far worse than anything I could do. Your customers just wait for a while to pick up the same garment very cheaply, so why would they pay full price. If I take them and change the labels, well your regulars are not going to shop here anyway, so we both do well. What do you say"?

"Well, put like that, I suppose we have nothing to lose by showing you what we have available". Hilary sweetened the pot. We pay cash on collection. All we ask is that you accept returned faulty goods with no argument, and give us credit for those goods on the next invoice". The woman agreed. Hilary asked How Su to go along to the manufacturer with her, to get her opinion on styles, prices and anything else she did not have expertise in.

Hilary informed a meeting with Barry, Millie, How Su and herself, that How Su and she had visited a manufacturer and had come away with samples of their stock. She then compared them side by side with stock from the Thrift Shop. It was obvious immediately that they needed to change and fast. Millie took notes from How Su regarding prices, then cleared Hilary to buy up to 400 Pounds worth of stock as an opening trial. If they sold well, she could raise the limit, but to speak with her first. It did not take long for the regulars to comment on and buy the new stock. After getting a new label made up – Antonino's of Milan – the old labels were removed and the new sewn in. More mannequins were found and adorned with the new clothes along with some stunning scarves, sashes and hats from How Su. Some of the brooches from Jean's jewelry section came in handy also.

Jean suggested to Hilary that the shop may be liable for misrepresentation with regard to the label. Hilary explained that Antonino was indeed the label maker, and that his store was in Milan Lane, Shoreditch. They had a laugh and a cuppa. "What else can we take a look at"? "Looks like we now have a bigger and better range of clothes than ever before. I can't wait to see if it works", said Hilary.

CHAPTER 44

It was not every day, that sea trunks got left at the back roller shutter door, but today was the exception. There were three of them. Reggie asked Jean where she wanted them. "Are they open"? "I don't know, I'll check"? The first two were without padlocks and were empty. The padlock on the third smaller trunk was brass, large and formidable. Reggie tried everything he knew including brute force accompanied by a hammer and crow bar. Still it defied Reggie's best efforts. Jean came out to check on progress. When Reggie said he had given up, Jean said, "I'll be back". She went to her shoulder bag and from an interior pocket she produced a set of lock picks. He watched her work her magic. First the thin flat blade was inserted into the key hole. She jiggled something inside the lock. Over the top of the flat blade she inserted a jagged blade and moved it in and out until the hasp clicked open. All in all, about twenty seconds.

"Blimey, on the weekend I'm going to change my front and back door locks. Tell me which ones are pick proof?" "None really. I would need a little more time with some of the latest locks. Even the most sophisticated electronic locks can be opened with the right equipment and the maker's algorithm".

Reggie reached down and flipped the domed lid open, to reveal on top, some old fashioned men's clothing including two suits. Jean put on rubber gloves and laid the clothes next to the trunk after checking the pockets. Next was a thin leather briefcase, with papers inside that she did not inspect. Under the briefcase was a flat parquet inlaid box. She couldn't wait to find out the contents. It was a Colt 45 six shooter with pearl handle. It was not in mint condition and there was a bullet in every chamber. She gingerly removed the gun and found a plastic bag to put it in, but not before she had released the barrel and removed each shell carefully into another plastic bag. Under shirts and under-wear, clearly old, they found old Bank of England white paper issue 50 Pound notes. Jean estimated about 60,000 Pounds in all. She told Reggie what she was going to do, and for him to take photos and act as a witness. As Barry was away, she dialed her Inspector mate at the Station. He sent two detectives over to file a report and to take the trunk away, with a promise to get back to Jean as soon as they knew anything more. Jean wrote out a report for Barry, signed by her and Reggie, and left it on Barry's desk. As far as she was concerned, case closed!

Two weeks later one of the detectives walked into the store and asked for Jean. Jean asked Barry if the detective could come into his office, and that Milly should probably be a witness also. He explained that they had finished their tests on the trunk and contents, and it had belonged to a Henry Rhodes, who apparently travelled around the world looking after his diverse interests in North Africa, Italy, and America. The trunk was his personal sea trunk. They found identifica-tion, letters of introduction and visas in the briefcase. The hand gun was registered in his name for personal protection. He had a mansion in Baltimore, but it had been sold several times since he died, and it was no longer in the family. He had stayed in hotels when he trav-elled, and the Baltimore mansion was his only permanent place of res-idence.

There were next of kin, but they were twice removed and as such had no claim on the trunk or its contents. It transpired he had lost a great deal of money in the Great Depression due to the bank that he used had folded, and he no longer trusted any bank, so he paid for most things in English currency, as it being the only one he would trust. His word was his bond, and the trunk had been left at the back of a chandler's warehouse for the past fifty years, presumably after he had suffered a fatal heart attack, until they sold off job lots when the warehouse closed down recently. It would seem that the person who bought the trunks couldn't open one of the locks, so they left them all outside the Thrift Shop as a donation, so title to the trunks legally passed to the Thrift Shop once they were taken inside. The bank notes totaled 54,000 Pounds, and they were now in the large carry bag that the officer handed over. He advised that they could be exchanged for legal tender by taking them to the Bank of England along with proof of identity and a Police Report – which was also in the bag. Whether or not they were worth more as collector's items the detective could not or would not say.

The detectives also left the gun – in the case, but had kept the bullets which they would destroy. He handed Jean a packet full of papers, to do whatever she liked with, as they too could trace no relatives. Jean thought she might contact the local museum to see if they had an interest.

Barry was left with a dilemma. Whatever the bank note exchange amounted to, the funds were legally the Thrift Shop's, but it seemed unfair to make a profit from a donation of that size, so he assembled all the staff and explained. "The Thrift Shop came into approximately 50,000 Pounds. It was found in an old trunk. The money now legally belongs to the store. I thought about putting the funds in the profit column; then donating it all to a charity; but now I think on this occasion it should be treated as a one off windfall and shared equally amongst all the staff including the two van loaders, so it looks like Christmas has come twice in one year. I'm setting a limit of 1000 Pounds for each of you, and that includes office staff and Management, with any balance to go to Mind Games. Millie will control the distribution". There were cheers all round, with much chatter as to how each would spend their share.

CHAPTER 45

One of the Thrift Shop new girls, Bree Spencer, was hired on the premise that she probably was not a good fit for the store, considering the median age of the clientele, but they were willing to give her a trial. Jean was now in charge of staff hiring and firing, and her instincts had been on target up 'til now.

She liked Bree, because she was a scattier but better educated version of Sarah, who had mellowed somewhat since starting and taking on more responsibility. It was Bree's idea to make a calendar. She approached Jean and Sarah in the lunch room, and put forward the notion that other calendars including the London City Firemen, The Calendar Girls, and the Country Womens Association all had calendars, and it seemed they were a cheap way of not only publicizing a store or an event or a charity even, that it might be worth considering.

"But it's been done to death, and anyway, who wants to see a lot of old women parading around in cast offs," said Sarah.

"Ah, but I've got an idea for a twist, said Bree. "What if we featured it as The Four Seasons, and called it the Four Seasons of Charity. As summer will be with us very soon, we can get it ready for sale in the autumn. If we dressed up in skimpy tops, short dresses, cleavage and ass showing enough titillating bits – bits I said - not tits, then it would probably sell to all those pervs out there. All proceeds to go to the Mind Games charity. Every piece of clothing being from The Thrift Shop. Every 'model' on show already works at The Thrift Shop. Every picture is taken in The Thrift Shop, and maybe with a wide-angle lens so we can get more clothes in the shot. That way we kill three birds with one stone. Good for the charity, good for business, and publicity. We could even start to give them away in the autumn, or we could sell them to raise money. It should also generate enough publicity to get some of the girls on radio and telly too – especially me – I want to be a super model. What do you think ladies"?

Sarah retorted, "With assets and a face like yours, I could be forgiven for thinking this idea is to launch your fashion model career". "Well let's say it does. There's no harm done and maybe plenty of good. I can look after the fashion side of it. I just need a good photographer".

"Well the store uses Kirsty Evans, Barry's new daughter in law, and she has her own photographic team headed up by Mark, so you need to ask the rest of the girls first, then ask Barry if he approves. Tell him that he'll need to put up the money to produce the calendars, and I suggest before you do anything else, you contact a calendar printer to get some prices, because that's what Barry will ask – what's all this going to cost me", – mimicking Barry.

"Hang on. You saying this is all down to me"? Asked Bree. "Well you bloody well want to become a model. This is how you start. Go on and ask the others if they want to be in it. As for me, I can still flash a slim pair of pins and Jean here reckons she's still hard muscled due to her gym work". Jean looked at her in horror, turned and walked away, muttering, "I don't want any part of this".

Fortunately, Bree managed to convince most of the others in both branches that the photo shot would be a laugh, and, "who knows, you might be famous one day".

She contacted a couple of calendar printers, who gave her quotes that were not far from each other's prices. They quoted for 500, 1000, 5000 and 10000 pieces, on the basis that the art work was finished to a professional standard. They would add words as required.

"Ok, what's next? Girls ok. Tick. Printers ok. Tick. Kirsty on board with her photographer for 600 pounds – reduced rate. Tick. Sarah said something about marketing. I'll see if I can get London TV7 interested".

She phoned and asked for a reporter. "It's a matter of life and death". "Basil Edwards here. How can I help"? "I don't want you, I can only speak with a woman. He clicked the phone and a female voice asked, Jodie Graham here, how can I help"? Jodie its Kirsty Evans here. I want you to talk with Bree. "Hi. Bree Spencer from the Thrift Shop here. We are creating a titillating girls calendar for Charity and we want you to cover it. You know, get us some publicity. Can you help me"?

Jodie had heard some lines in her time. Everyone wanted publicity for something or other, and she remembered that Mind Games had been in all the papers and on tele earlier on in the year. "Is the charity Mind Games"? She asked. "Yeah. Do you know about it"?

"My uncle recently left the service, and he was telling me how much one of the Counsellors had helped him and his family to adjust to civvy life, so yes I do know about it. Give me your details and I'll see what the manager thinks about running the story".

Bree added, "All the girls are going to model Thrift Shop clothes only, and there will be some flesh showing. We will be giving many of the calendars away, and many will be sold. All proceeds go to Mind Games".

"Well it sounds like a winner, but there are many similar calendars around as you know. I'll get back to you soon".

Bree was on tenterhooks for the rest of the week. She received a call from Jodie. "I've spoken to my boss, and he says the story is not amazing enough for him to run on The Project – you know the early evening show, but it probably would get some attention on one of the morning chat shows. I suggest you do what you need to do, then call me nearer the time, and I'll see if I can slot you in somewhere. If you have an additional amazing angle it would go better for you".

OK time to front up to the boss. Bree asked Sarah and Jean if they would come with her early next morning before work started. Jean said she was busy, Sarah said she would hold her hand, but she better had done her homework, because, "Barry likes all the questions answered, before he asks them".

Bree asked Barry if she and Sarah could talk with him. He asked if there was a problem. She answered that they – she - had an idea, and wanted to run it past him. "Ok, I've got fifteen minutes max, let's have you". Bree crooked her finger at Sarah, who walked over and in and sat down next to Bree.

"I put the idea to Sarah and Jean, and they said I had to get all my facts straight before you would even consider it", she blurted out. There was a silence when Barry asked, "Would you like to tell me what it is?"

"Oh yes. Silly me. Well I thought we could do a calendar, using the Thrift Shop girls as the models. We only use Thrift Shop clothes. We show a bit of skin. We give away and sell the calendars. I've spoken to Jodie Graham from London TV7, and she thinks she can get us on to a morning chat show, and even more publicity if we come up with an amazing angle. I've talked with Kirsty Evans" – Sarah told me to. "She and her photographer can do the work for a discounted 700 Pounds. The calendar printer has given me quotes", – she handed him a sheet of paper with many figures on it. "It looks like we can make each calendar for 2 Pounds and sell them for around 2.75 Pounds each. We need an initial investment of 1700 Pounds for 500 calendars or 1900 Pounds for 1000 calendars. All profits to go to Mind games. What do you think?"

"I think that Sarah has asked you to do your homework before you approached me, and she was right. Seems you've done a good job, so far. What do you think of the idea Sarah?"

"All of the girls are behind it. They think it would be a lot of fun. Some don't want to model, but that's ok, we have enough with the both stores, and some doubling up. They don't want paying. It's only Kirsty and the printers where the costs come in. The bottom line is it's for charity, but it could generate a lot of good publicity for the stores and the charity, and we can think of a great publicity stunt, then we'll get even more coverage. I think Bree has done a great job, and it wouldn't surprise me if she didn't get an offer for modelling work after this, so be prepared to lose her".

Bree jumped in looking offended. "Sarah, do you really think I would do all this just to get into modelling?"

"Yeah, but if it does us some good on the way, then I say good luck to you. With your ambition you'll go far. We can always claim that we started you on your career".

Barry said. "If you Sarah, can keep an eye on Bree, and over-manage her, and keep her on track, then you have my permission to get a thousand calendar run under way. But remember that these things take time and if they are not ready way before December 1st, then you've missed an opportunity to use them wisely. There are a lot of calendars out there, and ours must be something special or it won't work".

Bree burst out of the chair, went around the desk and hugged Barry tightly. She kissed him on the cheek and said, "Thank you boss, and thanks Sarah for believing in me. I promise I won't let you down".

Sarah gave Barry a grin as she left. Sarah knew that she had lost Bree from that moment on.

Bree put her heart and soul into the project. Selecting all the clothes for each month. She also approached each girl she thought would be right for that particular dress or outfit. She asked Kirsty if she could have the photographer's number so that she could discuss just how the scenes were to be set. Mark invited her to a pub one night and they discussed until chucking out time, just what this calendar would finish up looking like. After another two nights at the pub, where Bree took a large notepad, and every finalized scene would be transferred onto a single A4 sheet in a tantalizing freehand style that smacked of having been taught. She confessed that she had always been a gifted amateur artist, and that fashion had been a passion for ever.

Mark took the sheets, and suggested a change of plan. "You know I've been a photographer for a long time, and frankly I've never seen anyone bring so much passion to a meeting as you have. I think that you need to be the star of this show, as quite frankly, your fellow workers, lovely as they are, will only serve to make this a family affair, not a great calendar".

"I can't do it. Those people who I haven't known very long, are trusting me to do the right thing by the stores and them. I can't steal the limelight just to satisfy my eagerness to get on in the modelling and fashion world. Let's just stick with what we've agreed and use the people we've chosen eh?" Mark shrugged, "Your two pennies worth".

The next week saw chaos reign at both stores, as an area was commandeered for a green sheet to be strung up, and the selected girls dressed and fancied up by the hair and makeup girl – who just happened to be young Monica – Bree's friend, co-opted in, "As I've got no work, an this is like trainin' for me you know, cause I'm goin' to Beauty School next February. I don won payin. I just need some experience. I got all the stuff right here, Mum set me up wiv it". Barry agreed to pay her 10 pounds a day to cover use of her 'stuff'. Monica did a really professional job on all the girls.

Like a well-oiled machine, each shot was set up, taken, scrutinized, and then taken again and again until it was as good as it could be. Bree had to do two of the shots as one girl got stage fright. At the end of the week, Mark went round to both stores and showed the girls who had participated in the shots the proofs, in order to get their reactions and comments. On every single occasion, the comment was exactly the same. "Compared to Bree's two shots, I'm in a different league. I'm withdrawing. That girl needs to be the star here". Or comments along those lines. Mark asked to see Barry in his office. He explained his dilemma, and how Bree didn't want to betray her friends and colleagues. Barry waked into the store and asked Bree to come into his office. He asked Mark to explain the situation, then asked Bree if she would consider becoming the star, as all her mates had either pulled out or wanted her to take their place.

"You know, I've always dreamed, that someday I would be up on stage in a beautiful dress parading before an audience. It's like my only goal. If the girls and you Barry don't mind, I'd like to do this". "There, sorted. Go talk with the girls and re-shoot. They all only want the best for you, and you are a most beautiful person. Now go before I get all emotional". Barry masked his wet eyes by turning away, seemingly to carry on with business.

Mark photo shopped the green screen panels behind Bree with a different hue for each month. A central side box explained what was in the picture. January read. 'Bree shows what can be done with an on trend fake seal print skirt. A flaming orange with silver threads long sleeved top with frilled cuffs, contrasts but compliments the silver in the skirt. A wide black soft leather belt tied to one side demands attention and projects an air of simplicity combined with chic. The long black soft leather coat over her shoulder will keep the winter chills at bay, but beware when that coat comes off'!

Bree is dressed in both new and pre loved clothes from the Thrift Shops at the Angel and Kentish Town. Total spend 21 Pounds. All profits from the sale of this calendar go to Mind Games. Helping to combat service personnel mental health problems. If you can help further, please go to www.mindgames.co.uk.

It turned out that Bree had to organize 10,000 calendars in total. TV, radio, newspapers and magazines all took up the story about Bree wanting to become a famous model, and how the girls had wanted her to succeed by opting out of the photo shoot. This was the 'angle' or 'hook' that they had been looking for, and Kirsty was right on the ball, feeding this fairy tale story to as many outlets as possible. Kirsty and Mark were also becoming famous in their own right as a dynamic duo in the field of promotion. So much so that they announced the formation of a business to be called PROMO, advising any future star that they could handle everything from go to whoa whenever they were on camera or in print. The Bree calendars as they became known, did not hurt their reputation one little bit.

It came as no surprise to anyone when Barry in February announced to the gathered Angel girls that Bree had been offered a modelling contract with one of London's biggest agencies. Sarah called out from the back, "Too good for us now eh"? Bree went and hugged her and pulled her to the front and facing the girls and staff and said, "Without Sarah's backing, I couldn't have gone through with this, so I have her to thank for giving me the strength to start it, and all of you for helping me get through it. Barry backed Sarah and provided the finances. I don't know if the calendars have helped the stores or the charity, all I know it has helped me get to my dream job. I'll never forget every one of you". Massive tears ran down both cheeks as Sarah wiped her own eyes and pulled a tissue out of the box on the desk for Bree. The box was handed round for all to use.

Barry asked for quiet. "Bree single handedly promoted herself into stardom. It was always going to be. We just helped her along. Everyone could see she was special from day one, and Sarah told me from the start that the Thrift Shop would only be a stepping stone for her. Not only do we all wish her the best in her new found career, we want her to know that apart from the magnificent publicity that the stores have received, the clothing sales have gone through the roof, doubled in fact. So my investment in calendars and in particular you Bree has paid off handsomely. Mind Games has received donations and receipts from sales of calendars in the vicinity of 26,000 Pounds, so I consider that a good investment. Well done Bree. We wish you every success. Here is a card from all of us and a Mont Blanc pen only to be used to sign those lucrative contracts and to make pen sketches of those amazing designs in your head". When the clapping had died down, Bree turned to Sarah to give her another hug, and to tell her that she was off to Kentish Town to tell the others her good news, and to thank them personally.

CHAPTER 46

During the refurbishment of the Angel and Kentish Town stores, Jean asked Barry if she could have some extra security measures built in. He asked what they were. She described her plans and he approved them. She didn't think the measures would come into effect for a long, long time, but it was an opportunity that presented itself and she took it.

She thought about it as she walked to work, listening to the news on her phone. "Two brazen armed bandits, one slim female and one tall male, terrorized the three staff at the 7-11 on High St. Highbury, 30 minutes ago. They were armed with a sawn-off shotgun and demanded cash and cigarettes before striking one person to the head with the rifle butt, and threatening to kill the others if they moved, or set off the alarm in the next five minutes. One assistant raised her head enough to describe the partial number plate, make and colour of the SUV getaway vehicle. Police are looking for a maroon Mazda CX5. The index plate starts with 1DEF. Police advise the public to report only. Do not come in contact with them.

Half an hour after doing her rounds at the Angel store, Jean got a call from the Manageress at Kentish Town. 'Jean, you know that couple who robbed the 7-11 at Highbury, I think I just saw them walking along outside. I think they may be casing the garage on the corner across the road. Do you want to come over and have a look"? "Sure. I'm on my way". Jean hailed a cab, gave the address and asked the driver to hurry. "Luv. If you hadn't noticed, its rush hour, which means no one's rushing anywhere. I think it's called an oxymoron". Jean thought he was a moron, but buttoned her lip. Fifteen minutes later he dropped her off. Maureen opened the door for her, and pointed the couple out, sitting on the bench just down from the shop and almost opposite the corner garage. "What do we do"? "Well for starters we don't know that's them unless we had a better description, but the news said it was a man and woman dressed in black and that she was slim. If it is them, and neither of them are in black apart from his trousers, then they would have either dumped the SUV or it's in a car park somewhere nearby with possibly new plates. All we can do is keep an eye on them. If they make a wrong move we call the police. I'll stay by the door. You go about your work. Just remember our safety drill".

As Jean observed them, the woman turned and looked in the direction of the shop. She looked up and down. He spoke to the man, who slowly got up then pretended to do up his shoe lace by placing one foot on the seat, whilst all the time looking at the row of shops that included the Thrift Shop. His long fawn coloured jacket could have easily concealed a weapon she thought. Then she saw the inside lining. It was black. Could it be a reversible jacket? That would make sense. The woman had picked up the coat that was lain - with the white lining outwards - over the back of the seat. 'I bet that's black outside too', she thought.

As the woman lifted the coat, Jean noticed that she was lifting something else with and under it, and they were moving this way. The slightly tinted window, prevented them from seeing her, but that would change very soon. She ran over to Maureen. "Get ready to take a hold of those four people if I raise my hand. Keep in the back". She turned and walked towards the door which was flung open with such force, she thought it might come off its hinges.

The man shouted. "I want valuables from the display case. I want money from the charity box. I want all monies from the till and the safe, and from your handbag – NOW!" The woman started to withdraw something from under the coat. Jean raised her hand. That was Maureen's signal to push the four shoppers back and into a room, where the door locked behind them. "The woman shouted at the door. "Silly cow. When we're finished here, I'm coming for you. Get your money out and jewelry off, and stay away from the lock when I blast it. Now you. Start getting what he asked for or you're first". Jean pressed the remote control in her hand. The front door latched with several locks clicking at once. When their backs were turned to look, Jean slid into the change room, where the door locked behind her. A red light and siren started up outside, and a notice in the window, flashed on and off. 'Robbery in action. Police have been called. Stay away'. Jean activated the third button which allowed her to talk via loud hailer in the shop. "The police have been called. All doors are steel lined. They have all been locked. You cannot escape. When the police come, I can fill the shop with tear gas, or you can put your shotgun down close to the front door and go quietly. You have about one minute to decide. Please come again". She had always wanted to say that.

Sure enough the police came with a paddy wagon. Jean looking at the various monitor screens in the change room and advised the police whilst they were outside by loud speaker, that two robbers - one armed with a shotgun - were being held captive, and did they want her to activate the tear gas. The police went back to the car boot where they donned gas masks, then came back to the store as Jean filled the store. The two were overcome easily, then Jean let the police in to capture them.

Jean was interviewed by the local paper reporter the next day, and asked if she could tell them how the robbers were able to be detained whilst the police were on their way. "Let's just say that any wannabe crims in this neighbourhood had better watch out, The Thrift Shops won't put up with being threatened. We aim to keep our staff and customers safe at all times, which is why we invested heavily in this technology".

More great publicity for the stores. Maureen and Jean were commended by the Police Commissioner for their vigilance and assistance to public safety. Jean had several enquiries for the same system. Jean was now contemplating if this was the right time to change careers, so she gave many of them high quotes, some of whom took up the offer. The new work entailed teaming up with a builder and a security supplies company. She would get the quotes then invoice for another

50%. She needed only to supervise. "Let's see how this pans out part time first".

CHAPTER 47

Jean didn't know how it was happening, but Milly informed her that here was a discrepancy between takings and stock, after the end of month stock take, but only at Kentish Town. Jean went to see the Manager Maureen and explained the problem over a cuppa in the lunch room.

"I'm not sure either", said Maureen, "But I will keep my eyes open. I thought our system was pretty much foolproof. As the item gets put through, the item is deducted from stock and the tag registers the item as sold. The takings are supposed to tally with the amount on the item. Where is it going wrong"?

"I'm not sure yet, but if the stock take tells us that stock is not here now, then it must be being pinched, but how. Is there any one new here, or anyone you don't trust"?

"There is a new girl, started four weeks ago, but surely it would be too soon to start those tricks, and she would know that it would show up on the next stock take – and that she would be the most obvious suspect".

Maureen said she would keep an eye out for any strange things and especially keep an eye on Tanya the new girl.

Customers came and went and still Maureen could find no reason for the discrepancy. The second in a row. The total amount missing from two months was 1200 Pounds retail value, and it was clear that the thieves were targeting the Asian collection. The higher end of the price range.

Jean fast forwarded hundreds of hours of video tape to see if she could find a connection. What she did notice was that more Asian clients were buying from that section. That was not an issue as such, but the same faces kept on coming in, and even if they had plenty of money, they probably would never buy that amount of clothing for themselves.

She then looked at the camera facing the change rooms. Then it became clear. Some women were taking in four or five items at a time to try on. It seemed that they didn't come out with as many, so there was only one answer, they were putting one or more on, then putting their own clothes over the top. They would come out, throw the remaining clothes on the desk, then buy one item, but not pay for the hidden others. It all looked legit from the outside.

The problem was that every garment had a security RFID tag that was only cancelled once the garment was waved in front of the reader, where the price would also be shown on the register monitor.

It was obvious that either they had removed the tags and stowed them in the changing room or that they had RFID cancelling equipment in their handbags. When it was quiet, Jean took a portable RFID reader into the change room. It was not recording any tag, so it must be the latter ploy.

Jean set a trap. She was pretty sure now who the culprit/s were. Two of them came in together. Jean asked the assistant to surreptitiously wave the items they had selected, in front of her portable reader. It had been turned down low so no sound was heard as she did as she and Jean had practiced. Jean made sure that instead of one camera pointing to the change room there were now two. To ensure there were no loopholes Jean had had two pinhole cameras installed in the two rooms, with the monitor at the front desk recording in real time and dated.

The two women acted exactly as they had done on many occasions in the past – according to the CCTV. Once in the change rooms, they quickly removed the RFID cancelling device from their handbags and waved the garments they intended to hide in front of it. They stripped down and put the new tops and dresses on, concealing them with their own clothes, then boldly walked out together in order to confuse the assistant, and throwing some of the tagged clothes on a pile, whilst declaring that they would take one dress and one top and pay now. The assistant was obliged to take their money rather than engage them. They walked quickly to the front door, which when pulled would not budge.

"Excuse me, could you let us out. Seems like the door is jammed". Jean and Maureen walked up and asked them if they would mind accompanying them to the staff canteen. "I don't want a cup of tea, I just need to get home to my kids".

"Fine, then if you are refusing to accompany me then I am calling the police to report you both for stealing".

"Look, I don't know what you mean, but I suppose we can talk". Jean led them in and sat them down. She turned up the heat and closed the door. "Here's what I have. Our stock has been going missing for two months now. I have been watching you both on our video cameras, and I know there are two more of you thieving from here also. Today, you took six garments each into our changing rooms. You knocked out the RFID tags with a portable canceller. You put on the clothes you wanted to pinch. You both came out at the same time, threw the rest of the clothes on to the bench, then you paid for one item each. The total amount all four of you have stolen over the past two months amounts to 2500 Pounds retail. I presume you are selling them to your friends and making a nice profit".

One of the women started to get up. "I am feeling unwell. If you had proof of what you think you know, then you would have called the Police by now". "I think you'll find that as an ex Police Inspector, a security officer with The Thrift Shop, and having gone to great lengths to record you both in many different ways in order obtain absolute proof, that I have the right to make a citizen's arrest, which is what I am doing. By the way, if you want to cool down, feel free to remove some clothing.

Jean made a move to pull out her mobile phone. She pressed a speed dial number and her Inspector friend answered. "Hi Jean, what's happening". "I have two women suspected of stealing clothing over a two month period amounting to approximately 2500 Pounds. They won't give me their names, and they think I'm bluffing, but I've got plenty of video recorded information, and they are wearing some of the stolen clothes under their own. What's the best way to handle it"?

"You've done all you can. If you are sure you have plenty of evidence that will lead to a conviction, I'll get the duty Sergeant to send a car round for them. Just sit tight".

The women were clearly becoming extremely agitated. One of them made a bolt for the door, but it was firmly locked – with customers outside wondering what was going on. She shouted at them that she was being held captive by a mad woman. The patrol car arrived, and after Jean had explained the circumstances, told the officers that the women were still wearing the stolen clothes, and that if they call her from the station with the tag numbers, she would verify that they belonged to the store, and describe the item to them in order to offer proof. She would also be making a full statement, and they would have it in an hour. The women were still cussing her as they were cuffed them placed into the back seat.

CHAPTER 48

Although Furniture Fashions was doing well by supplying all of Barry's and thousands of others gee gaws that helped lift refurbished furniture, it was just jogging along. Not setting the world on fire, and when Barry thought about it, the business wasn't lighting his fire either, so when Herr Gunther Maxx, the owner of Euro Refurbs, after visiting the London Furniture Explorium where Fashion Accessories had been exhibiting, then having dinner with Julian Morrow, Gunther had asked for a meeting with Barry next day.

Barry organized for a limo to pick Gunther up from his hotel, and they met at the new headquarters of The Baines Group. 14 Paternoster Row. London EC4M. 7th floor, or so his business card said.

As lunch time was looming Barry suggested they go to a nearby bistro called Happy Tommy's. Gunther had been relatively subdued up to the time lunch was served. "Gunther, you and I have known each other for some time now. Why don't you come right out with whatever is on your mind. If it's something that Furniture Fashions is not doing well, just tell me and I will fix it".

"On the contrary Barry. I wanted to meet in person to tell you that I think your idea is amazing. I do however feel that your heart is not in this venture. I know you manage several other businesses, and from your company tax returns I see that Furniture Fashions is but a minnow. Now, I have this opportunity in Russia. It seems they have more money that ever since getting rid of the satellite states that literally drained Moscow of funds. They are producing millionaires third only to the USA and China".

"The new found semi-capitalists are all buying up mansions and re-furbishing them. Our group is big in Russia, buying up the old furniture and refurbishing it. We also add your accessories to give it a contemporary look. I could go on buying your product, but the truth is I would be better off owning it". And there it was – out there at last.

"I have done my math. I can buy up similar machines to yours. I can train people to run them. The whole exercise would cost 450,000 Euros. However, If I offer you 250,000 Euros, hopefully some of your workers will either move to Germany or be happy to be teachers for say six months, plus I will have the list of other clients that buy from you, and that will help us get through the first year. My offer is good for two months. After that I must inform you that we would start the process of getting our own plant up and running. So you have three options as I see it. 1. Tell me to go jump, and six months down the track, I will have become your competitor and you will lose your largest client. 2. Accept my offer, and work with me to a smooth takeover position, or 3. Now that I have tipped my hand, throw me out and find other clients. It would not be easy for you to get a hold of the Russian connections though, as our families have a long history of doing business together".

Barry looked long and hard at Gunther. "Well that was a surprise. I'm pleased that you understand how good a range of products we have and the potential they have to change mundane into magnificent. I also admire the fact that you have given considerable thought to your options. I also love the fact that you came to me as a business man and a man, and came right out with your thoughts. So thank you for that. It is refreshing to deal with an honest business person".

"I have an option to your plans. That is I retain 25% of the business for the sale price of 300,000 Euros. You and I know that those machines were new when purchased. We make sure they are regularly serviced by the manufacturers, and the amount of work they do, is only a fraction of what they are capable of - I am sure you know all this, which means that you can expand ten-fold from day one if you wished, and from what you tell me, you will need much more product than you buy currently. As for my workers becoming teachers or moving to Germany permanently, I can guarantee nothing, and it is not part of any deal we might do, however, I am happy for any people you may wish to send over, to be trained by my guys, but your company would have to find accommodation, meals etc. for them for up to six months".

"The business turns over 2.6 million Euros currently, with an after tax net profit of 200,000 Euros, so your offer values the business at 1.5 times profit. The current average multiple for a successful and growing business like this is 3 times, so the real value is 600,000 Euros. Again, I am happy to become a 25% silent shareholder for 300,000 Euros, what do you say". He put his hand out to be shaken. Gunther left his on the table.

"I think Herr Baines that I have met my match. I will take your counter offer back to my board, and let you know in two weeks' time. I also admire your Mind Games charity commitment. Personally, I couldn't find any spare time for such an undertaking, but if the deal goes through on either of our terms, I will give your charity 30,000 Euros, as I believe it to be one of the best in the world. I would also like you to consider expanding it into Europe. Now we can shake".

Two weeks later to the day, Gunther 'phoned. "Well Barry, my board met last night and the offers were tabled. Your counter offer was knocked back to 200,000 Euros if you wanted to retain 25%". Barry immediately railed. "Then I am sorry my friend but it is worth more to me to carry on and to expand the business, rather than give it away cheaply, besides I already have another suitor, Guilia's of Rome, is asking questions. Maybe one of your board let them know about the deal"?

"Barry. In your excitement to tell me what a miserable bastard I am, I was going on to tell you that I took your side against the board, and convinced them that your business was well worth the money, and that we would be better off having you as a partner rather than as a competitor. So, if you are still willing, we are prepared to make a formal offer to you – on your terms, and to offer you a seat on the board as an advisor. What do you say"?

"I'm sorry I jumped in. I thought all your board wanted to do was shaft me. But I am happy with your offer and wish you to go ahead with the paperwork. I will continue to be a customer of yours, but now I suppose I will have to pay you instead of me". They both laughed, then said their goodbyes. Barry had an ear to ear grin that could not be wiped off, especially when he phoned his wife Denise, who was really pleased if for no other reason that she thought Barry was stretching himself too thin lately. He wasn't getting in 'til late, and she thought at one time that he might have a mistress.

The Furniture Fashions deal went smoothly. It worked out that three of Barry's workers wanted the chance to move to Germany for six months to start with, then if it worked out well for them, maybe to become a German citizen - or at least a dual citizen. Three of Gunther's men in the meantime, would go to Barry's factory to start training for as long as possible, before the machinery removalists came to dismantle, pack, then ship the machinery to a section cleared especially to house the new venture at Euro Refurbs. The remaining three men were not machine operators, and they were invited to stay on whilst Barry organized his latest venture. In fact a container would arrive in the next few days, so he wanted the warehouse cleaned out and pallet racking with shelves fitted placed around two of the walls, so the three men had their work cut out.

CHAPTER 49

The CFO of Guilias, Paulo Centauro, whilst trying to find out if Furniture Fashions was still for sale, told Barry why the business would have been a good fit for them. They were the leading coffin manufacturers in the world, and Barry's adornments for furniture would make their coffins look more expensive still. After looking at Guilias potential offer - if Gunther's had turned bad, Barry decided it was too low and advised them of Gunthers offer, which Paolo suggested Barry take, as Euro Refurbs had far more upside than their company did, and so the offer died. Barry offered to introduce Paolo to Gunther as soon as the factory was in full operation in Germany. A feather in Barry's cap. More business for ER and more profit for the shareholders, which now included Barry.

Barry asked how many coffins they sold in the UK. "None my friend. We have just completed fitting out the largest woodworking centre solely dedicated to coffin making in Rome, and when it is in full swing, we will have enough stock to enter the UK, which quite frankly is supplied by three European companies and four small UK companies. We have done our homework, and know for sure that we can supply a larger range at a better price, and all from the one source. I think the market will change rapidly once we get a foothold. We are looking for a warehouse in the UK at this moment. Maybe you could let me know the best place to set up distribution. I have been looking at the Brighton area as it's reasonably close to the port".

Barry immediately jumped at the chance. "Paulo, we really don't know each other well, but the facts are that you are a well-paid CFO of a large Italian corporation. You have position and influence. Your company wants to expand into the UK. I am an owner of three businesses, and my bank balance has been buoyed by funds from selling another of them. I will soon have a cleared warehouse in Chadwell Heath, Essex. It is no accident why I chose the location. It is located where traffic is not too bad and not too far from the European access ports. Then there are access roads to all major highways not far from there. The workforce is reliable and the wages are not excessive. Is there some way we can work together"?

"Mmm. Interesting Barry. Let me talk with my CEO first. I will get back to you soon'. "Paulo, I do have other plans for the warehouse, if there's not a deal to be done, don't sweat it. If you can let me know within the week it would be appreciated".

At 9 am Monday Barry took Paulo's call. "My CEO likes the idea of working with a British partner, plus you have the know-how regarding logistics and distribution. Is it possible for you to come to Rome this week? We can fly you out on one of our jets from Stanstead and have you back the same day if you wish. The offer also extends to your lovely wife if she's free. My wife Angelina will take her shopping whilst we talk". It was arranged for Wednesday – after a quick call on the office telephone to Denise, whilst Paulo waited - at 6am when a driver would pick them up and take them to the airport. "We can have breakfast together. I am looking forward to our meeting as is my CEO, Roberto Guilia".

Wednesday came quickly, and spot on at 6 am the car arrived then whisked them through the early morning traffic to Stansted Airport. The vehicle entered the airport through a large sliding side gate, and came to a halt outside a white painted hut marked Customs & Excise. A uniformed woman came out and asked for the passengers identifications. She bade them a good trip, then waved the car through and into a hanger, where a Lear Jet with 'Guilias' in large red cursive script along the body of the fuselage greeted them. The pilot, co-pilot and a hostess were at the foot of the steps saluting and shaking hands as they boarded. "Welcome to Guilias", said the pilot in an Italian accent. The hostess also welcomed them aboard, and facing each other in Chesterfields with a table between them, they were buckled up and the plane started to taxi.

As the plane levelled out the hostess offered coffee and cakes, advising them that they were due to breakfast with Mr. Guilia at 8.30 am. After small talk with the hostess who advised them that the company owned jet - the Cessna Citation 9 seater - could be converted to many different layouts in about 15 minutes, and that it was pretty much airborne most of the time, flying Guilia executives all over the world, along with their favourite clients.

At Rome airport, a limo picked them up and transported them to La Dolceria in Fregene, as the town hall bell struck once for 8.30 am. At 8.32, in walked a large man flanked by four others, two of whom were well dressed women. Four small tables had been placed together to allow all eight to sit facing each other. Paulo introduced M. Guilia, He looked to Barry. You know me of course then turned and held his hand out to Denise and kissed it gently. "Paulo Centauro. Please call me Paulo. May I call you Denise? This is Adrielle Cormo our Director of Overseas Operations, so she will be dealing with you if we do something together. This is Sofia Fussani our Chief Procurement Officer. Jack Romano is the Company Secretary who will be taking notes, and as you know, I am the Chief Financial Officer.

The three women sat together with Denise in the middle. Roberto opened the conversation with, "I hope the location for breakfast was to your liking. Our offices are on the other side of the city. This luncheonette has a fine reputation for good food, especially breakfast, so may I suggest we order first then get down to some business.

As the breakfasts were being prepared, Roberto explained just how Guilia's had started and grown exponentially over the years, and how It may be that Barry had stumbled across them at exactly the right time. "I understand from Paulo that you are ready to take on another challenge. Maybe one that is more rewarding than the last. Here is my – our plan for our company's invasion of Britain. We now have the capacity to ship into the UK, five thousand coffins per month. We can ramp this up to 15,000 within the next six months". "Just how many people die every month in the U.K"? Barry asked. "Around 45,000, so you could take a reasonable share of the market to start with, whilst gearing up for say 20 – 30% of the market in a year".

Barry could not believe his ears, and put one hand up. "Stop right there. 45,000 people die in the UK every month? I'm finding it hard to get my head around. "For those not involved in the business of the dead, the figures are hard to comprehend. What you do need to know is the market is divided up between ten to fifteen players, and only a couple are of any size, and every one of them is but a fraction of Guilia's size and capacity. In fact, put them all together and we still outstrip them all, so if we do business together, you will know that we are the strongest of them all", explained Roberto.

"Now, before we eat, I must ask you Barry if this is a business you feel comfortable with, as not everyone is". "I look at it this way, everybody has to die – number one. Number two – someone has to supply them with a casket. I view our meeting as a potential business opportunity, nothing more".

"Well said, now let me pass the questions over. Who would like to go first"? Sofia spoke first. "Hello. It is nice to meet you both and welcome to Rome. I came along today not only as Procurement Officer but also I am in charge of Logistics. I understand that you have your own vehicles, that you use to transport furniture around Europe is that not so". Barry explained both the Vans and the Trailers are his and the prime movers are hired as required. "Ah, I see. Do you think you have enough capacity to pick up from our factories in Italy on a regular basis? The caskets are supplied as flat packs. Some funeral parlours prefer them to be assembled. When we start up in the U.K. we intend to go one further, we will establish make up factories where the caskets can be assembled, lined, trimmed and handles – we call the brass fittings furniture – are fitted also, which means that their staff have nothing to do but open a fully prepared casket according to the family's wishes. This is why we will be more successful than anyone else, because no other company is doing this. However, this will be part of your work. Firstly to pick up, then to store, then to prepare to order, then to ship to all of the parlours in Great Britain. It is a big undertaking, so our partner needs to be fully aware of the scope of the operation and be capable of fulfilling all facets in a timely manner".

Barry was impressed. Denise asked how many variations of coffins there were, and how many different types of linings they would have to cater for. "Denise, those are very important questions, because that goes to the space your company needs and how big your workforce needs to be. What Guilia's decided to do only last year, was to make only one size coffin. It is 1800mm long x 500mm at its widest. If a client wants a different size, then we suggest they shop elsewhere. This brings incredible economies of scale, and makes us basically the casket suppliers to the masses. As for trimmings, there is a range of products that we can supply to you, so that your staff have everything they need in one set of cupboards close to them. They simply roll out the desired lining fabric, cut it, lay it in and staple it to the top edge. There are a few stages, but they are easily taught. What you would be offering, is a one stop shop. You will need to invest in local transportation - yours or others". "But it needs to be discreet as casket deliveries seem to upset some people", answered Sofia.

The frittata di funghi – mushroom omelet - was placed before Barry. Verdiccio red wine poured all round. They all ate in silence for a while before Adrielle asked Denise what she did for a living. Was she involved in the day to day business with Barry? "I am the Editor Of Furniture Magazine. I was just thinking how I could get an article about coffins featured in it", she laughed. "Maybe you have a version that doubles as a wardrobe", she asked. Adrielle raised a glass. "You make a fine couple. I understand you have not been married very long"? "It seems like Barry is a soul mate". "We are a very good fit". My daughter does a lot of work with Barry's charity. Maybe you have heard of it. Mind Games". Adrielle shook her head slowly. "No, I'm afraid I haven't, sorry".

At that point Paulo chipped in. "I learnt about Mind Games last year. It was being featured on TV, and I understand it was a complete success. I suggested to Barry that he expand the concept to Europe. He hasn't given me an answer yet".

Roberto asked Barry to explain what Mind Games was all about. Afterwards he said, "I am very impressed by your answers and by your civic duty. We will ask more questions, and expect you to have many of your own. After finishing my breakfast I will leave you if you don't mind, then my colleagues and I will meet up later to discuss the matter in more detail. Please ask any questions you wish, and be as blunt as you like, then we will all know where we stand".

"Paulo will make sure you are returned safely to Stanstead by this afternoon. Feel free to discuss everything with my colleagues. After breakfast, Roberto bid 'Ciao' to all, and expressed his delight that Denise could come along. "A breath of fresh English countryside air".

As soon as Roberto had left, Barry came straight back to the subject. "Look guys, I don't like to beat about the bush", and seeing puzzled expressions explained, "I would like to get down to figures straight away, so that I can determine if I am wasting my time and yours, or if there is a mutually beneficial proposal to be worked out". Paulo explained that he and his colleagues had worked out that a per casket arrangement would be best for all, as they all then had a solid figure to work on. Paulo suggested that Barry buy every coffin from Gulilias. He nominated an amount of between 150 to 650 Pounds as the cost of each casket – dependent upon type of wood used and finish, ex works. He would have to abide by their nominated Price List for unfinished and finished caskets of which they handed him a copy. He would also make money from linings, trimmings and furniture, but they must be within the current price guides.

Barry did some quick calculations on a napkin. He listed transport. Loading / unloading. Storage. Unpacking and assembling. Local transport. He showed those figures to those assembled. "It seems at those prices, that I would be losing money for at least the first year. After that economies of scale kick in, then we can start to see a small profit. I thought Paulo that you said this would be a better proposition than our original business venture - just picking up and delivering flat packs". Paulo looked at Barry's figures. "I think we need to subsidize you for the first year then. I propose we drop our prices by 10% for the first year".

"I propose that if you don't drop your prices by 25% for the first two years, then it doesn't make sense to me". "Let us go away to consider your proposal, and we will contact you after we have looked at our figures. Either way, we will talk further", said Paulo. After more small talk and coffee, Barry asked if Paulo could arrange for them to return to the U.K. They arrived just in time for an afternoon snack and a welcome cuppa, back at Barry's office.

Barry contacted the largest casket supplier in the UK, which just so happened to be 5 kms away, so he suggested that he drop Denise either at home or her office, then he would go round to see Charles Tait of BFS (British Funereal Supplies). After dropping Denise off at home, he called in and re-introduced himself.

"Call me Chas", he said. "My old man was born and raised in Melbourne. He bought this place three years ago, and I run it for him. All the family live here now, although I miss the sun and surf something terrible. Now what can I do for you. You mentioned that you'd like to know more about the funeral supplies business. I have to ask what your interest is, as I don't want to give away any trade secrets, and don't try to bullshit me mate. I can tell a bullshitter from a cricket pitch away".

"Without giving my angle away – yet, I would like to know who owns the market for coffins in the UK". "Well that's in the public domain. We have about 30%. Corrigan's have about 23%. Rich Palmer Group has about 15%, and the rest are about twenty smaller players. Why do you ask"?

"Well I've heard a rumour that a company based in Europe is about to come into the UK and take most of the market. I wanted to know if I should buy their shares".

"Ok that's bullshit for a start. The only company big enough is Guilia's and they are a private company, so now start again, what's your game"?

Barry was surprised by the speedy retort and knowledge of the 20 something before him. "Well, the truth is that I heard a rumour that they are coming to the UK, and as I have a timber mill in Romania, I was looking to supply them, if indeed they were as big as my friend had told me they were, and if they were expanding, I presumed they would be looking for more timber. There, now you know".

"That's a little closer to the truth, but I happen to know that they own their own lumber yards throughout Europe so you wouldn't get a look in. Do you want to tell me what's really going on"?

"You Aussies are cruel. Give a man a break. OK. I have been asked if I want to distribute their caskets. Happy now"?

"Why the bloody hell didn't you say that in the first place. I could have told you, a. that the European Commission is going to launch an investigation into their nefarious practices relating to child labour in their mills, and b. many of their suppliers of fittings and furnishings haven't been paid, so if they are doing so well, what's happening to their cash flow and profitability".

"They say they are going to provide a casket fully assembled and trimmed for a bargain price, and that most of you guys will be out of business within a year".

"Barry, Barry, Barry. I don't know which planet you're from, but this is the third time I've heard this story in the past two years. It's true that many undertakers want finished coffins now, but the vast majority want to buy the flat pack, and do the rest themselves. The Brits are a mean bunch of bastards – you being the exception of course – and they don't want to pay anything more than they have to, so their plan won't go down well at all. Secondly the current suppliers have been around for dozens of years, that's why the only way we could get into the business is because my Dad's Brother died and he bought it out, but it still retains the family name and newcomers are definitely not welcome. I've seen two newcomers give up in the past year".

"What about price though. If Guilias come in with rock bottom prices, surely the funeral directors will buy them".

"The old boy network still works better than price. If one buys better and competes on price, the others will squeeze him out. It's all about maintaining profitability and the status quo, because they don't want to put the price of funerals down. It's all about up-selling. That's also why they don't encroach into others territories. It's a clique, a bloody British upper class clique mate, so good luck to Guilias, and good luck to you if you join them. I'll tell you something for nothing. I bet they asked you to pay for the caskets up front". Barry nodded. "That's because their cash flow is shit and shot. You would be doing them a favour, not the other way round".

Barry thanked Chas. "You might just have saved my bacon. Thanks for the information. You might also be telling me all this to frighten me off, but I don't think so. If you are, then it's the best double bluff I've ever seen".

Chas winked at him and waved. Barry was as confused as ever, but at least he now had a different perspective. He vowed to contact numbers two and three in the U.K. funeral supplies business tomorrow. Tonight he would go home with his head spinning, and discuss things with Denise. "What a day"!

Denise reminded Barry over dinner that there was never a shortage of patronage in the funeral business. Barry was wondering how he could be a part of it, but not with Guilia's, unless! "Hey, Denise", Barry suddenly exclaimed as he lowered his fork full of spaghetti bolognaise. "What if Guilia's is kosher and they are set to become the biggest in the world, and the guy I spoke to was giving me a load of flannel, while at the same time pumping me for info? If that's the case then I've said way too much. I wonder how I can find out if Guilia's is in dire straits or not"?

Barry called his Group CFO Michael Stanning. "Sorry for calling you so late Michael. Can you give me a few minutes"?

"Sure Barry, what's on your mind"? Barry explained the dilemma he was in, and asked if Michael had any suggestions. "Let me make some phone calls. I'll see what my financial friends in Italy know". "Thanks Michael. It would certainly make my decision easier if I have some more information and concrete facts, and by the way, ask if they know what expansion plans Guilias might have, that involves the UK if you can. Thanks again. See you in the morning".

Barry phoned Denise with the news mid-day next day. "Hi Hun. Just letting you know that Michael came good regarding Guilia's. His buds tell him that they are all looking to buy shares in Guilia's once they go public - supposedly not public common knowledge yet – and get this – the funds will be used to conquer first the UK then the USA funeral supplies businesses. Apparently they are buying up more lumber mills in Eastern Europe to cope with the expected demand, and are talking to some Canadian mills for supply to the US market, so that lying Chas is going to get his ass kicked, even though I blabbed, I suspect he already knew. Strange thing is, he will be getting a better deal from Guilias than from his old pals. Anyway I'll see you later". Denise asked what he was going to do about the Guilia offer. "Probably take it, but with a twist".

Now that Barry had enough information to formulate a plan, he wrote the salient points on paper and handed them to Michael. "I want to have a long term interest in Guilia's. I will earn hourly rates on the long haulage; daily rates on storage and piece rates per item picked, and piece rates on local deliveries. Not exactly millionaire making, so I'm proposing to you, that I do all the above, PLUS take a %age of my future earnings in Guilia stock before it floats. At the IPO I can sell off half my stock, and the other half should reap a handsome yearly dividend.

Barry drafted a letter of acceptance that Michael perused, corrected and added a few figures and lines. "That should make someone think", said Michael. Barry sent the letter direct to Roberto's personal e-mail. Roberto was not slow to welcome him on board. The covering letter and agreement cemented Barry's future with Guilia's.

Barry immediately began with a major investment in leasing trailers and depots close to Guilia's current and new mills, and on the outskirts of Slough, a large clear span building that used to belong to Amazon UK, and which they had grown out of, was leased for two years with an option to purchase at today's value at the end of it, or continue with the lease with a 3% per annum rent and price increase purchase option. The building was complete with heavy duty pallet racking and a small ultra-modern office space, with all the telephonic and internet systems ready to connect into. They had even left the six offices and reception fully furnished.

Every funeral parlour in Britain received a glossy brochure from Guilia's, showing an impressive array of caskets and trims. The brochure was in fact designed so that the directors could hand them out to clients to take home and talk with the family about their wishes. At the rear, was a form that helped list all the options, along with a space to add the prices as shown on a separate Price List. The exercise meant that the bereaved could price the casket exactly. By returning or scanning that page, the funeral director could then make contact and discuss the service, transportation, burial and or cremation.

Guilia's had another ace up its sleeve. 4 very pretty Italian women were drafted to London to become the follow up campaign. Sultry Italian accents asked if they could call on the funeral home Manager or Owner to discuss, "another lucrative deal – if they can find the time. I'm in your area Monday. Would 9am or 2.30 pm be best for you"?

When the lust and the eagerness had worn off from looking at her high skirt and low neckline, the sweetener was offered. "The reason for my visit Signore (heavily emphasized), is to advise you that if you take a certain number of Guilia caskets, linings, trimmings and furniture amounting to over 5000 Pounds in a month, then you are entitled to a rebate. The rebate goes into your personal bank account as a commission. If you reach the first target, we will give you 4%, which is 200 Pounds. If the orders amount to say 10,000 Pounds then you will receive 400 Pounds. You must however reach the lower threshold of 5000 Pounds".

"Would you like to participate"? If so, please put your personal banking information on this form and sign below, after reading our offer". She left her business card, "Just in case you need me any time".

Pout, Pout. Shimmy. Shimmy. How many older Managers or owners succumbed? – Most!

CHAPTER 50

Reggie Green, had been growing on and in the job. Every time Barry made a move, Reggie backed him up with anything he needed in the transport and logistics spheres. He was officially given the title Cargo Master – after the U.S. logistics whizzes in the U S Air Force – but Barry added International, because Barry's businesses were indeed all reaching.

BB LOGISTICS was born the day Barry signed the logistics deal with Guilia's. The warehouse vacated by the sale of the Furniture Fashions business now housed new offices with all the mod cons in them.

Reggie's problem –as Barry saw it – was that Reggie was always griping. At every opportunity he would tell anyone and everyone, especially VIPs that his was a lot that no one else would want. "Too demanding. Working all hours. Never get to see home", etc. Barry had been as gentle as possible in telling him that the half glass empty attitude does not help get the others infused with hope, it just attracted other whingers, and Barry certainly didn't want VIPs to get caught up with his negativity, which is why Barry left the end office empty.

He advised all at a meeting that Reggie was now officially known as the Cargo Master, because that had been his forte – getting impossible loads from one end of the earth to the other, however Reggie understands that the group under our new name BB Logistics is now in the multi segmented businesses that are logistics, namely FREIGHT: Local, county, national and international freight encompassing, air sea and land. WAREHOUSING: Providing safe, clean storage for goods either in transit or in long term storage. FULFILLMENT: The act of removing part or all of a consignment from our storage, packing it and making it ready for pick up to the customers clientele.

"So you see, Reggie handles the movement of goods extremely well. We need others to help in the other segments, so those of you who are doing those jobs currently, may or may not continue in them, dependent upon how well you adapt and learn, remembering that I am always willing to pay for any TAFE tuition anyone needs in order to better themselves. Lastly, I am actively looking for a CEO for BB Logistics. We have enormous expansion plans, so expect to see other warehouses, more trucks and trailers, and a greater diversity of products".

"The ONLY thing that matters in the end is that the client is satisfied. You therefore have what I'm calling LESAC - Limited Extent Satisfaction Action Capability. If you can fix a problem to the client's satisfaction at no or limited cost – let's say up to 200 Pounds, then you need to record your actions and bring them to the attention of your Supervisor, but you needn't refer to them first, so you have limited decision making authority to bring about excellent service. Let's become the best in the business". A thunderous applause greeted the news. Maybe because Reggie was not going to be the top dog?

Barry had someone in mind for the top job, but now was not the right time to spill the beans.

CHAPTER 51

Barry's son Trevor and Kirsty Evans had stolen more than a glance at each other after Trevor had arrived at The Mind Games finale as special guest of honour. Given leave specifically to attend, from the United Nations Peace Keeping Corp in Afghanistan.

Kirsty had latched on to him. Firstly to extract his stories for use in promoting Mind Games, but as she heard of his exploits, she realized that here was a man of integrity and conviction to help his fellow man, especially those who were suffering from the effects of war.

She heard him talk reluctantly about his work and what it entailed. She was able to slowly coax any information she needed from any person and that he or she was not aware that they were being slow grilled. Kirsty looked radiant in her long black gown with gold thread running obliquely through it, and gold shoes to match. Her hair in a stylish bun at the rear of her head. She listened to tales of heroics – all by others, and how Trevor thought that the United Nations was doing a great job, especially considering how underfunded they were and how they seemed to always be the whipping boy of both sides.

They obviously liked to be in each other's company, and apart from that first night which was formal, they agreed to meet again next day, after which Trevor had to make his way back to his unit. They breakfasted, lunched and dined, with walks around the capital in between. They found out that they had plenty in common and exchanged phone numbers. He told her that she should not worry if he didn't answer straight away, and his reply might only be a text – as coverage was poor in parts – but he definitely would like to continue corresponding with her – "provided her boyfriend or husband didn't mind". 'Up until now, I haven't found the right person that I have wanted to be with full time, and you"? "Same really, my interest has been helping people, and that means spending a lot of time overseas, with little time for commitment to a single person, however, my time there is almost up, and I will be leaving to take up a position in Dad's business – I hope. What that is yet I don't know, but we have discussed a number of options, and I'd like to take one, if the offer is still available when the time comes".

Six months went by, and everyone settled back into their routines. Trevor and Kirsty had sent e-mails to each other with general interest topics discussed, but Trevor was keeping one bit of news back.

The departure from the United Nations Peace Keeping Force was low key. Trevor had seen eight years of service in various parts of the world, and recently felt that he was not making the impact he had expected to when he first joined at 22, and as his 30th birthday was looming, he took the time to ensure he had as many telephone and e-mail contact numbers stored as possible before attending a passing out parade where several others were presented with medals and thanked for their time and efforts, "in what must be the most frustrating job in the world, but thankfully, we have the best and brightest souls in the world, trying their best to bring peace to the world, whilst at the same time, bearing witness to man's inhumanity to man", said the Company Commander.

Trevor had deliberately not informed anyone of his homecoming or of his quitting the Force. The first person he called from Heathrow was Kirsty. "Got time for a coffee". "Trevor is that really you? Where are you"? "I'm at the airport. Want to meet up for breakfast"? "How about I see you at Freddie's at 10"? "Oh, that would be wonderful. Do you need a lift from the airport"? "No, I'll get the tube. See you there". Before she could ask him anything more he had rung off. She could not contain her excitement and started to wind down her latest story, so she could be at Freddie's on time.

Freddie's was heaving with every professional, but they managed a corner nook after ordering at the bar and taking a number on a stand. With a look of wonderment she asked Trevor why the secret visit, and did he have to go back soon. "I wanted you to be the first to know, that I quit the peace keepers yesterday. I got my service medal last night, and jumped on the first plane out this morning – very early. Secondly I would love you to marry me".

Kirsty was mulling over the words. Firstly Trevor had left his amazing work, and what next, OH, OH, he's asking to marry me. Trevor thought the delay meant that she was considering his offer but was going to turn him down, so he blurted out. "You know I've loved you from the moment we first met at Mind Games, and it took me a while to learn that you were single, but I felt a spark between us, and I've been thinking of you every waking moment. I couldn't expect you to marry a person involved in war zones, so I had to make a decision not to sign on again, and I hoped it would not be too late. Please say yes".

"Trevor, I've felt the same way about you. I knew we would come together again one day, and it looks like it's here now. My answer is a thousand times yes. Yes. Yes. Yes". They pulled together and kissed a long lingering kiss. Lips just touching in order to protect the ambiance and delicacy of their situation, even though the throng around them was excessive to say the least. Trevor stood up and began ringing the side of his glass with a knife. The couples next to them looked at them, Trevor indicated he needed help. They started up, and one by one the whole restaurant was ringing with glasses.

Trevor walked out from the corner booth, and slowly lowering his raised arms caused the cacophony to ease to a murmur. In his loudest voice, he announced. "Trevor Baines – that's me, and Kirsty Evans – that's her, are announcing to you, that we are in love, and will soon be engaged to be married. What do you think of that then eh"? A cheer went up and someone started off with, "for they are jolly good fellows". When that died down an older woman piped up with "My old man said follow the van". The whole joint rocked for a while, then it settled down to its decibel rating of 90.

Trevor said, "I'm so relieved you said yes, now I can go tell my old man. Wanna come"? "Wouldn't miss it for quids". They jumped in a taxi and made their way to the Angel. When they walked into the office, Millie jumped up and greeted Trevor like a long lost son.

"When did you get in"? "Not long ago actually". "Barry has just gone out for a sandwich. He's due back any minute now".

"Ok, let's have some fun. How about Kirsty sits in dads chair and when you buzz the phone as dad walks in, she can pretend to be on the phone to an employee, telling them that she's taken over the role of Managing Director. She can have her back to the door. Then I come out from the bathroom after he's cooled off.

The plan worked like clockwork, with Barry standing there nonplussed, as Kirsty swung around in the chair, pretending that she ruled that world now. She looked him square in the eye and announced that the board had voted him out and her in. He would be found an office very soon. That's when Trevor walked in and the two of them accompanied now by Millie burst into laughter.

Trevor bent over and sighed. "You bastards got the better of me for a minute. In fact right up to the point where I realized that we don't have a board. Hello son". He hugged Trevor tightly. "It's so good to see you. To what do I owe the pleasure"? Millie started to walk out. Trevor asked her to stay. "Firstly I no longer am employed by the United Nations. No more tours of duty. Secondly Kirsty has agreed to marry me. That's what's news"!

Barry put his arms out wide and brought the four of them together. "Son, Kirsty, you just made me the happiest man in the whole world. Two of the nicest people I know are going to get hitched". He kissed them both on the temple. As they broke away, Barry said to Millie, "What do you make of that then Millie, eh"? Millie reached for a tissue and blew her nose several times, in between crying. She had no words but her actions spoke volumes. She hustled out to get more tissues from her desk.

"I suppose you'll want to tell Denise your good news. Are you waiting 'til tonight or are you planning to go to her office. She's there. I just spoke to her". "I think we might make another surprise visit", said Kirsty, and pulled Trevor out the door. Denise could not have been more pleased for them both, and announced the news to all and sundry. "How about you both come round for dinner tonight". Trevor retorted. "How about we go see Les Mis. I have four tickets just for this special occasion. I've also booked a bistro for 6 pm, so that we can have something to eat before the show. What do you say both of you". They looked at each other and said in unison, "we say yes". "Then Denise, would you mind calling dad and let him know what's happening, then I will arrange for a limo to pick you up at 5.15 from home".

"That's a wonderful end to a shitty day. Thank you both". She gave them a hug and they parted ways. There wasn't a lot of time for them to go back to Kirsty's apartment, after Kirsty invited him to stay, and Trevor picking up his giant kit bag and suit bag from Central Storage where he'd dropped them off earlier. He wasn't sure if he would be staying with Kirsty, his dad's place, or looking for a space to rent.

Denise and Barry arrived at the bistro, to be led to a table with tall candle furniture and even taller red candles. The rosy red glow spreading a warmth conducive to the occasion. There was much talk about how Trevor had been planning both moves for a long time, and hoped that Kirsty hadn't found someone better in the meantime. He was indeed. "Lucky to have a partner like Kirsty; a Mother in Law like Denise, and a wonderful dad as well".

Les Miserable was a resounding success, especially when Alfie Boe made a guest appearance as Jean Valjean, as the current singer in the limited time west end run had taken a bad turn. The audience went wild, with a two minute standing ovation. It seemed like Alfie was singing directly to them. There were no dry eyes in the theatre.

The four retired to Barry's house for drinks and snacks and the answering of hundreds of questions, before Trevor and Kirsty bade them goodnight. Barry's last thought before retiring was, "somebody brought him home safely to me". He could not stop humming 'Bring him home', until he fell asleep. Trevor and Kirsty had other ideas.

CHAPTER 52

The bomb was deafening. The front pillars holding up the first floor from the car park had been blown clean away, and the front façade of the building had formed a V where the pillars had been as the bricks moved down then out to leave a gaping hole.

The red Perspex lettering forming the words MEDIA MOGULS had been shattered into a thousand pieces. It and thirty or more disintegrated glass panes from the floors above and across the road, rained down onto the pavement. Some passers-by were caught by the shards and debris, and were calling out for help. Witnesses at first stunned, then realizing what had happened, started to run to the aid of those trapped under the rubble,

A desk was precariously half hanging from the second floor, and strip blinds were waving out in the stiff breeze, where windows had previously been. A pall of dust hung around at floor level, Confusion reigned until a couple of Police cars pulled up and the officers started to take control of the situation. Firstly they thanked the helpers, then asked them to go behind the tape that they had set up thirty feet each side of the explosion. They didn't want to say it, but they feared another possible explosion as was often the case with terrorists, waiting until police and help arrived, before detonating a second bomb.

The Fire Brigade came next, then the Emergency Control Unit, then an armed SOG unit – just in case. The SOG's moved watchers and bystanders even further away. People were streaming out of the damaged building, being directed by the Fire Brigade, some of whom donned breathing masks after interrogating some of the residents coming out.

As they wandered through each floor, it was clear that the damage and any casualties had been confined to the front middle section of the building. One stair well was out of action from the second floor, and one pair of lifts in the front of the building had been shut down by the security woman on duty, whilst the rear lifts seemed to be unaffected.

Denise had an office at the front of the building on the sixth floor – of eight. When the middle collapsed inwards, it stopped at the fifth floor. When she heard the explosion, she was the first to move back from the window, shout at her secretary to run to the rear, then went around to the other offices, telling everyone to make for the rear stairs immediately; waited until they were all out, then moved to the back stairs – and went up! She repeated the exercise on the seventh and eighth floors until she was sure everyone had gotten away. The stairs were clogged, but they all kept their cool and met the firemen coming up as they were going down. They told them that Denise was going from floor to floor getting people to move quickly.

The firefighters checked each floor to make doubly sure. They met Denise trailing an older lady who was having trouble traversing the stairs. "This is Mrs. Kitson our tea lady". One fireman lifted the older lady from Denise's arms. "I've got you now love. You'll be fine". Mrs. Kitson, never short of a word, said. "If I'd have known a young fireman was going to rescue me, I would have set this up myself long ago". Denise asked the fireman whose name was Dennis, what had happened, he explained that two supporting pillars had been blown away, and that the front of the building had collapsed into a V shape. Levels six through to eight were looking very precarious. "It may be that the whole front at least may need to be pulled down".

Denise called Barry as soon as she had been checked out by the ambos, declaring that she was fine, as was everyone else in the building, but unfortunately a couple of passers-by had to be taken to hospital with cuts and bruises. She would have to work from home for a while, and that it was just as well her work had been uploaded to the cloud every half hour. The Police were investigating a possible motive, and checking nearby CCTV cameras for clues. She asked Trevor to call Kirsty and Trevor to tell them she was ok. Right now she had to get back in if possible to retrieve 'stuff'.

The Fire Investigation Unit was on the scene, and an officious officer declared her insane for wanting to go back into the building. "Madam, you attempt to return to your desk and I'll have you arrested. Not only could this building collapse at any moment, but there's also a terrorist alert on, so would you mind placing yourself behind either tape – if the Police have finished with you". The officer closest said. "We have your statement, thank you Mrs Baines. If there is any chance that your chattels are recovered, we will make sure you get them, so don't worry".

Specialist builders were later called in to prop up the front of the building whilst police and other investigators scoured the scene for clues, before the clean-up began 24 hours later.

Video from a nearby building showed a man leaving a modern looking trash can between the two main pillars, earlier in the day. No one had thought to question it. They merely started to fill it up with rubbish. The picture of the man with his head facing the other way, was circulated and shown on TV in the late news, but no leads were forthcoming.

Barry decided - on Denise's behalf - that the time had come for her to work from home on a permanent basis. She didn't argue, especially as she had made a list of most of the personnel in the building and was constructing an index of names, phone numbers and e-mails for all to share – from their homes. Life went on for the staff. Not just all in the same building.

Barry then asked if she would like to become the company Secretary of BB Holdings, so that they could work together. Denise thought about the offer and said, "That's a wonderful compliment. That you think I have what it takes to look after an ever growing company like yours. Frankly I don't think I'm the right person, whom I see as needing to be steady and a long term decision maker, whereas I live for the ever changing and fast paced world of magazines. Besides, I need to be with my colleagues right now. It would seem as though I'm deserting the ship that just came under fire. So, lovely thought, but no thanks". She kissed him on the cheek and said, "You know they have to find the person who did this, don't you? We don't know if it was a threat against one of the magazines, or against a particular individual, or even the building's owners".

Denise's phone rang. The number was unknown. "Denise Baines", she answered. "Hello Mrs Baines, this is Detective Constable Edward Price. We have obtained footage from a couple of the CCTV cameras in the vicinity of your office, and would like to show the footage to you. Can we meet somewhere at your convenience"? "How about you come over to the house, and gave him the address. "Thank you Maam. Would half an hour be ok with you"? "Fine, see you soon".

She turned to Barry. "A Detective Constable Price is calling round soon to show footage of the office. This might be interesting". Her investigative reporting background now coming to the fore, even though she now enjoyed the comfortable position as Editor of Furniture Magazine, it wasn't always so. She missed the cut and thrust. The stealth. The late nights. The undercover work. She was wondering just how she got to be so dull, when the front door bell rang. Trevor and Kirsty walked in. Trevor asking if they could stay for lunch as they had just picked up a cooked chicken and salads from the supermarket.

As Kirsty was preparing the chicken, Denise let DC Price in. He introduced himself. With a cuppa on the breakfast bar, and helping himself from the biscuit tin, he opened his tablet. The camera from obliquely opposite showed a male wearing a dark blue windcheater, pulling along a modern looking trash can, which had been fitted with wheels on the rear only. He had dark hair, with what looked like either highlights are streaks of grey above the ears. It seemed incongruous that the man wore white and black checkered top trainers, with the Nike whoosh clearly seen. Denise was concentrating on his dress manner – strange to wear a windcheater in the summer – when he glanced round to face the camera.

"Shit. Sorry, but I know who that is. It's a bloke who called himself Rosie Greenhaugh. He said his name was Rosie due to his family wanting him to be tough – like a boy named Sue. About two weeks ago, I was called up to the reporting room for Hunters and Shooters –

another magazine in the group. There was no one in the building that could take this man's statement. He told me a story about how he had been discharged from the Grenadiers after being accused of stealing several weapons from the Army and selling them on to enthusiasts like the magazine's readers. He told me that he was set up but couldn't prove it at the time. He now had proof – he said.

He accused a Sergeant Tom Woolf. He said he had evidence, as he had tracked down one of the missing weapons through some amateur sleuthing on his part, and he needed us to expose this Woolf character. I took down all his information and contact details. They are still on my computer at work, but I might be able to bring them back from the cloud.

Maybe I made a faux pas, because I told him that his best option would be to contact the Police and lay his story bare to them. He said that he had tried, but nothing was being done. He said that they were still investigating and didn't hold out any hope after six months, so he came to us, in the hope that we would publish an expose".

"Was he similarly dressed when you interviewed him"? "No. I only recognize him from the grey steaks in his hair and his facial and physical features". "Thank you Mrs Baines. You have been a great help. If you manage to get the information on Mr. Greenhaugh it would help, but we have extensive records and will start the tracking process immediately. Thanks for the tea and biscuits. Much appreciated". He handed her his card and was escorted to the door.

Police did not waste any time looking for and finding Rosie Greenhaugh. After intensive questioning and denying everything accused of him, they confronted him with two objects. One was a trainer, and the other was a windcheater, both remarkably similar, to those the perpetrator was wearing at the time of the explosion, "wouldn't you say Rosie"?

"They look like mine and they may or may not be, but you've got the wrong man and I can prove it. I was up north. Liverpool to be exact. I went to see a promoter about a boxing match coming up, and I had to get into the ring and show him I could mix it with one of his lads. The guy's name is Eddie Jewell of Solomons Gym on Lacerell St. Go on give 'im a call. Then ask any of the lads there". This revelation gave the need for a pause, and the recording was halted.

After ten minutes, the DC came into Interview Room 2, to advise Rosie that he would be taken back to the holding cell pending further enquiries by Liverpool CID. "But if you are giving me the run around, I'll make sure we add wasting Police time to your charges".

The investigation now focused on testing Rosie's shoes and windcheater for evidence of another wearer. After 12 hours the breakthrough they were looking for came in. "We found several hairs on the jacket that do not belong to Mr. Greenhaugh. The DNA information doesn't show a match on our database". DC Price knew just where to look next. He made enquiries through the Camp Commandant at Aldershot, where Sergeant Woolf was still stationed. He explained to the Commandant where the investigation had led to this point, and that he needed to take a DNA swab from Sergeant Wolf, "In order to eliminate him from our enquiries".

"You understand, I think DC Price, that the Army prefers to deal with sort of thing in house. National security and all. Don't want to scare the natives what". "Sir, as much as I appreciate your position, someone – maybe from your company - planted a rather large bomb in a trash can under a building, bringing down the front of it. Fortunately, no one was killed, but it could have been a very different story. Now, I suggest that either myself or a colleague comes along to the camp, where your Sergeant will present himself for a DNA swab voluntarily. If he refuses, I will be armed with a warrant to compel. If you would kindly advise me if the Sergeant is on camp, then we will make the necessary arrangements to call on you first. I will hold whilst you find out if he is still there". The Commandant came back on line and advised DC Price that, "Yes he was still there. Yes he would await their visit the next morning. Yes, he would make sure he didn't leave camp in the meantime".

"Commandant, would you please also supply to me a list of any possible missing weapons and explosives from any store that Sergeant

Woolf may have access to. It may be that records have been doctored also". "I will get that audit underway immediately. You say that you know of at least ten weapons that have gone on sale on the black market. That is serious if true".

Next morning the DC and a female constable were introduced to the Commandant, then taken by an orderly to the clinic. The duty nurse had been apprised of the situation and took the test kit from the constable. She was about to open it, when the constable asked her to wait until the person of interest was in the room and had been read his rights. She may or may not be required as a witness in any future case. She nodded.

The orderly brought Sergeant Woolf in who immediately asked, "What's all this about then"? DC Price, advised the Sergeant that they had obtained a warrant to compel him to supply a DNA swab to them for the purposes of eliminating him from an investigation they were conducting into the matter of stolen armaments and possibly explosives. "Do you wish to volunteer a sample Sergeant"? "Sure, I've got nothing to hide". DC Price nodded to the nurse who pressed the lever to release sanitizing gel onto her hands, and after a quick rub in, unsealed the kit, removed the swab container, then the ab, and asked the Sergeant to open his mouth. The constable asked the nurse to make sure to get a sample from under the tongue also. As the swab was loaded back into the plastic tube and sealed, DC Price asked the Sergeant to write his name and sign it along with the date on a sticky label, with space for three other names and signatures, which included all present. This label was attached to the vial, with one part of the label forming a tamper proof seal, which he pointed out to all present, and that this sample would be sent to the Police testing facility at Hendon for analysis. The constable then asked the Sergeant to place his hand onto a tablet. The tablet would record first his left then right hand finger prints, which he acceded to. DC Price then thanked the Sergeant who was escorted out by the orderly. He then thanked the nurse, who it seemed, had seen a little excitement in her day for once.

As DC Price suspected, the swab proved conclusively that Sergeant Woolf had worn Rosie's windcheater at some time. He now had to place him at the scene of the crime. He let Rosie free, asking him to stay local until 'this' was over. If he had to go to Liverpool to fight, then to let him know first. He gave him his card.

Obviously Sergeant Woolf had gained access to Rosie's place, then had to quickly return the windcheater and shoes, so DC Price visited Rosie's block of flats along with the same female PC. She was sent to the floors above and below, door knocking. DC Price concentrated on both sides of Rosie's place. There was no success until as they were leaving a dark skinned girl with pig tails said, "I saw you over at Rosie's place. My Mum said I had to tell you what I saw once". With that, a large, black skinned lady trudged up onto the landing and puffed until her breath steadied. Ok honey, tell the man what you saw". With a tilted head, and an air of ultra-concentration, the girl who introduced herself as Molly, said, "I told my Mum that a man who looked like Rosie had come out of his flat in the morning as Mum was putting out the washing - she pointed – down there – where a row of lines were evident. "She told me to wait up here". The man came out of Rosie's flat with a white plastic bag. I waved, but he didn't see me. I didn't see Rosie for two days, but the same man came back with the plastic bag after lunch. It seemed like he couldn't find his key, 'cause it took him a long time to get in". The constable told the little girl and her Mum, that she needed to get a statement from them both a bit later, and that they had helped considerably with their enquiries.

DC Price knocked on Rosie's door. There was no one home. He called Rosie, who advised them that he could come home in about twenty minutes. Meantime, DC Price called in and requested a SOCO team go to the premises, looking for evidence of an intruder. When Rosie arrived the SOCO team were also outside his flat. He let them in. DC Price advised Rosie to leave the flat for tonight – they would pay for a local hotel, and in the morning he could come to the station to pick up his key. He told Rosie that it was part of the ongoing investigation to clear his name. Rosie accepted that. He left them to it.

Sure enough the team came up with evidence of fingerprints in some of the most unlikely places. Places where the non- professional criminal would likely leave some evidence. A rush job in the crime labs resulted in matches from some of the hairs on the windcheater. It was enough evidence to subpoena the Army to release Sergeant Woolf for questioning by the Metropolitan Police. The Commanding Officer refused on the grounds that a Military misdemeanor had been occasioned first, by a) the stealing of weapons, of which their MPs had gathered sufficient evidence, and b) the removal and use of military explosives, in the abetting of a felony, and c) the impersonation of a former serving member with intent to cause distress, and d) actual harm to civilian property with potential for bodily harm using said explosives. It was therefore a military jurisdictional preference, and that police led civil actions could take place afterwards. "So, no, Sergeant Woolf would remain in an Army lock up pending a Court Martial. After we have finished with him and he has served any sentence that may be imposed upon him, you may have your turn, and when you have finished with him, any civil suits can then be lodged".

DC Price had to refer the matter 'upstairs' for a decision, Meanwhile he had done his job. His team would continue to build a case against Sgt. Woolf, and on the basis of the evidence gathered it was agreed that Rosie could return to his flat, and that the owners and occupiers of the business premises that had been disrupted, were now free to take any reconstructive measures they saw fit, and to prepare any case they wished for future action against Sergeant Woolf once all the evidence had been gathered.

The buildings insurance company upon receipt of the Police Report, agreed to fully reinstate the front of the building including two new support pillars, and because it had been scarred, new aluminum façade panels were purchased to make the building look like new, along with a classy new sign. After five months all the building work had been completed and the staff moved back into their newly refurbished offices.

After just two months the Lord Mayor's office called to ask Denise if she would attend a function at the Town Hall. She accepted in front of her workmates and family the Fire Brigades Bravery Medal, for her part in making sure that the people in the floors above hers were gotten out safely and without panic.

CHAPTER 53

"Barry, you gave me a wonderful opportunity to manage House & Garden Accessories, and I've had the pleasure of travelling around with Michael Stanning getting to know the European suppliers. I know you look at the figures regularly, and you would know that over the past two years we have trebled profits. That shows we have the right mix of products. We have repeat buyers. We are on trend. We are successful. Now you need to open up some more centres around the country".

Barry leaned back in his reclining back office chair. "Well, haven't we come a long way in a short time? Here you are telling me what to do and how to expand, Well, Barbara Charming, I have only one thing to say to you".

Barb looked worried, she had taken her pushy ways to new extremes. She was about to get fired.

"What are you going to do about it"?

Barb was relieved. She half thought it would happen like this, but you never could tell. She had hit the bullseye. She pushed her luck. "I've been speaking to Michael and to Millie. I asked them to keep quiet about it until I spoke with you. They have crunched some numbers. Mike has investigated four potential sites in strategic locations that give us about 50 miles between each one. Far enough away from each other, and a large enough catchment area for each centre.

I was enquiring about franchising and got some background figures if you preferred to go that way. We even have two possible franchisees, who agree that a buy in figure of 140,000 Pounds and a royalty of 15% plus advertising at 5%, based on the figures we are producing at our first centre would be a viable proposition. Or, you may prefer for the group to run them ourselves".

Barry asked Millie and Michael if they would mind attending a meeting in the board room where a sandwich lunch and coffee would be provided. Barry grilled them both, then congratulated them all for doing a fine job of progressing the centre and for looking into its future.

"Now, Michael, Barb tells me that you have figures relating to expansion based on two premises, a) we continue as we are going – or should I say growing, and we add another store when we have sufficient funds, or b) go the franchise route. Let me hear your opinion".

"If you want plenty of stores relatively quickly, then franchising is the way to go. It gives us a healthy 15% clear margin as against a 30% margin right now, but then we have to take overheads and staff from that. We can buy in bulk, making our costs lower – remembering that the centres can only buy from us. We select the range - and Barb has done an outstanding job so far in that regard. We get an immediate cash flow from the buy-in figure. We get an additional 5% for group advertising which buys a lot more when you have a greater number of stores. It usually takes at least six months to produce a franchisee bible, but Barb has done most of that work and has already implemented most of it at the centre, so it would not be hard to formalize it. The franchise experts will need to organize the implementation documentation, but it just means tweaking existing document formats. When Barb came to me with the idea, I thought this is too much too soon, but she convinced me that she had done her homework, and by looking around we still have very little competition, so by growing the business fast, we actually prevent others from copying the format, so my recommendation is to franchise rather than to grow organically".

Barry looked at Millie. "Now Millie, your two cents worth please". "I've watched Barb grow into this job, and she has taken it very seriously. She has come to me for advice on dozens of occasions. Every one of them to help progress the centre. Michael and Barb have done some terrific research and I think they have enough information to make it work. I also think franchising is the way to go. I also think that if it goes ahead, Barb should be made Operations Manager of the centre and of the franchisees. If we need to start a company run centre and if we do not have a franchisee available, Barb can organize everything, get it up and working, then sell it as a franchise when it is running smoothly – that's an easy sell to any business person. So there is no need to wait, we can build and sell, using our company run centre or centres to provide a benchmark for the franchisees, and show we are in it together".

"You see, that's what's so terrific about every one of you. It's not about you, it's about all of us and our futures. You come up with an idea. You research it, then if it looks viable you come to me for a decision, and that's just about how every business should be run, with you guys having the balls and the ability, and me to make decisions that foster your enthusiasm, so well done".

Barb piped up. "When I first started here, you promoted me to Thrift Shop Manager straight away, because I was the only one with retail experience, but you told me, all you expected from me was that if I saw that things needed doing or improving, I was to investigate; come up with three options; then argue for the best one. Everyone in this business knows your credo and it works. I'm only doing what you told me to do".

"Well, Barb, Michael, Milly, you lot have all been under the pump this time. I have nothing but admiration for you all, and of course I am taking on board your recommendations. Can you work out management and processes between you, or do you need expert advice to make this happen"?

Michael spoke next. "I suggest Crockford Franchising Systems are our best bet. They can put all this in train. Meantime we three can get together and work out the nuts and bolts and report back to you say every month regarding progress, and by the way, I second Milly's idea of promoting Barb – providing Barb is happy to take on new responsibilities". They all looked at her. She raised both arms. "What can I say? I was born to lead". They all laughed and left chattering. A new chapter in the newly agreed upon BB Enterprises empire had begun –

to go alongside BB Logistics. Barry pulled Barb aside. "Welcome to Upper Management, Operations Manager, H&GA and Franchises".

Barb and Michael agreed to meet up at the local pub that night, and after a few drinks, had a plan of action agreed to. They worked out all that Barb needed to do on one side, and Michael's responsibilities on the other. Michael confessed that he had a couple of young assistants who would take on much of his work, but Barb needed to have a hands on approach for her tasks. Her first job was to contact her existing suppliers, with a view to supplying greater quantities of goods – at a better price – more often. They needed to gear up for change. "If they couldn't, she would have to find alternative suppliers". Most agreed that it would not be a problem. Some offered an immediate discount of 5% for container lots. Other said they needed to come back to her re pricing. One said that they could not possibly expand and certainly could not do a better price, so they agreed to part company there and then. She thanked them for their service so far. Barb had another supplier in mind and began the task of contacting them, and that, "she would be making a trip to their region soon, to see for herself what their quality was like, and if their facilities meant that they could supply the volumes she needed". She had used this tactic before. It meant that they were either genuine, or they started making excuses why she shouldn't visit.

Michael's first task was to contact the two potential franchisees, to see if they were still interested. He gave them brief details, after which they said they were still keen, so he told them that someone from Crockford would be in touch. He passed their names over to the Crockford rep who was handling the preliminaries. He ensured Michael that they would follow through with them, then advise him when they had signed up – after all the documents had been drawn up and approved. Michael advised the rep that they had already picked out four locations but no sites yet, and that the two could pick any one they wished – just let him know which.

A separate bank account needed to be set up in the name of 'House & Garden Accessories Franchises'. All fiscal dealings with potential franchisees would channel through this account, to ensure everything was above board and that the Tax Office could monitor the centres accounts easily. The company owned centres would still go through a company account, but the figures could easily be removed for comparison purposes.

Barb asked Arthur Wilson, the longest serving member of H&GC to travel with her, to the four locations they had selected from the map, as they showed the most potential, with similar household incomes as their current centre. The first was a dump. On the map it was ideal, but it was in the midst of an urban redevelopment plan, and the people with money were in fact on the periphery, making the median income range look good, but they needed to do better. Barb pulled in for petrol, and asked the woman behind the counter where the nearest garden centre was. "Well if you want cheap and cheerful, go to Worster Rd Garden Centre, up the road, turn left at the top and it's down about a mile. If you want posh (she pronounced it 'poshe'), then go the opposite way. Turn left at the first lights then second right. It's on the Causeway. I can't afford anything in there love". Barb decided to go to the Causeway first.

The Causeway Garden Centre was mainly filled with every type of plant and tree imaginable. There were a few ornaments, but they were all large and very high priced. They toured around the area, then started to make their way to Worster Rd. The Garden Centre was little more than a plant nursery with many small shrubs and plants in punnets. Very disappointing. A longer tour of the surrounding areas convinced them both, that the urban renewal plan area may just be the ticket, so they called into the Town Hall and spoke to one of the Town Planners who showed them the plans and depictions for the whole area, which was set into four distinct themes. At the intersection of the four segments, there was a small shopping precinct planned for. In fact, they had already seen that the development was well under construction. Barb asked if there was any chance they could secure a site for a House & Gardens Accessories Centre there. The man called up his boss who ambled in, listened to their idea, and stated. "Why not put in an application and a submission now and come to the next Council Meeting on Thursday the eighteenth, where all submissions are debated. If one of you are there, you can answer any questions that might arise, on the spot. Chances are it can be decided upon, on the night. You can't lose anything, and from what I know about your centre, it could make a good addition to the area and set the tone for the other developments in the area. It would take six months or more to get up and running if that's within your time frame. About a quarter of all the low rise and single dwellings will have been finished by then, and as you would have seen, there is a large quantity of traffic passing through the intersections at all times".

This place, if it went ahead, would not be their second site, but if they were able to secure it, it would be in a perfect position for a Centre later. Barb diarized the next council meeting date and would organize things when she got back, along with the form filling exercise, along with a note to contact the owner of the development too.

Arthur suggested to Barb that they still had time to get to the next location if she was willing. As it was getting on for lunch, she suggested a stop off in the town centre on the way. Sure enough, a sandwich bar appeared and they both walked in to give their orders. They waited in line behind a few people. The woman in front turned around to Arthur. "You remind me of my Uncle Alec". "You mean good looking and with a full head of hair"? "No. He looks half dead. Is there something wrong with you too"?

The road to their next destination was all Motorway, so they made good time. They toured the area someone suggested as a maybe option, but they were not impressed. They found a Home Improvement Store and went in for a look around. They had what every other HIS had around the country, but in the 'Gardening' section she was amazed to find some of the types of things that she had brought in from Yugoslavia. She looked at the labels on the back and sure enough they were from the same supplier. She knew the supplier did not manufacture them, but she had an arrangement where they could not sell to any other company in the U.K. She asked Arthur to take down the details of those items she pointed out. Apart from those, there was not a lot of competition as far as she could ascertain.

Right across the road from the Home Improvement Store, a large derelict warehouse was being demolished. They drove over and into the yard after opening the double wire gates. They sat inside the gates until they got the desired reaction. A skinny bloke wearing dirty jeans, black polo shirt and a hi-vis vest, threw open the door of the dozer he was driving and had come to a halt right in front of the car. "You're not bloody well allowed inside the gates. You could get injured. What do you want"?

Whilst Arthur was content to sit tight with the window up, Barb wound hers down and fluttered a 10 Pound note in the air. The young guy got down from the cab and came closer. "What's that for"? "I am looking for a place to rent, lease or buy and this spot looks to be ideal. Who do I talk to"? "Ten quid aint buying you nuthin". "That's fine, I'm off to the town planner's office. They'll tell me all I need to know. You were just going to save me some fuel". She started to wind the window up as the guy pulled the tenner from her hand. She wound the window down again. "Smart lad". The developer is Knight Moves. Mark Knight. He's thinks he has a big furniture retailer interested. I happen to know they've signed a lease on a new place the other side of town. My brother told me". Barb, pulled out another tenner. The guy went to grab it. She pulled it back. "What's the number and address of Mark Knight, and if I want to see him right away, where would I find him"?

Arthur jotted down the information as the guy scoured his phone. "He's at another site on Johnston St in Caulston, but he leaves in about thirty minutes. You'd better give him a ring first". Barb handed him the tenner. "Thanks love". The guy looked over at Arthur. "By the way, are you alright mate, you look very pasty faced"?

As Barb sped out of the gate after typing in the next location details in her sat nav, Arthur called ahead. Mark Knight would wait for them, but they only had a short time to talk once there, as he had a kid's party to get ready for. The mechanical voice said, "Turn right on

Johnston St. In 50 yards you will reach your destination". They alighted and walked towards the site hut marked OFFICE. As they walked in, a deep voiced, well-tanned man of about fifty said, "You must be Arthur and Barb, come and sit here". He dusted off two plastic chairs with a tea towel. "Sorry about the dust, it gets everywhere". "No problem", said Barb. "Look I'll come straight to the point as you have to go soon. We are looking for a site to establish a garden centre, and you have one opposite HIS in Brockham. What if I say the only changes you need to make to it are, 1) a new front entrance, 2) Big Ass fans throughout – I see it already has heating, and, c) A roller shutter door at the rear. There will be other minor stuff, but not much. I also know that the tenant you think you had, has leased elsewhere – the other side of town. You can check while we wait if you like. I am prepared to take a 3 year lease with an option of 3 then another 3, at a rental of 6 Pounds per square foot, with 2% annual inflation. You pay council taxes. We pay everything else. When will it be ready to occupy"?

"Jeesus lady, you caught me on the hop. Firstly I just heard about my prospective tenant moving on. Secondly, your rental assessment is exactly what I had in mind. Thirdly, we can fit the front and rear and the fans as you request, and fourthly, if you are prepared to take it on in two months' time, you have a deal – provided you pass the credentials tests that my secretary will send you details of". They exchanged cards. Mark looked at Barb's card. "I know of your business and I know Barry Baines he's a good operator, and it looks like he's got a firebrand for a Manager. I'll call him tomorrow. The only problem is he'll hit me for a donation to his charity. Gotta get to my kids 6th birthday, or I'll never hear the last of it. Nice doing business with you". He glanced at Arthur. "Do you need drink or something mate? You look seedy"!

Barb suggested that they find a motel – with separate rooms, and did Arthur want to go see a Doctor, as he did look pale. Arthur nodded. He thought that the nearest hospital might be better as the docs would be closed, so Barb dialed in the hospital which was fortunately only five minutes away. The Emergency Triage on- call Doctor, asked Arthur many questions before a nurse took Arthur away to an examination room. Barb had been busy meantime asking people in the waiting area where the nearest motel was. She was busy making reservations, when a nurse came out and asked for a Barbara Charming. She held her hand up, then said into the phone, "I have to go, I'll see you later".

The nurse said, "Arthur had asked that you be informed that he has to go down straight away for an emergency appendicitis operation as it was on the verge of bursting, and would she phone his daughter. I have the number here".

Barb took the slip of paper in disbelief. "You mean that poor bugger has lived with this all day, without complaining once. What if it had burst"? "Well you and I would be having a different conversation now. Most appendix related operations are successful, but he will need some hospital bed rest between 1 and 3 days, and home recuperation time of between 2 – 3 weeks". "Thanks nurse. I'll give his daughter a call now".

"Hi Jodie. You don't know me but my name is Barb Charming. I work with your dad at the House and Garden Accessories Centre". "Hi. I do know of you. Dad is always telling me about how great it is to work there and for you. "Aw that's nice. I have some news for you that straight away is not serious so don't worry. Arthur and I have been looking around for new garden centre sites, and he has looked pasty all day. We finally went to Caulston General where the Doc declared he has appendicitis, and just to be sure, they suggested operating on him right away. The nurse assures me it's all routine, but he needs a couple of days in hospital and a couple of weeks resting at home. I'm here in the waiting room".

"I'll come up right away, although it'll take me two hours to get there". "How about I stay here and wait for the op to be finished. I already have a room booked at the Caulston Inn, a motel nearby. You come up in the morning after the rush hour. Take your time. I will wait for you. My number's in your phone now. We'll go in to see him together, then you can take my hotel room for one or two days until your dad is ready to go home. I will make sure the room and any meals you have there are covered by the company. I'll call you at home a week after you get back. How does that sound"?

"Oh Barb, that's so good of you. That would certainly suit me better, as I can make better arrangements for the dog to be looked after. It seems like dad is in good hands, so thanks again. I'll see you in the morning". "Oh, by the way, the company has a good health scheme, so any costs should all be covered. See you tomorrow, and hey, don't worry, it's all good".

Barb drove to the motel. Parked. Cancelled one room. Went for a meal and checked out her room. She pulled the battery clock from her holdall – they had been prepared to be out all night - and set the alarm for two hours later. She didn't know which way was up until the fog cleared and the day's events unfolded up to the realization that Arthur would be out of surgery and probably sitting up in bed.

She walked to the hospital, and introduced herself as a friend of Arthur Wilson. The nurse looked up the name and frowned. "Is everything all right"? Barb asked. "Just a minute please". She picked up the desk phone and punched in a number. "A Doctor will be with you shortly, and as if she knew what was coming next, she said, "I don't know any details, but the Doctor will explain everything".

A white coated doctor with a name tag announcing Dr Wesley Grainger, asked Barb to come though as the door which automatically opened and she walked through to be guided to a room marked Consulting 1. The Doctor pulled the large office chair from behind the desk and placed it in front of the chair that he had indicated she should be seated in. His hand rested on hers, which was on her knee.

"Mr. Wilson". "Arthur", corrected Barb. "Arthur would have been in intense pain all day. He had been leaking toxic fluids from a rupture in his appendix for some time. You may have noticed him in pain and he would have been very sickly looking". "No. He looked pasty but said he was fine. He only went to the hospital after I nagged him."

"Because the poison has permeated his blood stream, he has acute septicemia – sepsis or blood poisoning. He is on the critical list. Truthfully, he may not survive this ordeal. We have pumped him full of powerful anti-biotics, and it's up to his body to fight the infection. The odds are about 25% when it gets to this stage, so pray as hard as you can that he is strong enough to fight it. Sorry for the bad news, but he really should have seen a Doctor way before today".

Barb messaged Jodie with the latest news. She advised her to stick with the original plan, because there was nothing anyone outside of the hospital could do for Arthur.

Jodie arrived around noon next day. Barb told her that she had been in to see Arthur and that he was heavily sedated. She suggested they go for lunch, then go visit. She showed her to her hotel room where she unpacked. Barb had already packed her things. After lunch they both went visiting. Arthur was awake and barely audible as Jodie explained to him what had happened, and that she would be staying close for the next few days whilst he recuperated.

The Doctor explained to them outside of Arthur's earshot, that he was now over the worst and that he should make a complete recovery if he continued in the same vein. Jodie turned to Barb as they walked back to the motel. "Thanks for everything Barb. It seems he was worried about letting you down, so he didn't complain. Silly old sod. You know, when I was in Uni, I worked many times at the House & Gardens Accessories centre with Dad. He always told me I would never be paid, but I loved going in at weekends observing and just to get a feel for commerce. He was so glad that I took an interest. He is so proud of that place".

"What do you do for a crust", asked Barb. "I just finished my degree in Accounting, so I'm looking for a position. The problem is that accounting is so boring, but I'm good with numbers and want to use that skill in a more interesting way, so I was thinking of Forensic Accounting or even importing, something along the lines of your job". "Blimey, I've only known you five minutes and already you want my job. Tell you what. When you're ready, come down to the centre and we'll talk. Ok"?

"Your dad's holdall is over there. I'm not sure if he needs anything from it, I'll leave that to you. I'm off. Take care and give Arthur my love. Tell him to take all the time he needs.

The weekend passed and Barb reported to Barry about the events on Thursday and Friday, and how she had Arthur's job covered at the centre. "Would you be prepared to sign a three year lease on that new property Barry, provided it all checks out with Millie"? "Let Millie do her homework, and I'll let you know. Well done for starting on our – your expansion plans". Barb left the best 'til last as she walked out. "By the way, Mark Knight said he would be more than willing to become our first franchise holder when we have the site fully established, and if it goes well, he may well be in the market for one or two more". He said he would call you to catch up this week, and he expected you to touch him for a donation to Mind Games". They both laughed.

Barb wasted no time in getting in touch with the supplier in Yugoslavia about the items she saw in the garden centre. "Mr. Jurzoc, I am just about to cancel our arrangement, which at the last count was worth 650,000 Euros last year. I have proof that you are supplying more than one garden centre in the U.K. with products that I have sole distribution rights to in the U.K. according to the agreement you signed when I first set this up. I can give you the names and descriptions of three items along with their product numbers. They come from Speggzi with whom we also have an exclusive distribution agreement. You have 5 minutes before we say goodbye, and before I initiate a formal complaint with the Yugo Chamber of Commerce, who will surely revoke your license. Then I will pursue you personally for breach of contract. Then I will make sure that your name is mud everywhere. Your time starts now".

Anatol Jurzoc came clean immediately, but it wasn't what she expected. Mrs Charming, you and I have had a cordial relationship for two years now, and I have acted in good faith on your behalf, acting as the consolidator for your various manufacturers in Yugoslavia. Now that you have bombarded me with this tirade, I believe I might be able to shed some light on your problem. About six months ago, a driver by the name of George Bendic, spoke to my Logistics Manager about filling up your pantecs. He told us that you had authorized him to add any items that we had in store – that is loose boxes that would fill in any spaces at the rear of the truck. He said he was acting on your instructions and that you had given him written authorization to make sure the trucks were fully laden. Usually as you know, it is full of pallets and there may only be a quarter or half pallet space left over so we hadn't bothered up until then. When my Manager showed me the letter of authorization, I presumed it was legitimate, so I suggested they keep many of the smaller crates or cartons aside - to be added to the truck load – if there was any space. Usually it would be smaller items in cartons, not the larger expensive stuff".

"It looks like I jumped the gun. I'm very sorry. Apart from not checking with me first, I can understand now why this has happened. Obviously, this George Bendic has taken the goods out of the truck when he's arrived in the U.K. and is selling them to garden centres. Would you mind finding this letter of authorization and sending me a copy. If this George fellow comes in, just do as you usually do. Don't let on to your staff either. We will catch him from this end".

"Would you really have ruined me, if I had been complicit"? "You can bet your balls on it, but right now we are best buds, and I owe you a drink next time I'm in town, which by the way will be soon, as we plan to expand our operations. So expect us to double our throughput in about three months' time, then double it again in another six months after that. Just keep in touch with Reggie Green about supplying sufficient trailers to cope with it, I suspect that George Bendic will not be picking up after this next time. Again, sorry about the rant, but it was the quickest way to the truth".

George pulled up outside his lock up, then unloaded the 'extras' into his lock up, then closed the door.

Jean had given the trailer tracking company, permission to relay the truck's movements to her computer. She had told her cop friend what was happening. He had arranged for a plain clothed constable to meet Jean down the road from the lock up. As soon as George had walked around the corner, the constable who was equipped with a flexi cam that slid under the gap at the base of the roller door, advised Jean that images showed pallet racking full of cartons. The external markings were identified as belonging to House & Garden Accessories.

Jean confronted George in front of his truck. He seemed resigned to the fact that he had been caught in the act.

"It was good while it lasted", he admitted, as the constable stated that a) he had been tracked taking the truck to his lock up. b) They had pictures of House & Garden Accessories stock on the pallet racking. c) He hadn't paid for the goods. d) Police had receipts from two stores that had purchased goods from him - and would find more – they were sure. e) The lock up was in his name, and, f) his bank account was showing a healthy increase in funds over the last six months, to the tune of 120,000 Euros. "So George, we will photograph and document every item that belongs to Mrs Charming's company. Each carton will receive a number and an officer's signature. They will remove the goods to their store, where they will be held pending your trial for forgery, deceit and theft. After you have been convicted, the goods will be released to the company for sale. Do you understand? If so, I will read you your rights". George nodded.

Barb took the Inspector aside before the Constable received the nod from the inspector to go ahead. "What if I get George to pay the company 120,000 Euros, and take the stock back, and you charge him for some road traffic infringement that will hurt his back pocket even more, then threaten him with all sorts of violations if he gets cheeky again. How would that sit with you"?

The Inspector thought about the offer. "Give me a minute with him". He walked over to George and pulled him by the arm to where they were against the wall. Five minutes later. "It seems that Mr.

Bendic was acting in the interests of your business after all Mrs Charming, and this may all be a mistake. Mr. Bendic it seems was about to pay House & Gardens Accessories the sum of 60,000 Euros as monies built up in his bank account on your behalf. He also understands that the goods in this lock up also belong to you. He apologizes for any misunderstanding that may have occurred. Isn't that so George"? The constable never got to read George his rights.

George looked crestfallen, but then looked up at the two and nodded. "Much better than ending up in jail, with no money and no prospects. Thanks. I was only making a few quid on the side you know". "George it was theft, you idiot. You're just lucky you got caught early". Barb agreed to come down to the police station to witness the statement, and to oversee the transfer of funds bank to bank. Reggie Green would send another prime mover to uncouple then couple up to take the trailer to the warehouse, and a van with two men to pick up the goods from the lock up.

CHAPTER 54

It was many months since Lonely made her debut as an international supplier to The King Group. Their cuddly lions were so successful, that the company had ordered shipments to be despatched to their branches in Ireland, the USA, Canada, Germany and Australia. All she had to do was to make sure each bear had the appropriate web address on its back. She insisted that she got the exact sample that they were going to supply, before they could ship even one bear, and if subsequent shipments varied in any way, they would be sent back at the manufacturers cost.

Lonely was treated to a dinner by Jonathon King. He wined and dined her, then asked if she wanted to come and work for him. Lonely appreciated the flattery, but deep down she was a simple soul, but one that had been earning good money from her position and had recently put a deposit down on an apartment in Kentish Town, close to the Thrift Shop store. She felt very good about herself and her prospects. Jonathon King however was just a bit above her station she thought, although she loved the attention.

She made her way to Harrods. The buyer was non-committal, and advised her that they had their own buyers in China, and that the suppliers, "Had to meet a very strict 'Code of Conduct', and meet very stringent 'Guidelines for Manufacture', before they could even think of supplying Harrods". Lonely was going to go to Hamleys next, but suspected she would be given the luke warm shoulder there also, so she sat outside the café drinking a latte, thinking about how best to make more sales. She reasoned that if she sold them to other stores, they would be competitors of sorts, even though the high-end stores would take different stock at higher prices.

She kept coming back to corporate. The King Group started her off, and other corporate s had followed in the wake of her advertising. Jonathon King had known exactly what he wanted. She was trying to sell others, using an image of Jonathon Kings bear, which she now realized was selling the King image. Each corporate pitch needed a toy and a story specific to each company. "Why didn't I see that before"? She phoned Milly, and told her of her dilemma, and would she mind if she spoke to Kirsty Evans, as she had experience in these matters. Lonely took down the number, sipped her coffee, ate a piece of custard tart, and then dialed.

Before the tart had cleared her throat Kirsty answered with, "Kirsty Evans"? Lonely coughed then apologized. Hi Kirsty, you probably don't remember me but I am Lonely, the Manager of Kentish Town Thrift Shop, I am also Import Manager – Toys". "Yes of course I remember you. We met at the Mind Games do, and secondly, how could I ever forget a name like Lonely. Your Mother must have been the wisest woman in the world to give you a name that no one would ever forget".

"Thank you. I am looking for some professional guidance in the field of corporate marketing, and I believe that is what you do, is that right"? "Well, yes. Is this a private request or does it come from The Thrift Shop?". "I've spoken to Milly, who tells me I need to get a quote from you for your time. Can you do that"? "How about we meet for a coffee first and discuss your needs". They agreed to meet at JoJo's in Holborn at 11. "Forgive me Lonely, but the thought, 'How will I recognize you', came into my head". The two laughed. The ice was broken.

At 10.45 am Lonely was seated outside and was partaking of a glass of water, when Kirsty rolled in on an O Bike. She removed the helmet and locked it to the bike frame. The bike was then locked to the lamppost by an extendable lock. She smiled at Lonely and said. "Hang on a sec Lonely, whilst I de-register this bike. She punched a code in, and a beep told her that the bike was free at that location and ready for the next patron.

They shook hands. "Love your mode of transport", said Lonely. "When I work in the City, this is the easiest, fastest and cheapest way of getting around – provided it's not raining. I use them all the time". "Brilliant idea. Now tell me what's on your mind". Lonely told her of her success with the King Group, also that she couldn't duplicate it to the same extent since, and she hadn't been able to penetrate the bigger retailers. "So I need some professional guidance".

"Ok then. I usually come from a different angle. I am mostly in magazine advertising, but it is also my job to convince businesses to advertise in them, so I have to be ready with a WIFM and a story line – preferably with pics. It's the - before you ask – What's In It For Me. Professional sales people the world over run WIFM through every presentation before even considering spruiking it to a client. It means that we are looking at the proposition through their eyes. It's not about what we want, it's about what they are going to get out of it. If they believe that the benefits outweigh the cost, they will at least consider it, but without it, you have nothing to grab them with. Let's take a hypothetical client. She looked around the street. Let's say I am the boss of UTA, that building over there, and you wanted to sell me soft toys, where would you start"?

"When you put it like that, I don't think I could. What is UTA anyway?". "Well that's your very first lesson, what is UTA? I happen to know they are United Trades Assurance. They insure the various trade unions around the world against lawsuits brought by business owners. You have to get into their psyche. You need to know what drives them. How are they different from their competitors? Where does their revenue come from? What symbols do they use in their current advertising? Who would be the best person to discuss a proposition with?"

"This is why I need you. I don't have a clue about any of that stuff. I think I got lucky with King Group because the bloke knew what he wanted. Can you help?"

"Lonely, I can help to a certain degree. I can give you, or get, answers to any questions you may have. I can then help you formulate a plan. We can then discuss together a WIFM. I can then bring it to life with a story and pictures – even a video. What YOU have to do is, when I identify a target, you have to get a sample made to suit that target. When all the pieces are in place, you need to make an appointment to see the person in UTA that can make a buying decision or at least push the idea up the line for you. Can you do that?" "I can definitely do that, although I will probably take our CFO Mike Stanning in with me for moral and company support".

"Very well then. I will send you an e-mail this afternoon, with my fees and scope of work on it. When it has been approved, I will get to work. Please remember, and this is very important, that with the best plan of action and with the best presentation, you still may not win any work from them, because a million reasons may be in play behind the scenes, but what this exercise will do for you is, a) give you a blueprint that you can use on any corporate entity, b) show you what research is required to get to first base, and c) how to present yourself, the product, the WIFM, then get the sale - if it's there to be got. So all of this is a learning exercise, but one that will be invaluable to you for the rest of your career".

"I have to get to Highgate by twelve, then head back to the office later, when I'll send you a proposal. Do you want to ride in a taxi with me? I can drop you off at work at Kentish Town if you're going back there". Lonely agreed, especially as she could discuss things whilst they went along. After they had settled down, Kirsty asked Lonely. "You married?" "No. I was, but my husband left me after our son was killed in Afghanistan. He couldn't face looking at me, as me and my son were very similarly featured". "I'm so sorry. You really are a beautiful woman, in fact I would say model material". "Get away with you. Me a model, no way"! They talked about the stores and how they were doing. Kirsty told her she was one day, going to be Barry's Daughter in Law, when she married Barry's son Trevor, and that Barry had married her mother Denise. "Well blow me down, I never knew". The time came for her to be let out in front of the store. "It's been a real pleasure meeting with you. I do hope we can work together on this project, but that will depend if they approve the funding for it". Kirsty held out her hand, then placed the other one over Lonely's. "Don't worry. I'll make sure it happens. See you soon".

Kirsty set out a plan of action and a Pro Forma Invoice for her services which were to run over six weeks and incorporate all that she and Lonely had discussed. She also wrote that there were no guarantees of results. She emailed it to Barry, then gave it half an hour before she called him. "Jeez you're keen aren't you. I've only just finished reading your five page submission, which by the way is very good. Do you think Lonely is up to the task"? "Frankly, I don't know her well enough to give you an informed answer, but if her enthusiasm is anything to go by, then yes. She has the King Group business under her belt, and by all accounts it's been a profitable venture. If she can replicate that many times, you have a real business woman on your hands. It will be my job to teach her why it worked, and how she needs to go about getting new business. What do you think of her"?

"I love the woman. She's smart, funny, friendly and eager to better herself, so I'm ready to support her. It looks like you've got all the angles covered and the price seems to be right – especially if it pays off, so go and take her on the journey of her life, but don't forget that she still manages a store and she still buys in for both, and I don't want the stores to suffer if she's distracted".

"Don't worry, I'll pace her, and I'll look after her. Thanks for the work. Love you". The last two words pleased Barry. They had been getting along famously since the first day they met, but since becoming closer to her, he felt a real affection for her. He stuttered out the words. "Love you too".

Kirsty phoned around for a soft target for Lonely to tackle first. One that she at least had a better chance of winning. The UTA did not have a reputation for largesse, let alone spending on frippery. One of her friends worked at Channel 4. They specialized in promoting kid's shows, games and films. They often put on or promoted, outside shows. These acted as reminders to the kids to watch their favourite kid's shows on Channel 4. Often, they would have larger than life animals roaming around, allowing the kids to cuddle them. The front and backs of the costumes always bore the Channel 4 logo, so the kids could identify it on TV.

'So', she thought, three of the main criteria had been established. 1. The company being targeted was big enough to afford any promotion. 2. They had the funds to do so, and, 3. They had an inside contact, who could point out who to talk to. Not a bad start. She kept up the sleuthing until with information in hand, she called up Lonely one week later. "Hi Lonely, it's Kirsty. I'd like to start our first lesson. Can you make it here by 9am tomorrow"? "I have a meeting at 9, could I make it at 11"? Good for you thought Kirsty. She's managing her turf, whilst planning ahead. "11am it is. When we've finished the first session we can go to lunch, then back here for another two hours, what do you say"? "I say great. See you then". She spoke to Milly, who said she would organize a taxi for her, then handed her a taxi card for use any time she needed to see Kirsty or clients. Just to keep a record of each trip on her expenses app, so she could check the invoice when it came in.

Lonely's guest just happened to be a potential new Chinese supplier, who had brought with him many soft toy samples. She had asked him to meet her at the Angel store, where How Su could listen in to the conversation between her, the supplier, and his colleague who he introduced to Lonely as his son, "educated in Philadelphia". Mr. Sung Ling ("call me Sunny, please") and Po Ling ("Call me Paul, please"), asked if Lonely would check their merchandise, "to see if we can do business". Sunny gave Lonely his card – two handed and with a bow. LINGLO was the name of the company, with a head office in Shanghai. Lonely handed him her business card – two handed with a slight bow. He smiled and perused the card.

Lonely also asked Sarah to call in to view the display of goods. She looked them over and picked them up. "They look all right to me", then left. How Su had a more measured and respectful approach to their works. She admired the cloth used, the stitching and finish. She asked about being suited for children under the 'Fit For Purpose'

Act and the 'Children Safety' Act, where there were not supposed to be any parts that could come loose and hurt a child, or be swallowed. Sunny asked Paul in Cantonese if their goods complied with these two Acts. Paul relayed in English that they had been tested against the codes and that they could issue a Certificate of Compliance and a CE mark for each product. Lonely replied that they would need to include that information on any label. Paul said that it was not an issue. "By the way, we only use virgin, cleaned materials for the outside and the stuffing. That will also be on the label".

Lonely advised them that she would consider the range and the prices and let them know if they could do business. Sunny presented her with the samples with a bow, Paul bowed also. They all shook hands. The men left.

"What do you make of those two then How"? "I think they have integrity. It seems they have a fairly well established business, and although they supply some stores in the UK. They seemed happy to supply you with your own exclusive range, so I suppose that suits you – doesn't it? Just so you know Lonely, as they were leaving the building, the old man commented on the fact that they had never dealt with a black woman before. It was just a passing comment, with no bias to it".

Lonely was keen to get to Kirsty's place. She scooped up the samples into a Sainsburys bag, as she wanted to show Kirsty the types of toys she dealt with. Kirsty was pleased to see her, and led her to one of the comfy armchairs away from her desk in her office. On the desk was a coffee maker and pods. "Want a cup"? "Yes please, I haven't caught up with myself yet". Kirsty explained why she had shifted tack regarding the target. "You need to give yourself every chance of succeeding, so the first lesson is to choose your best target first. This means researching those companies that fit your list of criteria, which is here. I drew this up, so you would have a check list for the future. You'll see that under 'Contact/s' I have put in Marie Swanson's name. She is my friend, but you need to contact her to find out who the buyer and the promotions officer and the managing directors are, so that you can have all that on file. Get their e-mails and contact numbers too if you can. So, that is your first task. Here's Marie's number. She doesn't know you are calling, but mention my name as a friend and go from there.

At exactly 11.45 Lonely had secured all the contact information she needed. Kirsty was impressed. "I'm pleased you remembered to use the phrase, 'I'm hoping you can help me'. As I say, it disarms and creates a desire to assist. Let's go to lunch and get back in an hour. They walked out and around the block to a row of food trucks, with many tables and chairs set up under the trees and in the park. Over kebabs and rice, they discussed the next phase of the programme.

"So, you have the names of potentially those who can help you get into Channel 4. What do you think is next"? "Find an appropriate soft toy I suppose". "Well, actually we have to find the right person to talk to first, so when we get back, you work the phone using this script". She handed her a paper, which she perused. "Practice it in your head".

Back at the office Lonely got to work. After just two calls she got an appointment to see Peter Rasmussen, head of Studio Promotions. He, she was told, had the final say on how all programmes were promoted to the public. They agreed to meet two days later at his office, and would it be ok to bring her publicist Kirsty Evans. "Of course, Kirsty is well known in my world. I'd be happy to meet with her and yourself of course. So Thursday at 8am then. Bye for now".

Kirsty congratulated Lonely on a good job. "Now that question again, what's next"? "A soft toy"? "No, a credible story with a big WIFM. Let's do some research about what he does and what he's working on or promoting at this time or in the future, then we can work a plan". She took her phone from the coffee table and dialed up Marie. She explained that they had gotten on to Peter Rasmussen and that they had an appointment next Thursday at 8 am. Marie was impressed. She asked Marie if she could find out what he was doing currently or about to do, so that they could get a proposal up. Marie promised to call her back.

"How about we look at Channel 4 for some background"? The content was typical of the age range for that time of day – stay at home littlies and Mums. What was more interesting was the channel promos featuring Purple Pig. The hero of The Farm. They saw an image of a purple pig with a cape on and a gold sash with PP on it. He was flying though the fields, preventing one catastrophe after another. They looked at each other. Kirsty took a screen shot and immediately messaged it to Lonely's mobile. "That's what we need. A Purple Pig and a credible promotional story". That's it for today. Go home and think about it, then call me tomorrow. I will do the same in the meantime. You need to get soft toy replicas made up asap, because we are going to hand them out on Thursday to everyone we see in Channel 4. You have less than one week to create a miracle. I will be creating the story".

Lonely racked her brain about how or where she could get these soft toys made up, when it occurred to her to give the two Chinese that were in town a call. First she called How Su, to ask her if she would make a dinner date with them, at a restaurant close to their hotel, then she and Lonely would meet them tonight as say 7.30. "That's if you are free, and willing, of course". "Actually, I was thinking of Paul this afternoon. He is quite a handsome man". "Well then we can kill two birds with one stone – so to speak. Please call me straight back with any news". It was only a few minutes later that How called and said that all was arranged for the Chariot of Fire in Kensington. Lonely told her that she would be in a taxi outside her house at 7 and that the driver would toot the horn.

After cordial greetings, they were shown to a round table where How somehow sat closer to Paul than Sunny. After some small talk and the first sip of the ordered drinks, Sunny asked, "why the urgent meeting. Lovely as it was to meet you both again so soon. Have you agreed to our range and prices already"? He asked.

How Su looked at Lonely, then after her nod, began to explain in Cantonese how they had an opportunity – for both parties – to make some money, but they all needed to participate fully and quickly in order for it to work. The men were intrigued and appreciated being spoken to in their native tongue. The waiter appeared and they all ordered. How resumed. She told the story of how they needed some Purple Pigs urgently and could they help. She nodded to Lonely, who took out her phone and showed them both the picture.

They spoke to How Su in Chinese for a while. She asked Lonely how many she wanted for the first run. Lonely suggested that 100 would suffice, but she would need a price for 5000 units very soon, to see if an offer to the station would be feasible. After a few minutes talking with his father, Paul spoke to them. "We have considered your proposition. We will have our head seamstress make a mock up for you – please transfer your image to my phone. He jotted down the number. She will send the pictures to you in the morning. There will be no charge for this service. Please check it out, then let either myself or my father know if it is suitable". "I want to add one more thing, apart from the PP on the sash, I also want screen printed on the cape, the Channel 4 logo".

"If we get your approval tomorrow, we will guarantee that you receive 100 pieces by air next Wednesday. The price will be 5 pounds each including the cost of the courier. It is higher than usual due to the urgency and the limited number involved. So your promotional bid to Channel 4 will cost you 500 pounds. In the meantime, I will get a price to supply 5000 units to you in the next few days. What do you say", said Paul.

Lonely was ecstatic, and agreed to their terms on the spot. Dinner arrived and they all engaged in small talk until the coffee was served, then they repaired to the lounge bar for a couple more drinks. Over a Martini, How got the answer she was hoping for. Paul was not married, and had been working his way through his father's business since leaving Trade College in Shanghai. How told them her story and that of her parents. They were intrigued. "Are you going back to China"? The old man asked. "You mean, 'CAN I go', as I haven't been before. I think so, as any problems my father and mother may have encountered were before I was 10 years old". Paul spoke to his father. He nodded. Paul asked if How would like to meet with him the next evening, and they could go to the theatre together as Wing Shu was in town with their traditional juggling and dancing acts, and would Lonely like to come also. "I'd be a third wheel", she said, "And besides, I have to get this promotion rolling, so thanks but no thanks". Paul asked what a third wheel was, and they left laughing. The men to walk back to their hotel, and Lonely and How to hail a cab.

Kirsty and Sarah agreed to meet two days later, when they would discuss their plan of action. This time it would be at a pub close to Lonely's part of town. The Ploughman's Widow was selected. They met in the dining room, and over dinner and a pint, they discussed the events to date. Lonely was able to show Kirsty the mockup of Purple Pig. "That's really great. Can I suggest you get them to fix a ribbon in a loop at the back of his neck? My idea is that as we go through the offices at Channel 4, we hang one of them on every hook in every cubicle, and give a quick spiel as we do so. It will be ideal too, if kids can hang them from their belts. It could start a craze. This could go viral.

Lonely texted Paul with the idea. He confirmed that he could fix a 50mm long purple ribbon loop to the 100 units, and was glad to hear that the mock up was perfect, so that they could start making up straight away. He would be sending an invoice to her office the next day. "Don't worry, its procedure so that we can start the work. You pay upon inspection of the goods when they land".

For the rest of the week, Lonely and Kirsty exchanged messages, and met twice more. On the Wednesday of the following week, Lonely signed for the carton from LINGLO, then inspected the contents. Every PP was packaged in a sealed clear plastic bag. She opened one and inspected it. She took in one to Barry, then one to Milly. Both wished her well for the next day's presentation.

Kirsty and Lonely had been working on a script for the past two days. Lonely had to memorize every part of it, and had been practicing in the mirror. She texted Kirsty to advise her that she would call at her place in the taxi at 6.45 am the next day.

When they arrived at the Channel 4 offices, the security guard checked their credentials and advised them that they could go up to the fourth floor and wait for Mr. Rasmussen, who apologized for being around 30 minutes late as his plane was in late from New York. "He must have caught the Red Eye", said Kirsty. They went up to the fourth floor where many cubicles were already being used. They stopped at the first one. Purple Pig is coming to Channel 4. Would you like a free mascot? The mantra was repeated at every occupied work station. 20 PPs were off and flying, with the girls hanging them up on hooks so that all passing could see them. They sat on padded chairs in front of the man's closed door office. When new workers came in, one of them would take a PP to them and give the spiel. By the time he arrived most of the forty cubicles had a PP. A couple of women had sent pics of PP to their kids, and came over to the pair, asking if they could have more, "as one kid would kill the other, if there was only one PP available".

Peter Rasmussen strolled in and immediately apologized to the pair. They introduced themselves. "How about we get ourselves a coffee, before we go in and sit down? The coffee bar is over there". After grabbing coffee and biscuits, they settled down around a small meeting table. "Again sorry, but I was in a meeting with FOX to promote our upcoming series of Purple Pig. I don't suppose you know anything about it, eh?"

"Matter of fact, that's exactly why we are here. I run two Thrift Shops in the Angel and Kentish Town. One of the things we have become known for is our amazing range of new soft toys, made exclusively for us in China. One company, the King Group gave us a trial order of a mascot for their company – a King Bear, with a crown on, and their web address on the chest of the King. They started out with 1000 bears and have to date given us orders for over 100,000 bears, and we have shipped them to five countries in the King Group territories and to their subsidiaries. They give them away, and every customer has one. No charge. The feedback has been amazing. For the 350,000 Euros spent with us, they believe the promotion has generated over 5 million dollars in free media advertising alone. Their mascot is the highest front of mind toy in every European, Australian and US Company, and their mascot is changing hands for up to ten Euros on e-bay".

"I want you to experience all of the same joys and benefits with your own mascot". Lonely, pulled out a Purple Pig from her carrier bag. We made this especially for you, to promote your new series. Imagine how well this will go down everywhere your Purple Pig programme is shown. At the end of each programme, you have a contact point to receive one for free or two or five dollars, whatever it takes. She handed it to him. He looked at it and said. "Ladies, I could have spared you a lot of time, heartache and expense if you had pitched the idea to me when we first spoke. He pulled out from his suitcase a Purple Pig. Their faces dropped. They looked at each other. Kirsty said, "Mr. Magnussen, I have made a major blunder. I should indeed have checked with you first. It seems we both had the same idea at the same time".

"Let me compare the two. Firstly, yours has a hanging loop. That makes it much more versatile - but there's nothing to stop me from adding one to mine. Secondly, you have put the Channel 4 logo on the cape. Great idea, and one I can also pinch. Let me compare the product quality. Mine is a rougher version of yours, but it does the job. I will be up front with you. I would get mine from the States. It would be US$3.00 plus a little more for the additions. Freight from the USA is a little cheaper than from China and they usually demand outrageous minimum quantities. So ladies what are you offering".

"I must admit that I – probably we – are flabbergasted. Not that you wouldn't have thought of the same thing, but that we hadn't taken the time to talk with you before committing to our plan. As you can understand, we are totally committed to making this work for you, and you are correct, we have spent many weeks planning this; making the prototype, and the first 100 units just to impress you. The good news is that we can supply them to you, well made, guaranteed virgin materials, and guaranteed to conform to all British child safety laws, at a price of US3.00 + VAT, delivered to your store under this building. We can have the first 5000 units to you in one month exactly, after receipt of your order. You do not have to pay up front – only on delivery, and you do not have to concern yourself with minimum quantities. We will also hold a buffer stock of 5000 units so that you can never run short. I only ask that if you cancel – which you can do at any time – then you pay for the buffer stock upon delivery. What we have going for us is that we are probably the largest customer for a vast range of soft toys from one – now two - factories in China. We guarantee the quality, which is something you would find hard to do. We ship twice a month, so shipping extra for you is no problem to us. We have cheaper shipping rates as they will come by road, and the logistics company is owned by my boss. All in all, I think it is the best deal, and even better, we do all the work, you just place an order. By the way, we took the liberty of passing around freebies to most of your staff. It seems they love the idea and the product".

Peter Magnussen told them they had a promise for an initial order of 20,000 units, provided they were in his warehouse in one month from the order date. They shook hands. Lonely and Kirsty were escorted through the office, with many shouting out, "Great idea, boss, my kids are gonna love this", or "Fantastic toy. Any chance of another"? Lonely dished out a few more on the way through. Even the receptionist asked for one. "Seems we have a hit on our hands ladies", as he showed them to the lift.

Barry organized for all the staff of both stores to attend a reception at the Kentish Towne Reception Centre, to celebrate Lonely's and the others successes over the past two and three years since the stores opened. It was a rousing night where all of the staff received accolades and recognition for their services.

Channel 4 reordered twice more, just two weeks and three weeks after the first order, which now totaled 60,000 units, due to the vibe going round the station about the Purple Pig and the mascots, where kids when they came to the station with their Mums were wearing from their belts – as Kirsty had predicted. It was even the talk of FOX

USA. Peter had contacted Lonely for the rest of the toys she had on her – which he was willing to pay for, so that he could send them to FOX executives as soft sell gifts.

Lonely and Kirsty celebrated together over a beer in a pub. They congratulated each other. Kirsty said. "Forgot to tell you. The first rule is never to jump in without the facts". They laughed until their sides hurt.

One month later and Purple Pig debuts on British TV. The kids go wild. The promo at the end of the show tells kids how to apply for their very own Purple Pig. 60,000 units sell out- for 4 pounds each - in one week. The executives had to put out an apology. The Chinese manufacturers worked day and night to get another 10,000 units in a week, with the station ordering another 50,000 to follow on ASAP. TV and radio stations were bombarded with complaints that Purple Pig had gone missing and it was a conspiracy by Channel 4 to ensure publicity – which the shortage achieved magnificently. The Manager of Channel 4 appeared on no less than fifteen shows, trying to placate the kids who said he was mean – and much more. Some too explicit to read out. Even late night TV weighed in, calling him mean and short sighted. Anyone would have known that Purple Pig the soft toy would be a hit. Many texters and e-mailers called for him to be sacked for incompetence.

Peter Rasmussen called Lonely. "Hi Lonely, it's Peter from Channel 4. I just wanted to let you know that the Purple Pig series has been sold to the USA, Australia and five other countries. The best news – for you – is that they only get the series if we supply all their Purple Pig soft toys. Now we could go to the manufacturer in China and do our own deal. We are talking a million toys here, but you did everything right. You pulled out the stops when we needed you to, and much more, so we still want to buy through you, but two things need to happen. 1. You reduce the price, based on a guaranteed order of 1 million units over the next year, and 2. That you ship them directly to the stations in those countries included in the price. The minimum order will always be one pallet, so you know what your shipping costs will be. If you're interested, please let me know by the end of the week. By the way, would you like to come to dinner on Friday? Let me know both answers soon. Bye"

Lonely, could not believe her ears. 1 million units. She placed the mobile back on the desk and stared into space. When she awoke from the dream she phoned Barry. Milly answered. Lonely told her what had happened. Milly said, "Hold on, Barry has just walked in, I'll put you on speaker. Lonely repeated the sentence. Barry looked at Milly. "I can't believe what I've just heard. This could well be the largest transaction anyone has done in the Thrift Shop. Bloody well done Lonely. I'm so proud of you". Milly shouted, "Me too. Well done girl. What are you going to do now?"

"I'll have a quick word with Mike Stanning, then formulate an e-mail for Sunny and Paul. I just hope they can come to the party on price". Barry interjected. "Gotta go Lonely, but I've got complete faith in you, and by the way so does Kirsty. She reckons you've got what it takes to get to the top. Run with it girl". Milly congratulated her again, and asked that she let her know how it progresses. Mike Stanning helped formulate the e-mail, and Lonely sent it off. Mike asked if she was free for dinner Friday. Lonely told him about Peter Rasmussen's offer. He castigated himself for being too slow. "If it doesn't work out with Peter, you know how I feel about you – don't you"? She said her feelings were mutual, but they had not had a discussion about his personal life, so she did not know where she stood with him, which is why she accepted Peter's offer – or was going to.

Po Ling (Paul) telephoned Lonely about an hour after receiving her e-mail. "Hello Lonely. It was lovely to receive such good news, and we would be proud to continue to be your supplier. I have spoken with my father and he advises me that we can drop the price by 15% for a written order, taken off over 1 year. By the way I am in London next week. Would you like to have dinner with me"? Lonely could have burst with pride. So much achieved in so little time, and some of the nicest and probably wealthiest men are asking me to dinner. Geez.

"Can you give me a call when you get in? It's very busy at the moment".

The deal with Peter Rasmussen was signed sealed and settled on the Friday morning. Dinner at Claridges in the evening. Was she game to go any further? She liked Peter very much, and he had expressed interest in going much further with her – even to New York next time to see FOX. She reciprocated with touching, kissing and making out, but said she would see how their relationship developed – as she had not been intimate for some time now, and wanted to be sure. Peter said he understood entirely. Lonely asked the question that she thought would be on everyone's lips. "How much difference would your life be if your partner was black"? He pondered for a moment. "I don't see colour. I see a beautiful, intelligent woman, who I would be proud to be seen in public with. I have a question for you. How much difference would your life be if your partner was white"?

"Touché. I wouldn't be here if I wasn't comfortable in your company, although I must tell you that two other very eligible men have asked me to dinner in the past few days, and I intend to go out with each of them. Ahhh. Life is very difficult".

CHAPTER 55

Barry had not been sitting on his hands. He had sent Sarah on a mission. First he had scoured the map of London, and determined that two demographics fit the bill for a Thrift Shop. They were Brixton and Ealing. Sarah had the unenviable task of getting to each tube station, then walking around looking for suitable areas, then sites. The day was selected and although the weather looked threatening, she rugged up and took her brolly to the first on her list – Brixton.

Brixton had two reputations. One as being not a safe place to be – especially at night time, and two – as a major centre of African centric peoples – one of the largest concentrations in fact. Neither of these was a deterrent. Barry and Sarah both knew that the shops needed a certain socio-economic mix, a large local population and access to public transport.

She turned left out of the station and walked about 500 yards down. There were a couple of likelys which she entered the details of in her notepad. She crossed over and walked back the other way. There was one other possibility, but she decided that it just wasn't doable. She walked past the station on the opposite side until she came to a double fronted shop that had new window glass, and it looked modern compared to the others. It was next to Poundland and something called Fun Exchange. She mused that both of these shops were going to bring customers in for sure. Could Barry afford this good looking shop though? The glass had a misting of whitewash over them, but fortunately the door placed centrally was open. She walked in to see three tradesmen sitting on milk crates, round a central one.

The most rotund looked up. "Sorry luv, but we got our quota of professionals here. Come back next Wensdee, we'll be gone by then". They all chuckled. "So you're the clown of this outfit eh. Woss your

247

name". "William Masterton the third, at your service madam". He rose slowly, then bowed. "Wot can I do for you then".

"What you can do for me Sir Masterton, is to tell me who owns this shop. I'm looking to rent in the area, and this looks likely". "Well why didn't you say"? He drew up another upturned crate, and beckoned her to it. She sat down. "Now take this name and number down. William Masterton. 041 204 5690. Give him a call and he'll tell you all you want to know. Sarah dialed the number. The portly guy picked up the phone and answered, "Bill here". The lads cracked up.

"You silly sod. You mean this is your place"? "It is. Me and my mates are just doin' a refurb. Unfortunately for you I just took a deposit for three years rental. Nice bloke too. Says he's into hardware. I told him there's a Mighty Boy Hardware about a mile up the road. He tells me that his stuff is every nut, bolt, screw, nail, fixing you could ever want, along with cheap power and hand tools and that's it. No lawnmowers, shelving and stuff. He seemed a genuine bloke", Sarah gave him her card. Sarah Walling. Manager Thrift Shops.

Bill looked at it and tears began to well in his eyes. Sarah asked if he was alright. He turned away from her and reached into the tissue box on one of the counters. He blew his nose, and with anther wiped his eyes. He then turned back. In a cracked voice, said, "My brother Tom came back from serving in the air force. He was a fighter pilot, but his main job was to support ground troops under attack. One day they gave him the wrong co-ordinates and his bombs blew up a school full of kids. He was exonerated but he couldn't go on, so they sent him home for rehab, which was unsuccessful until he heard about Mind Games. Tom was one of the first to sign up. The difference it made to him, especially when he teamed up with another pilot was amazing. They went from pub to pub until they settled on one out of the City. It became an outing for them both. They were shithouse with the games but had the most fabulous time together, with Tom inviting Charlie home to meet us all, and us getting to know him too. I can't tell you how much my family owes the Mind Games. Jodie, one of your nurses comes round every week. You should see his eyes light up. He gets her a cuppa, sits her down and from her asking about him, he now asks about her, so we think he's over the worst".

"Sarah asked for a tissue". The other two men went off wiping their eyes. It must have been serendipity's birthday, because Bill received a phone call right then. He came off the phone with a smile on his dial. "Well, if that don't take the cake. The geezer that gave me the deposit for this place, just called to say he found another place down the road that is cheaper, so he has canceled the cheque. The rent here is 10 pounds per square foot. There are 4000 square feet and a roller door out the back onto the service lane. Newly fitted toilets and a tea room. I want 4500 pounds per calendar month for it".

Sarah, pulled out her phone and dialed Barry. Milly answered. "Hi Sarah, Barry's gone to Spain for a couple of weeks, can I help you"? "Hi Milly, Barry gave me this job of looking for new premises and I'm in Brixton. The place I've found has been refurbished and it's just up from the station next to Poundland and a computer games exchange place. It's 4000 square feet and the owner wants 4500 pounds per month for it. I think it's great, but I'm worried that it's too big". Milly put on her official voice. "Sarah, you have worked at the Thrift Shop since it opened. You have brought on Kentish Town, and now you are responsible for all Thrift Shops. It won't matter if I speak to Barry or Michael, they will all say the same thing, that they have faith in your judgement and so do I, so do what you need to do and make a decision. Barry will stand by you no matter what".

Sarah said, "Thanks Milly. That's what I wanted to hear", and rung off.

She turned to Bill, and said, "Bill, I am afraid that your rent is too high for us. We would love to take on the shop but we have to also find another one in Ealing, so there's going to be a considerable drain on our resources until they are fully functional, what can you do for us"?

"What I can do for you lady is to make a phone call. Just sit tight. I'll put the kettle on. Don't worry I have disposable cups. "Ello. Bill Squared"? "Smee. Wodja want ya stoopid bugga". "You know that shop you're working on in Ealing Broadway, what size is it. What rent do ya want, an when will it be finished"?

"That was my best mate William Williamson – Bill Squared. He does what I do, refit shops. He's doing a shop on Ealing Broadway. Its 3000 square feet, on a corner, and the owner wants 3000 pounds per month. He finishes in a week's time. How would you like me to run you over there now"? "How far is it away from Ealing tube"? "It's about twelve shops up from the station. Just turn right. It's on the next corner. It's painted green and brown outside, but that can be fixed".

Sarah downed her welcome cuppa and accepted two Marie biscuits. "Bill, thanks for the offer, but you've got a lot to do, and I can make my way by tube quicker than you can drive. I'll have a look at the shop and let you know how I have gone. Write your number on my pad, along with your name. If you know of any other shops in this area close to the tube that are less expensive, please let me know".

The tube ride to Ealing afforded time to reflect. Should she have given Bill an ultimatum regarding the rent? If she didn't take it, some-one else surely would, as it was the right location, it looked fabulous and she felt sure that Bill would include other fittings she had in mind if she had said yes. She went on to Ealing Broadway, thinking about the potential of Brixton, and how great a store it would be. She alighted. Stood on the escalator that deposited her into the lobby of Ealing Broadway Station. It was easy to walk to the next corner where the shop described was being worked on.

"Bill Squared"? "He's over there luv". A skinny man with a mane of red hair caught behind the head with an elastic band, looked around. "Sarah? Bill called me. He said I had to look after you. As you can see it looks better inside than out, but we have new showcase windows and an aluminium framed door being fitted in a couple of days' time, so it will look schmik".

Sarah loved the location and the fact that it would look great when finished, and the time frame was ok too. Bill showed her the facilities. She said that if she took it, she would need changing rooms, a tea nook, a front service counter with desk behind, and that they would need more power outlets and internet connection to the desk. He assured her that he could do all that, but wasn't sure if he price would be affected. "So who do I talk to about the price"? "Bill", he answered.

"You mean to tell me that Bill owns this place too"? "Yeah, didn't he tell you? He's got about fifteen shops that he does up and rents out. Our Bill is a wealthy man".

Sarah went back to the station and left for the Angel. There she asked Milly and Mike to sit with her whilst she unloaded her news to them. Mike suggested that he have a word to Bill whilst they were all together. Sarah was glad of the help.

"Hello Bill. This is Michael Stanning from the Thrift Shop. I'm the CEO and I'm with Milly from Accounts and Sarah, who you've been talking with today. She has filled us in on your two premises, and I would like to put a proposal to you. Both premises suit our needs and we are prepared to take both on, but I need you to drop the per square foot rate to 85p per month. If you can do that then we have the opportunity to do business. If you can't then we must say thanks and goodbye". We can sign a three year lease with a three year option".

"I love your charity and I love that Sarah, so ok we'll do a deal. I'll have the papers e-mailed to you tomorrow". The line went dead. "Well that wasn't too hard. Well done Sarah, looks like you have two more stores to look after. When they are bedded down, let's talk again about getting another two up and running".

CHAPTER 56

The second Mind Games came and went with significant fanfare. The announcement that The Thrift Shop had donated the amazing sum of 240,000 Pounds to the charity was well publicized, and Kirsty made sure of it. There was only one other amazing announcement, that Mind Games was expanding its scope to include all public service personnel and their families who have been exposed to trauma, and were finding life difficult to cope with.

Many police and first responders had contacted the charity, to ask if they could come under the Mind Games umbrella, because the government did not have enough resources to properly help traumatized public service personnel. So all public servants were invited to participate in the coming years events. All they had to do was register, and a help and participation kit would be sent to them. The media were again praising Mind Games, this time for its inclusive nature to other services.

Another five trauma nurses would be trained up immediately.

Kirsty Evans and Trevor Baines, along with the permanent head of Mind Games Jodie Marshall, all had their work cut out for them just organizing the main event, but all went smoothly, especially as Master Of Ceremonies, Mike Bradford-Jones, volunteered to participate once again.

CHAPTER 57

BB Logistics was now firmly entrenched in the haulage of the timber for making coffins. Barry's fleet of trailers and pantechnicons covered every mill, every workshop, every warehouse and every delivery point on behalf of Guilia's, the largest casket manufacturer in the world and based in Italy. The mills were flung far and wide throughout Europe and Asia, as were the distribution points and final make up shops.

Spasmodically, over the course of one year, Barry and Reggie Green, his right hand Logistics Manager, had visited every point from mill to delivery, just to ensure all was working as it should, and apart from the odd incidence of people smuggling and petty theft, it was working well. They did however take notes on how improvements could be made.

They called in at Guilia's where Roberto greeted Barry like a long lost son. Reggie was asked if he would like a tour of the factory as he hadn't seen it before. He accepted Alfredo, the Factory Manager's offer with glee. The factory was well laid out. Alfredo pointed out the various points from the office balcony overlooking the enterprise, before they went down to the factory floor. Starting with Inwards Goods, the kiln dried timber in packs covered with heavy duty film were unloaded by forklift into cantilevered flow-through racking which separated the trucks from the guys needing stock, as they pulled it out from the other side of the racking. It seemed like there was a line of trucks waiting outside also.

He was then shown the cutting, thicknessing and sanding operation, where every board was cut to a predetermined size by computer. The machine spat out four sizes, that when assembled made up a certain casket size. 95% of all caskets were now the one size, so this particular machine only catered for those. The specials were made on another machine. When the pack heights were reached, the pack proceeded along a powered conveyor, where they were sent in one of five directions. At the end of each spur was a spray booth with plastic strips at the entrance. A hoist with two steel prongs came down and at the end of each door was a pre drilled hole. The prongs entered the holes horizontally. It then raised the board to a vertical position. B blowers fitted to the end of the spray booth started up to blow any excess dust off the panel as it proceeded into the booth on its side, where one of five urethane finishes would be applied by a robotic spray arm. Another booth at the other end, dried the coating using ultra violet light. It was perfectly cured when it was again presented flat then stacked.

Workers removed each board using a vacuum lifter and placed it into a jig. As the jig moved along, the casket was screwed together. The lids had been diverted to where workers added every manner of mouldings, insignias and name plate mounts. The handles were in a plastic bag and placed inside. They fitted the hinges and screwed the lid on. It was sent through a tunnel that applied a heavy duty plastic bag which was sealed then labelled. It was placed onto large pallets along with others totaling 18 caskets, then plastic strapped and placed into the despatch racking. Reggie was in awe of the level of sophistication of the operation. He was told that for places outside of Italy, the packs of treated boards would be despatched by the truck load, and local finishers would make up the caskets for delivery to funeral homes, although some funeral homes preferred to make up their own coffins from the board stacks.

Reggie asked Alfredo if there were any problems with their logistics systems. He replied that it all ran smoothly, with the exception that some of the mills in Russia found it difficult to despatch trucks in mid-winter, but as long as they had stock from other sources production would not stop.

They all sat down for lunch in the canteen and Barry asked Alfredo how they could grow their business together. Alfredo replied that

Guilia had just bought out Mid West Caskets in the USA, and was considering sending containers full of boards for making up in the mid west states, then hopefully moving into other regions. He was not sure where Barry would fit in, as he did not have a logistics role in the U.S., although his trucks would still take the containers to the docks.

Alfredo advised Barry that they would need more trailers in Europe to cater for the increase in demand for timber. Barry asked that he be informed two months in advance of any new mills opening up, or increases from the current mills.

Barry and Reggie left Italy later that day, arriving at Heathrow late, so Barry dropped Reggie off at home, and organized a meeting for the next morning. After the initial chat where Mike Stanning had also been invited to discuss financing of the additional trailers, Reggie asked the secretary to find Cedric Straughan. "Gentlemen, I want you to meet Cedric. He is employed in setting the timetables for pickups from the various Guilia supplier locations, after they advise us that they have a truck load ready. Cedric connects the closest truck owner or driver with the closest available trailer. He came to me with a solution to a problem that I didn't realize we had. Cedric this is Barry Baines the owner and Michael Stanning the Chief Financial Officer. Please tell them what you told me".

"Hello. I was looking at the stats and thought we might do a better job of matching up all of the pickup and delivery points with the locations of the trailers, the trucks and the load frequencies". Without waiting for approval, he said. "I have created an algorithm, which allows us to pick the nearest trailer to the job, provided that you invest in GPS locators on each trailer. The GPS locator can tell us its last position. If all the prime movers we use had them, we could marry them up. The good news is that most of them have them already. Those that don't we could subsidize them. When a call comes in from a factory, a trailer needs to be sent there for loading. If we can mix and match better and know where every trailer is at any point in time, we can do a much better job. There's more. Mr. Baines, you have Estates R Us and House and Gardens Accessories. These pickups and deliveries can also be integrated into the system, meaning you could save a lot of money and be better organized, and have full tracking capabilities". He sat down.

All three clapped the young man. Barry asked how long he had been working on this algorithm and when would it be ready to test. "I have been working on it since last summer, the day after I joined the business. I have to confess I am a computer geek, and it's my hobby to make up and test algorithms for all sorts of things". "What has it cost you to date and how much would it cost to implement it fully through-out our businesses?" "Not a penny. I could install it on your comput-ers any time. At the moment it's only running on my lap top. Here I'll show you". He opened the lid, punched a series of codes into the pro-gramme and up it came in all its glory. "What I've done is simulated where the trucks are located in our manual system. You can see that the programme picks up the nearest trailer, then goes looking for a Prime mover as soon as we receive a notification of load pick up. "If you wish, we could add things like life of tyres and expected replace-ment; service dates, nearest repairers, and more".

Barry asked Reggie what his opinion was. Reggie was beaming ear to ear. "If that side of the business was automated, we could add trail-ers as required by expansion, without extra manpower. We might even be able to use it in the USA". He looked at Cedric. "Absolutely, the only thing we need to do is to get different sim cards and North Amer-ican Maps and a GPS service company to set it up for us, but it is defi-nitely do-able".

"Cedric, would you mind giving us ten minutes. Please see Millie and ask where the coffee is stashed. We will find you shortly". Cedric left. Barry spoke enthusiastically about Cedric and how he had done all this without prompting, and how they had grown like Topsy but had given little heed to the Internet of Things. "I propose we make this young man head of IT for the group. He can tour all the establish-ments, bringing us all up to date. If he lacks expertise, we can pair him up with someone who has what he lacks. The recognition and a pay rise would be an excellent reward for his initiative, what do you think"? He looked at the other two for answers.

"I am totally in awe of this young man", Reggie said. I think that if we promote him and give him a title, he will want to wake up enthused every day. I'm all for it.

Barry looked at Michael. "It is a big responsibility for a young man. We might be giving him an opportunity to hang himself and the business too if he gets it wrong. I would prefer to have our local computer guy look over his shoulder to ensure all the right code is in place, and that we are not compromised by back door thieves. It would give me some piece of mind".

Barry asked Reggie if he would find Cedric. "Cedric, firstly let me congratulate you for having the initiative to help make our transportation systems work better. You've done a splendid job in getting to first base. Now none of us actually knows you, your background or your capabilities, but because of your presentation, I would like to give your system a trial run. Firstly I want to award you with a 1000 Pound bonus for your work to date. You will be shadowed by the tech guy from All Systems Go. We need him to advise us, I'm sure you will understand. I want Reggie and yourself to work closely together to identify and implement a system that maximizes our potential, whilst simultaneously working on a similar model suited to the North American markets. If you agree, I will give you the title of BB Group IT Advisor, and increase your salary by 40% forthwith. If this all goes as expected, I would be looking to give you more responsibility in the future. What do you say Cedric"?

Cedric looked Barry squarely in the eye. "If I were sitting where you are, that would be exactly how I would play it. We have a deal". Cedric shook their hands in turn, then picked up his laptop and left, saying goodbye to Millie on the way out.

"Reggie, can you find out how many of the prime movers we use have GPS, and how much it would take to fit GPS to all of our trailers then let me know".

When the men had left, Barry made a call to Roberto of Guilia's, and asked to be included in their US expansion plans. "We are also investing in GPS locators for all our trailers and the sub contracted prime movers we use, so that you will get even better service, and we intend to do the same in the USA and Canada. I wanted you to know that your business means a lot to us, and we want to be the best we can". Roberto was impressed, and thanked him for letting him know.

CHAPTER 58

Jean the ex-cop had been looking to retire for a while now. She had enjoyed her time at the Thrift Shop and had responsibility for overall security. She had kept her hand in, and had some good ex Police contacts in her black book.

When it came time for hiring another person for the Thrift Shop, Jean let Barry know her intention to retire, and that it might be a good time to introduce someone who could take her place as head of security at the same time. Barry agreed and asked if she could undertake the hiring herself. She said she could. She contacted her Inspector friend. She asked if anyone was unlikely to return to active duty and needed a job. The pay wasn't much, but it was better than vegetating, and she would train him or her in the security aspects of the job – if they had the right attitude. He said he would find out.

Two days later a Senior Sergeant Collins called her. "Hello, is that Jean Stone? I'm SS Collins. My inspector asked me to do a job for him, then to contact you with the findings. If you let me have your e-mail address, I can send you the list". She gave him the details and thanked him for his help. There was no reply. He just rang off. She wasn't sure if what he was doing was outside of Police procedures or he was just a grumpy old bastard.

She dismissed the first two as being unsuitable for any number of guessed reasons. The name. The reason. Length of Service. She wasn't sure, but she liked the sound of the third one. Her name was Glenda Reese Sprocket. The surname was amusing, and she would have had to take stick from everyone with that name, so she thought she would have to be tough to survive. She had been involved in a horrific accident in the Patrol Car. Her driver had been killed and she had been hospitalized for the past eight months. She had lost her left leg beneath the knee. Jean called her.

"Hello, my name's Jean Stone. I work at The Thrift Shop opposite the Angel tube station. I was wondering if you were looking for a job? Part time at first until you prove yourself. Sorry, but I'm an ex-cop and I'm retiring soon and I am looking to train someone to not only work in sales, but to also look after security for the group. Would you be interested in coming down to have a chat"?

"I'm not sure how you found me, but I'm guessing it's through the Job. I could be there at 2.30 today if that suits you".

"Blimey, I didn't expect a response so quickly. I'll have the kettle on". "Don't dress up just for me", she said dryly. "Oh, a comedian eh. You and I will get on just fine".

Jean informed Sarah that another comedian would be coming in for a chat at 2.30 and would she be there to check her out and give her opinion. "I finish at 2 today, but I'll hang about 'til about 3. Is that o.k."?

Glenda was tall and had a slight limp. She wore loose fitting black trousers, a burnt orange blouse with a light short leather coat. Jean introduced both herself and Sarah. They all sat down in the tea room. Jean poured tea from a pot on the table. Biscuits were passed around.

Jean started, "We are looking for a replacement for me, and an ex-cop is what we need, but the everyday job is selling stuff from the Thrift Shop. Security takes a back seat, but it does have its challenges and rewards. Can you see yourself working here? It's a far cry from Police work, but I understand you are not able to return and that you will be invalided out of the force soon. Is that correct"?

"Exactly right. I have been getting on famously with this prosthesis. I still limp, but every day it gets less obvious. I can't do any running – yet, and climbing stairs is awkward without crutches, but I get around without them for the most part, so if your thieves do a runner, all I can do is to shout, make a phone call – or shoot em in the ass with my pistol. Only kidding! Look I don't have any retail experience, so you'll be training me up for everything. You sure you want someone like me, who could in fact be more of a liability".

Sarah asked. "Got an old man, kids, pets then"? "Well that's very direct. No to all". "Do you think you can handle the general public, especially the old farts and the smelly kids"? "I can handle anything". We pay 12 quid an hour. Part time is 20 hours a week for five days, with a rostered on Saturday once a month. If you get to full time – if you want it. Hours are 40 a week. 45 minutes for lunch and two tea times of 15 minutes. Do you want the job or not"?

"Well, that's the fastest and most in your face interview I've ever had. I'll take it if it's being offered". She turned to Jean. "Sure". Sarah put her hand out to Glenda who shook it. "See you Monday". She then looked at Jean. "That's all you have to do, see. See you tomorrow. Bye". Jean and Glenda looked at each other. "That was Sarah. Let's sit a while and you can ask any questions". When they were finished, Jean said, "As Sarah, said, See you Monday".

Over the next three months, Jean showed her around to all of the shops and warehouses that belonged to the group. Glenda in turn, filled Jean in about the ever changing face of the Met Police, and how it all belonged to the young things who are on top of computers, and think like the young petty criminals who they hoped to stop becoming hardened criminals. Then there was the ever present threat from terrorism, which according to Glenda there was much more co-operation from Police forces around the world including Border Forces, for information gathering.

Jean told her that it was no use passing over her Inspector contact's name as he too was leaving the force at the same time. In fact, there was every chance that they would be getting together afterwards, "But keep that bit quiet"!

Milly had been given funds to make sure the Thrift Shop sent Jean off in a grand manner. She had an inkling but it was not what she expected, when a limo was sent round to her flat on the Friday of her departure. In it were Barb and Sarah. "Want champagne girl"? Said Barb, the second she got in. "Only if this limo is taking me home later". The driver told her that he was to go to the shop at 2 o'clock. "Let's party then". The Angel store was decorated with banners. One read, JEAN'S LEAVING – BOO HOO! Another read, FREE TEA AND CAKE. 12 -1. IT'S JEANS LAST DAY. Inside the girls had strewn loops of crepe paper across the ceiling in both directions forming colourful squares. Two mirror balls were rotating stars onto the ceiling. Music was blaring out. How Su and a new girl Andrea, along with new cop Glenda, were there to give her a hug and to wish her well. A couple of customers roamed around, soaking up the festive atmosphere.

Jean was handed a bundle of cards in envelopes, and one giant card with dozens of signatures inside, all wishing her a fantastic new life. Jean and the others all talked about her experiences before and after the Thrift Shop, Jean was happy to talk about many of the good times she had experienced with the force, especially the sillier and brighter moments, like the day a burglar had climbed out of a rear window, hoping to jump over to next door's roof. Instead he dropped down between the two brick walls. Four hours later someone heard his call for help and called the cops. It took us ages to find out where the noise was coming from. I looked out of the window that he had escaped from and saw him, then I called up Fire Rescue, who came up and looked through the window. They had to call in a mobile crane who put the boom out and over the next building, where a fire crew attached a harness. They shouted to the guy that they couldn't send anyone down as the gap wasn't wide enough – this guy was skinny. They told him how to fit the harness.

He tried for more than fifteen minutes, but he couldn't get the straps under his legs. In the end the Chief Fire Officer shouted down. Listen mate its breakfast time and we're going. Just grab the harness with two hands and we'll pull you up and over. If you fall off, that's not my problem. The harness started to rise and the bloke hung on for dear life, whilst they hoisted him onto the roof top. I was on the roof by then. I asked the bloke what he'd been doing – knowing full well that he'd stolen some jewelry from the flat – he said he had gone out of the window to get to work, as the front door had jammed tight, and that his lunch was in his knapsack down the middle of the buildings, and could they get it for him before they left. We all pissed ourselves with laughter at the cheek of this bloke. We had to send a rookie cop up onto the roof with a rope and a hook. He fished the knapsack out after three hours.

At lunchtime two vans arrived. The first contained trestle tables and chairs and tablecloths and flowers. They pushed the displays back and filled the tables with all manner of sandwiches and cakes, along with large urns of tea and coffee, even a small fridge for milk and cold drinks from the second van. Customers and staff helped themselves. At 1 p.m., Barry, Milly, Michael, Lonely, Sarah and the rest of the staff that could be spared, gathered round whilst Barry called Jean to stand next to him.

"Jean, as a founding team member and as one who has seen every aspect of this business grow and prosper, I have been impressed by your dedication, and by your skills as a security guard. You have combined both jobs well. You oversaw the jewelry section mainly and kept us secure and safe at the same time. You have been passing your knowledge of the Thrift Shop and our subsidiaries on to Glenda, who I must say has taken to the job really well – according to Jean. So the baton will pass on to the newcomer. Welcome Glenda".

"From the management of BB Enterprises, we all wish you the best for your future. Apart from a bonus, you will see that management had a whip round. It should be enough to buy you a box of matches". He handed the envelope to Jean, who firstly removed a cheque for two thousand Pounds. With it was a bundle of notes. Jean thanked Barry, Milly, Michael and all in management for their kind thought and cash – especially the bonus. Barry then invited Sarah to come up.

"Barry knows that the staff here wanted to show how much we all loved Jean, and how much we wish her well, so here's a little something from us". The envelope contained what must have been a thousand pounds. Lonely stepped forward and handed Sarah a silver handled wooden truncheon – full sized, engraved with, and read out by Sarah. "It says". 'To Jean from The Thrift Shop Girls. 'You can leave his truncheon alone now – you've got one of your own'. Merriment swept through the place as all the non-usual staff left the store, heaping good wishes and kisses on Jean as they left.

At 2pm the limo driver walked in and announced that, "Her Highnesses carriage awaits". She got in alone, but for her envelopes and truncheon and a bag full of goodies. She cried as she waved away two of the best years of her life.

What the Thrift Shop management and staff did not know, was that Jean and her Inspector 'friend' (Harry Parsons, who was also about to retire from the Force) were going into business as security consultants and had already registered the name StoneWall Security. She had a future in mind. It may also involve speaking with Barry sometime down the track.

Back at the shop, Ethel the down and out – who could read the 'free food' sign very well, was still tucking into the sandwiches and drinking tea. "Well Ethel, I hope you enjoyed yourself this afternoon. Here are some sandwiches and cake to take away with you. Don't say you never get looked after at the Thrift Shop", said Sarah. "My dear. If I had money, I would purchase a range of fine clothes from your shop. As it is, every stitch of clothing – apart from my drawers – which I get from Priceline – has been donated by you girls. I am ever so grateful. Let me know when someone else is leaving. This is the most nosh I've had in a long time. Bye". The caterers cleared away everything and the shop once again traded as usual for a couple more hours.

CHAPTER 59

The trip had been very successful. Barb had been back to Yugoslavia, and negotiated some fine deals in Macedonia and Serbia, before flying out of Belgrade. She was especially pleased with the new stock that they had not seen the like of before. She could not wait to show the staff at the H & GA the photos, plus the fact that the new store in Barnet was about to open in two weeks' time.

She would have to divert some of the buffer stock in the warehouse in the meantime, in order to stock the new store. She also needed to tell Reggie of her new suppliers and when stock would be available for pick up. All in all, life for her was good. She didn't need a man, but if one came along, she would seriously consider a slower life. She was no spring chicken, but then she loved the travel, meeting people and doing deals.

Summer was at its best. The sun streamed through the windows of the 737-300, which carried 150 but was only half full. Many passengers had pulled down the shades. Some had drifted off to sleep even though they were only 30 minutes into their flight, and after the attendants had offered drinks and snacks and cleared the debris away.

A tremendous shudder went right through the plane. She looked out to see one of the two engines on fire. An announcement came through. "This is your captain speaking. We have, as some of you can see, experienced a starboard engine fire. It will self-extinguish. This plane is designed to run efficiently on only one engine. Unfortunately we have to land at the nearest airport which is Ljubljana in Croatia. If we run into any serious difficulties, oxygen masks will drop down, and I will get you to attain the brace position. Please look at your Safety Card in the seat pocket in front of you if you are not sure. As we are over land there's no need to put on a life jacket. However, should we need to put down outside of an airfield, the flight attendants will open the exit doors. At their command, make your way to them without removing any luggage from the lockers. The air chutes will inflate, then you can slide down them in an orderly fashion. When on the ground, move well away from the plane. Hopefully we will not need to use these procedures, but better safe than sorry".

Shortly after the announcement the second engine flamed out and was extinguished. "Passengers, this is your captain speaking. We have only gliding power now, and we are a fair way from the main airport. We are however in gliding distance of a local airfield, and I am attempting to reach it. We have approximately ten minutes of glide time, so if you wish to send a text to a loved one, now is the time. We have no cell phone coverage for calls – only texts. Gather any small items that you need to take with you such as passports, money, etc. and put them in your pockets. If you have a jacket put it on. Sit back down and do your seat belt up. Remember, no luggage whatsoever".

After a few minutes an attendant's voice came over the speakers. "Ladies and gentlemen. Our pilot Captain Henderson and Second Mate Peters are very experienced. They will do their very best to see that we all land safely, but now is the time to prepare for the worst. Gliding is fine, but we will land heavily, so be prepared to be in the brace position. After landing, wait in your seats until an attendant calls you to the nearest exit. If you stand up, we will not be able to move around. Stay calm. Seat belts on please. Brace. Brace. Brace".

The aircraft belly flopped onto a grass runway. The landing gear thumping away as if the tyres had burst on impact. Clumps of earth were being plowed up and thrown over the fuselage. The plane was slowing, but it was running out of runway. It careened through a chain link fence, over a road and into a paddock sown to turnips which a farmer was busy harvesting with three machines in a line.

The nose of the aircraft buried itself in the soft soil as it came to a halt.

True to the pilot's prognostications, the attendants flew into action. The 'Unfasten Seat Belt' sign went on. The pilot advised the passengers that, "the plane has now landed", to which a cheer followed. "Please remain in your seat until an attendant tells you where to go". The cabin doors were opened and the air chutes deployed. Row by row, the attendants shuffled the passengers off and down the chutes. They started to congregate but were told to move well away from the plane - just in case.

The farmer and three of his workers came rushing over, asking what they could do. The attendants asked if the passengers could seek shelter in a barn or under a hay storage structure. He told them they must follow him. He would also make sure they had food and blankets, as he had started to ring around the other farms for help. A few of the passengers with minor injuries, and some of the older passengers, were loaded onto the flatbed trailer and towed by tractor to the farm buildings.

Almost immediately the air was filled with every siren type you could imagine. Fire Trucks raced to the road and played out long hoses to the plane. Fortunately there was no sign of a fire. Police had also arrived, but the passengers were en route to the farmhouse. Civil Emergency trucks pulled up. The plane was a mess, and the Police were instructed by the pilots to, "Secure the perimeter, then get all the luggage out of the lockers along with all blankets and pillows, they could find. They would all have to go to the farm buildings where the passengers could claim their hand luggage. The Aviation Authority would send vehicles and personnel along to remove luggage and freight from the holds. Anything lying loose on the floor needs to be placed into bags and given to one of the attendants, who were not allowed into the plane, even when it had been declared safe. Only firefighters, Emergency personnel and Air Safety Officers. No one else"!

Barb had sustained a broken leg, so she was taken by trailer to a small barn where the injured were gathered together. Two ambulances were outside, and medics were working on the injured. She was air splinted and taken to hospital along with a man of about 50 - she thought, who had dislocated his shoulder as a result of the sudden jolt whilst in the brace position. As they left, other ambulances were heard heading their way.

The Doctor looked at the x Rays and declared that Barb needed a plaster cast. The leg was straight and the broken bone would knit together on its own in about six weeks. She needed to visit her local hospital in the next two weeks, just to check on progress. "So who pays for the medical care then", asked Barb. "In these cases, the airline covers all costs and any out of pocket expenses. You will get a visit from a representative before you leave and where you live also. You were very lucky".

Barbs 'Send to all' text message read, 'No engines. Plane going down in Serbia near Ljubljana. Flight LH-205. I love you all. XX', sent her colleagues into a frenzy. Mike Stanning said he would make enquiries with the airline as he had flown there before. He got a recorded message stating that 'Flight LH-205 had experienced difficulties. Please call this number if you have relatives or loved ones on board'. Mike called the number several times until at last a human voice asked him which passenger or passengers he was enquiring about. When told Barbs name the operator said, "Just a moment please while I check the passenger list". The few moments seemed like an hour. The operator said, "Flight LH-205 was forced to land in Okic, about 20 Kms from Karlovac, after a double engine failure. All the passengers and crew are safe. A few have minor injuries. MS Darling has a broken leg. It is being set at hospital in Karlovac. She will be transported to a hotel in Ljubljana today. Please leave your contact number. I will pass it on to her and let you know which hotel she is staying in later. She can board a flight home when a Doctor gives her clearance to fly. Naturally we will pay for all expenses incurred until she is home safe. She should be able to get mobile phone reception easily from Karlovac, if her phone is ok.

Michael relayed the message to as many people whom he knew, knew Barb. They were all mightily relieved. Mike also had to find a way to get her back home. He looked up on Google, to find that 24 hours is the least time before travelling, so his plan was to ask Barb if she fancied staying at the hotel for three days before he booked another fight for her.

Barry got a call from Barb two hours later. "Hi Barry, sorry about the cryptic message, we weren't sure we were going to make it, but the bloody pilot did brilliantly, and I only got a broken leg". "Hi Barb. Sorry to hear about the leg, but boy I'm glad you made it out alive. That's a story to tell over a pint. Look if you don't mind, I'll pass you over to Michael, He's been tracking your status and movements. See you back here soon". He passed the phone to Mike. "Hi Barb, Glad to know you're safe. Sorry about the leg. How does it feel"? "Oddly enough it's just a dull ache. I've had medication, so I'm a bit dozy. Anyway, they are taking me straight on to Ljubljana, so when I get there, I'll call you". "You need to stay off the leg for at least two days, so I suggest you rest up at the hotel, then get a Doctor's opinion before flying back. Use taxis to get around. What's happening to your luggage"? "They said they would send it direct to my home – in about a week, meantime I need some bits and pieces to get on with, but apart from that it's all good. Thanks Mike, for checking up on me. I have my hand luggage so I can arrange a flight back". "Ok, call me if you need me".

Barb thought about that. She wanted someone – anyone - right now, but Mike hadn't made that move to go further. It was the occasional dinner, but mostly to discuss work. He didn't have a partner, or if he did, he didn't discuss him or her.

The minibus driver dropped her and six other passengers off at the 5 star Continental in the city centre. A porter brought out a motorized wheelchair for Barb and guided her to Reception, where after receiving a key card, she was handed a dinner menu advising that she could go to the restaurant from now until 9 pm. She opted to look in the chemist and clothes shops in the foyer, before going to her room to freshen up, then she would go to dinner. The receptionist asked if she needed the services of a female concierge to help her navigate her room and help her dress. "No love, but thanks. I'll be alright for now, but I may take you up on that offer tomorrow morning when I'll need to tape a plastic bag over my plaster cast. And don't worry. If a woman is not available, just send up a good looking fella". They both laughed, as Barb weaved her way to the elevator. The only problem she had was finding out where reverse was as the doors opened. She had to let one lift go, before a hotel guest showed her where the switch was.

Whilst waiting to be shown to a seat in the restaurant, the Maitre D asked if she wished to dine alone or with another guest who has indicated that they would like company. She said that company would be good. "Male or Female"? "Well male I think". He wheeled her chair to a table in the corner. "Mr. Sinclair, may I introduce Ms. Darling - your dinner companion". Mr. Sinclair rose and offered his hand, "Dennis is my name, what's yours"? "Barb – sorry Barbara. Pleased to meet you". They got chatting. Firstly, about the plane crash, which he found hard to believe that she had come through it so well. "I could have done without the broken leg, but I suppose it's better than being dead".

It turned out that Dennis Sinclair was - still is – a fine wine merchant, dealing in wines from the region into the UK and Europe. He was in the hotel to meet up with buyers from Germany – this evening, and from the UK and from France in the morning. "How long will you be staying, he asked Barb"? "A few days, then I have to get back to work". She told him who she worked for and what her job was. He was fascinated to learn that she had been travelling around parts of Yugoslavia looking for interesting products. He suggested that they might meet up again on his next visit to London. She agreed that would be nice. "Would you like to meet with the German wine buyers tonight"?

"No thanks. I don't know enough about wine to be able to discuss anything with them – or you, but when you have finished, maybe we can have a drink together, I'll give you my number". They exchanged numbers. In her phone he was Dennis Sinclair. Wine Man.

Three days after enjoying Dennis's company, Barb left Joze Pucnik airport for London, where Mike Stanning picked her and her crutches up, after being wheeled through the customs doors. Needless to say, she got a mighty reception from her colleagues. Barry told her to stay at home for as long as it takes. Barb replied that she can get around on crutches but might need to use a taxi more frequently. She was back at work. She told him about the successes in finding some really great new products and would be talking with Reggie about transport tomorrow.

She went home and couldn't stop shaking, as this was the first time that she had time to think about how lucky she had been. She had no relatives to consider, but still, alive was much better than dead. A hot chocolate drink helped calm the nerves before retiring to 18 hours of sleep. No one at the Thrift Shop bothered her.

CHAPTER 60

Brixton and Ealing Broadway Thrift Shops were now ready to go. It just needed Lonely and Sarah's co-operation to get things finished as far as the shop internals were concerned and then to stock them. Both stores were bright and airy, with plenty of display window space.

Far from the times when thrift shops or op shops were the cheapest and dingiest of any shop around, the Thrift Shops stood out and were in fact becoming the 'look' others needed to aspire to if they wanted to lift the tone of their shopping strip.

Lots of shelving and lighting capable of changing shade and colour, gave the ladies options never seen before. Demountable shelving allowed them to configure the insides as they wished.

Sarah conducted the initial interviews for the staffing of the stores, with Lonely coming in on the second wave. First up was Ethel. She was probably 80 if a day. She waddled in with her walking frame and plopped down on the wicker chair. "I 'aint been workin' for the past 40 years, but I was a shop assistant with Marcies Fashions until I fell down her front steps and broke both my legs. They 'avent been the same since. I sued the crap out of that place. They paid for my new car. Shame they had to close down though, I liked that place. Dead convenient it was. Not like this place. I 'ad to get a bus and a tube to get 'ere. I fink you'll 'ave ta pay me extra cos of the cost of transportation. 'An by the way, I need Wensdee orf, my cat as to go to the vet. So now, wot's me pay an if it's ok, wen do I start".

Sarah cleared her throat. "Ethel, that's good of you to come in for an interview, but I'm afraid we already have our quota of ladies. I have to interview a few more, but unless they are outstanding, we already have more than enough people to choose from. Look here's five quid to get you back home, alright"? She quickly moved around the desk and hooked her arm under Ethels, spun her around and out of the chair, and walked her out into the street. Putting the five pound note in her pocket, Sarah wished her a safe journey home. "I wonder how many times a day she pulls that stunt", she asked herself.

Richard was next in. "I only answer to Richie". "Ok Richie, why should I hire you"? "Well, I've been into dressing up all my life". Sarah then noticed the different coloured nail polishes. "Have you dressed down for this interview"? "How very perceptive of you. I usually wear more outrageous clothes and sometimes my hair colour will change – with my mood you know. I didn't want to turn you off though. Did I do the right thing"? "My only problem is, how will the customers take to your persona? I like it, and you remind me of me when I was a little younger and crazier. I'll tell you what. I'll schedule you for another interview next week. Would Thursday at 1 suit you"? "Oh yes. Thank you. See you then".

Cassy was overweight, that much was obvious, and she had trouble sitting in a small chair. As Sarah was about get another one for her, the folds managed to slide down between the arms and settled. "Hello, I'm Cassie, we spoke on the phone. I don't have any retail experience, but if you could give me a try, I think I could do the work. I'm an ex waitress. I got too big, and needed more and more rests, so they let me go. I love meeting people and get on well with them".

"Cassy, you're going to be on your feet all day. You can sit when there's no one in the shop, but believe me that's very rare. Will you cope any better in this job do you think"?

"I won't have to rush around, so it's got to be better. My goal is to save enough money to have lap band surgery to shrink my stomach, but it will take a while as it's expensive".

"Tell you what, you come back next Thursday at 1.30 for a second interview and we'll take it from there. O.K?

The day was full on until she had filled out a quota to return next week, when Lonely would also interview them.

Lonely and Sarah had walked around both areas, trying to get a feel for the vibe of each. Lonely suggested a new idea. It seems that there may be an element in both these new areas that may not like the idea of buying something used or pre-loved, "so how about we try one window full of new products only, to see what reaction we get. The trial doesn't have to last long, but I've got a feeling that some of the more well-heeled customers will be tempted by genuine offers and bargains, if we tell a good enough story".

"You know Lonely, you're not just a pretty face, there's a sharp brain in there too. Let's just do it. We can tell Barry after the event – if it's successful". They worked on a couple of lines first. One had just come in from Barb's trip to Bosnia. It was a hall stand made from Beech. Fully demountable and packed into a white carton. It looked tremendous, and although Barb could have saved them for the House & Garden Centres, she wanted the Thrift Shops to have something special of their own. The girls organized a display in one window. The signs read. New from our ethical labour factory in Bosnia. DIY Hall-stand in Brilliant White or Jet Black. Made from sustainable plantation Ash. Proceeds help towards rebuilding the local economy. Only 20 Pounds. Boxwood copies elsewhere, sell for up to 45 Pounds. Limited stock! White and black boxes formed the backdrops to the black and white assembled hall stands.

The opposite window was given to mainly Asian influenced dresses with some of the soft toys on thin vertical shelves on both sides. It would be a week before the windows would be changed again. All of the shop's offerings would be shown eventually.

It was a fact that fewer people wanted to by pre-loved items as the population was more affluent and cheap products flooded the shops everywhere, so they had to be pro-active, and less reliant on blow in's after cheap clothes, although there were certainly more items being left or dumped outside the roller door at the rear of the stores, and they had to remember that they did not cost them anything, but they still had to be selective in what they offered to the general public.

As before, the public, any staff not working in the stores, and local dignitaries, were invited along to the openings. One on the Friday and the other on the following Monday. Barry attended both and made a few short speeches before declaring the stores and the cakes and coffee open for general consumption. Kirsty and Trevor were roped in to interview the celebs and the general public.

Terry Styles was booked for the day, as was an upright piano. He played outside each shop, a selection of slow, fast, boogie-woogie, wartime, hit, popular in fact anything the public wanted him to play also. He was a hit. The TV cameras loved him too, with his lank shoulder length jet black hair jumping up and down every time he played a lively tune, as he jumped up and down on the spot, or his legs went wild. His accomplice Jenny would come in for the high notes, then she would revert to the bass section. At times, both were either jumping around crazily, or playing soulfully together the sweetest music.

The piano on the footpath was a stroke of marketing genius, thought up by Lonely, as she had seen the 'Play Me' pianos in the subways and in shopping malls, and Terry Styles had made several YouTube videos that extolled his prowess on the piano. During their breaks, the general public would tinker and so would the kids. Sometimes a player with heart, would capture the on-lookers imagination with a rendition worthy of genuine applause.

What no one had bargained for was a visit from Ethel, who at an opportune moment when the local TV camera was still working, butted in and took the microphone from the reporter. She was holding up a sign, saying 'THE THRIFT SHOP AGE DISCRINMATES'. She raised her sign and shouted into the microphone. "I came in for an interview, but she". The camera swung towards the subject her finger was pointing at – Sarah. "She told me I wasn't good enough for this shop. She said I was too old, and that I smelled. I can't afford nice clothes, that's why I came for a job, but SHE told me they were full up, but I saw them coming in all day after me. It's old age discrimination. I want justice. I want justice".

Kirsty knew that this was good TV, but she also knew Sarah and The Thrift Shop, so she knew a smelly rat when she saw it. Kirsty and the cameraman, walked over to Sarah. Kirsty looked into the camera.

"This is Sarah Walling, Manager of Stores for the Thrift Shops. Sarah has been here since day one. What can you tell us about this lady's accusations of age discrimination by you?

"Thank you Kirsty for the opportunity to reply. I don't think Ethel was counting on the fact that you would give me a right of reply. I suspect that Ethel does this sort of thing as a way of scamming money and sympathy. In the interview she told me that she last worked 40 years ago at Macies, and that she was glad they burnt down. Well Macies records of employment are still intact and there is no record of any Ethel by her name working for them. Ethel is 80, so we are not able to employ her due to insurance restrictions. I suspect she is trying to shame me and the shop in order to gain sympathy and some monetary compensation. She also can't spell. Another reason we couldn't use her".

"Well there you have it folks. I do have sympathy for Ethel, but I feel she might be lacking some sort of care". Notwithstanding Ethel's disruption, I feel sure that the Thrift Shop, with now four branches to their name will continue to offer the locals outstanding value for money products, with a portion going to that well known charity Mind Games".

Bill Masterton called in late, as he had been busy fitting out another store. He wandered over to Sarah, and asked how the day had gone. She told him she could not be happier with the shop and was looking forward to officially opening the second one on the Monday, and would he be around for that too. "If you're inviting me, I'll be there. In the meantime, how about you and me going for dinner later"? Sarah was not surprised, as she knew Bill liked her. "Well what did you have in mind then, eh"? "How about you choose". Sarah looked him straight in the eye. "Do you know what? I've always fancied a night at the dog racing, with dinner in one of the boxes. Would you fancy that"? "Tell you the truth I've never been, but if we could have a flutter on the hounds and have a good meal then that sounds great to me. You'd better let me have your address and I'll pick you up in the truck, say about 7". "I'm not going in some tradies smelly truck.

You'd better be joking". "Oh, I suppose I'll have to find something better for you – my lady. Give me your address". He pulled out a note pad and pencil.

They had both put on smart casual clothes, as the greyhound racing fraternity didn't usually dress to the nines. Bill pulled up in a huge Dodge Ram shiny black double cab utility. "Sorry gal, I've only got trucks, but it's a bit better than the work ute". Sarah was happy and climbed in with the help from bill's hand under her elbow.

The meal was superb. Her pan fried chicken breast with crispy skin; Irish colcannon potatoes and young string beans, sprinkled with roasted peanut nibs, plus a chicken jus foam went down well, with betting and drinking on each race throughout. Bill was pleased as he had two winners and a second. "That paid for the night out. We must do this again". He declared.

At the close of the evening's festivities, Bill and Sarah headed for the Ram. They both had a smile on their face but said nothing, as Bill wended his way back to Sarah's place. Bill went around the truck and opened her door. Sarah swiveled, then placed both feet onto the running board, then leaned forward so that Bill had to virtually catch her. The door was slammed shut. It seemed like the day had slammed shut too as Bill was preparing to say goodnight, Sarah leaned into him and kissed him gently on the lips. "That was a smashing night Bill. Thanks. If you'd like a reward then follow me". She got down and started to walk towards her apartment. Bill pressed the key fob and remotely locked the doors. His smile said everything. "I didn't think it would be that easy to get to first base". "Listen Bill, I don't muck about. We are old enough to know the ropes. Let's have a drink and we'll go from there. Come on".

CHAPTER **61**

Alexanderplatz in Berlin was where Trevor first encountered The Tiles. He was fascinated by groups of people standing around many of what looked like angled computer screens on posts. There were blocks of four, all facing outwards, and protected under a temporary shelter with sun sails. As he edged closer, he began to understand why the people were interacting with them.

The sign above each one read 'The Tile'. The screen was divided into 10 squares east x 10 squares north, making 100 tiles, each approximately 1.5" or 37mm square. The tiles were yellow with black outlines. Each tile had a number in the top left hand corner.

The sign reading 'The Tile' went blank, and instructions scrolled along. 'The Tile is interactive. Ask me anything. One person leaned in and asked, "How do I get to see the Berlin Wall". The Tile immediately answered, "You can take the 100 bus from the fountain, to get to Brandenburg Gate, or get a taxi from outside the square, or you can pick up a hire bike from Uno on the north side of the square". At the same time a map showing the route came up on the screen. "How did I do?" asked the Tile. "Great, thanks". "You're welcome".

As Trevor moved from Tile to Tile he heard another question, this time from a young girl. "Can you find my mother please"? The tile asked the girls name then the mother's given name. In a moment all the Tiles lit up and a flashing light pre-empted an announcement. "Hello from the Alexanderplatz Tiles. We have a Jenny Morton waiting at Tile number 8 on the south side. Would Jenny's Mother Elsie, please go find her, and by the way, bring an ice cream, as a reward for losing her". Everyone clapped. Everyone looked around to see if they could pick out a distraught mother, wending her way to Tile 8.

Trevor was intrigued by the human touches built into The Tiles. After lining up behind a woman who wanted to know where the number 17 bus stop was, and with the Tile saying, "Madam, if you walk towards the 24 hour clock, behind the clock on Reet St is where the bus stop is. Have the best day, but don't forget it's going to rain heavily in half an hour.

"Wow", thought Trevor. That's a nice touch. I'll ask it a question that will flummox it. "Hello Tile number 17. I want to be able to meet a nice young lady between 21 – 30 to act as a paid tour guide. Can you help"? "Certainly, but first I need your details; name, age, nationality, languages spoken". Trevor told The Tile. Miss Eva Brunther is available from the Tour Guide Centre in Potzdammer Place Here is her contact number and address. The details came up on the screen. "Have a nice touristy day, but remember to take or buy an umbrella, and oh, tonight we have the Moonglow Celebration in this square from 7 pm".

Trevor was very much into technology, and loved the fact that The Tiles were very much more human than any static and staid bulletin boards he had seen before, and which took ages to press a million buttons or a touch screen before getting useless information. He asked The Tile. "How can I get in touch with the makers of The Tile"? "Do you have a complaint? Maybe we can work it out". No, I want to become an Agent for The Tile for Britain". "Oh, that's excellent, here are the details. On the screen came all the information which Trevor exclaimed, oh, that's too much info and I haven't got a pen or paper". "That's easy. Place your phone or tablet under the light and the information will be transferred to your email account under 'The Tile'. When it stops flashing the information has been transferred. Have a nice day Mr. Baines". Trevor stood astounded for a second until he realized that he had given The Tile his details earlier.

The next question of The Tile was, "How do I get to the head office of The Tile in Berlin. I don't have transport". "Get the underground on the north side to Potsdamerplatz. Turn right out of the station. 150 yards turn left on Vienna Strasse. It is two doors down on your right.

Trevor couldn't walk fast enough to the station. He didn't want to waste time calling ahead. It was only a few stops away anyway. His heart was beating fast after the walk and the anticipation. He gave his name, then explained to the receptionist why he was there. He told her that he was in Berlin on business and had just seen The Tiles, and needed to speak with the owner about getting a license to operate The Tile in Britain. "Oh, in that case, please take a seat Mr. Baines". Trevor could not sit down. He was too excited.

A young woman came out after the receptionist. "Hello Mr. Baines, I am Elsa, how can I help you"? "I have just had the most marvelous interactions with The Tiles in Alexanderplatz and I want to know if The Tile is already in the UK and if not, could I look at getting a license to operate it there"? "Come in".

"I am the inventor of the system. My name is Elsa Meersch. I work with many colleagues in order to make The Tile as human as possible and we have some very advanced artificial intelligence operating in the background. Our expertise is in semantic computing, the next wave, where instead of machine learning which is accumulated knowledge, sematic computing asks various questions, then hypothesizes which is the best answer dependent upon the question, which is why we can link the weather to your planned trip or surmise options which are relevant.

We are very Berlin centric in our answers, but once we have inputted all of our knowledge of a city, we then let our semantic algorithms link all the pathways in order to become more human like in our responses. We have indeed been working on London and we are actively looking for a partner, but whether you are it, I cannot say. Tell me more about you, your business experiences, what plans you may have for The Tile, etc."

Trevor told Elsa about how Barry had built his empire, and that he had taken on many responsibilities in the business, and was actively looking for more opportunities to grow the group, and thought The Tile would be excellent. He was also partnered with a publicist, and that she and Trevor had started up in their own business recently, and how she was very well connected in the magazine, newspaper and media worlds, so publicity would not be a problem.

Elsa asked if he had the funds to take on say fifty Tiles straight away. She explained that The Tile generated income from the businesses surrounding the installation; the city council; any advertising placed into the computer via links. "For instance, if you ask for a taxi, it might link you to the nearest or available cab. Also when it is not activated, the screen scrolls down with paid advertising on a loop. If you ask for details of theatre or stadium tickets you are automatically made a re-seller and receive a cut. You could also place your own businesses on the screen for very little outlay. Another feature is that the squares can become smaller. Say it asks a question (in red) on line 1. Your response (in blue) is on line 2. The more you write, the smaller the box becomes so that we can get up to 100 characters on one line instead of 10. We can also produce place to place maps and have them transferred to your smart phone".

The more Elsa spoke, the more he wanted the Tile for the U.K. "O.k. you know all about me now. Can we do business do you think"?

"I'll tell you what, as we have only just met, let us do our due diligence on you, and in the meantime you can do the same on us. I will contact you by email in two weeks' time, then we can see what – if anything – we can do together". They swapped business cards. Trevor left somewhat deflated, but was rewarded by a visit from Elsa two weeks later at Barry Baines corporate head office, after she had ascertained he would be there through his secretary. They had lunch together, then went back to the office where Trevor introduced her to Barry and Michael Stanning. They discussed The Tile in the conference room where Elsa showed them the latest in semantic computing using her laptop.

Barry and Michael were stunned, especially after Elsa had explained the various revenue streams available through The Tile. Barry saw the potential straight away and envisaged one or more in every tube station, in every square, market place and mall. Elsa gave Trevor the Tile Price List, along with a list of terms and conditions. It was passed around. Michael asked the question. "Would the Baines Group be the sole operator of The Tile in the UK"? Elsa answered that she would have a problem deciding right now, as a) they had no sales, and b) if they didn't perform as to her kpi's (key performance indicators) then they would be holding back a more progressive company if she was locked in to them alone. "How about we commit ourselves to ordering thirty Tiles now for delivery in one month. That would show good faith. In the meantime, we could generate sales. When we get to 100 units, we could have a discussion about becoming your exclusive agent for the UK and Ireland. They all agreed this was the way to go. Barry asked Trevor to make up an order which he handed to Elsa.

Barry turned to Trevor. "I understand that you think this is a good proposition for the Baines Group, but we both know that it is an even better fit for the company that you and Kirsty own, as you are already a media outfit and this would fit well what you are already doing".

"Well Dad, you and I know that we don't have the money to start a venture like this, which is why I brought it to you. Firstly it is new and cutting edge and people like it, and secondly, I was hoping to buy it back from you some time in the future". They both laughed. "A chip off the old block eh? Here's what I'm going to do. I will provide the funds through the Baines Group, but you and Kirsty will run it from day one under your company name. You can pay me back when you have a revenue steam. I will let Elsa (who was still in the outer office, awaiting Trevor and Barry to come out in order to go to lunch) know of our arrangement so that they know where they stand from day one". Trevor gave his old man a hug and said, "Thanks Dad. For the first time since leaving school, I feel I am becoming the master of my own destiny. I won't let you down".

Kirsty joined them all for lunch, where Trevor told her what had transpired earlier. Kirsty went round the table to Barry and kissed him on the cheek. "What's that for"? "For being the best potential Father in Law ever". Barry smiled. He liked the sound of 'Father in Law'. One day it will happen, he mused.

Elsa announced that the Tile Group had probably made the right decision today, and would await the progress of the Fame & Fortune company (owned by Kirsty and Trevor), to show the amazing results that everyone expected these two bright sparks to produce.

Barry suggested that each Thrift Shop and each of the four House & Gardens Accessories stores should be equipped with a TILE. "So there's eight rented out already" said Barry. "Send your paperwork to my office for signing". "But Mr. Baines". "Come on Kirsty, you can call me Dad if there's no one else you call Dad". "Well, Dad. You don't even know how much we charge to rent a TILE". "It doesn't matter, I reckon that once we get them in, the crowd around those things will be great for business, so they will pay for themselves".

Getting back to her home office, Kirsty started straight away, contacting many of her business associates, and especially those in the media. Many of them asked if they could provide content for the TILES. Kirsty had to advise them that that was something she did not understand yet, but would get back to them. She contacted Elsa who was still in London. She was shopping and getting a late plane back to Germany. Kirsty asked if she had time to explain how the content got onto the TILE and who owned the rights to the content. "If you're at Harrods, would you mind if I grabbed a cab to meet up again"? Elsa agreed to meet up with Kirsty at The Bright Spark Brasserie round the corner in half an hour. Kirsty was armed with a list of questions and a foolscap note pad.

"So glad you were still in London. Thanks for meeting up. I hope I'm not interfering with your shopping"? "I like to see what's new in the London shops. German stores are a little too staid for me. So, what can I tell you"? Kirsty asked about how content got onto the TILE, and who owned the content. Elsa answered with a stare. "You have come to the crux of the matter in hours. Most people take months even years to understand how TILE is monetized. In Germany we own the rights to all content. We determine just how many times that content is played on the screens as rolling ads, and this is where the funding is generated. Then there are the interactive recommendations. If you ask for the nearest French restaurant, then you can pick from the list of advertisers that have signed up. This is not necessarily the nearest – unless you persuade all the French restaurants to come on board. You use the FOMO effect – the fear of missing out, to sell your advertising. All the other stuff supports the advertisers. In answer to your first question. You as the license holder owns the rights to the number of times and the price paid for content to be played, even though the actual content is not yours. I will have my office send over to you our advertising rates, which you will see lowers in cost for quantity. The client can send you new content any time, and I encourage it. The fresher the ads the better, and oh, here's a tip, if they make them funny, then people love to see them.

If you choose to make ads for others, then get together a first class team of copywriters, animators, cartoonists, video editors, because you can then offer a front to back, full service proposition. You will then have a skilled team like very few others. The TILE is your outlet, but content is King".

After their meal and talk, Kirsty closed her note pad cover after filling up four pages of notes. "I am so glad we could make this time together. Thank you for the kick start. Would it be possible for me to come to your office sometime soon, so that I can get a feel for how your people work"? "Kirsty, it has been my pleasure. Just let me know when you are coming. I will organize time with every department for you. I have to get my things from the hotel and get a cab to the airport now". "Then at least let me drive you there" said Kirsty. "No. London's traffic is getting heavier by the minute, so you go back to your wonderful partner, and I will see you in Germany soon". They kissed on both cheeks before parting.

Two days later, Kirsty had a Price List of all services ready to go, and had found her first customer by the end of the day.

The first eight TILES arrived in one week. Much content had been loaded into them already, but Kirsty had been working in conjunction with her German colleagues to set programmes for each of the eight TILE sites, which were ready as soon as they were switched on. All content was remotely fed to each TILE as it needed renewing. Revenue started pouring in immediately, and billing had to be done weekly in order to keep up with the flow.

As predicted, the TILES created a sensation, whipped up by Kirsty's contacts in the media. Local TV sent a reporter to find out what the fuss was all about. As the camera looked over the shoulder of a schoolboy asking the TILE where the nearest shop was that he could buy a vibrator from, the TILE answered, "I believe you would get satisfaction at Ruby's Sexuality, but you may need to ask your father to buy it for you". The crowd rolled up. "How did you know I was a minor"? I have a camera, so I ran your face through our recognition system. You are clearly a male minor. Plus I detected your voice pattern, your approximate weight and height and deduced. Was I correct"? "Too right. I'm going to tell my dad he has to go to Ruby's Sexuality for me". The crowd clapped.

A big man elbowed is way to the TILE. "Look here, I want to know how to get to Hampstead – now"! "Whereabouts do you want to end up sir?" "I have to get to The Archway Tavern by four". "Ok, there's not much time. Can you afford a cab?" "No". "Then get the tube from the Angel, get on the Northern line and get out at the Archway. Turn left, then run like hell 220 yards down the road. Turn right on Archway Rd, and it's about fifty metres along on the right. Go now and you'll be there by four. Good luck. Oh and say hello to her from me". "Whadya mean". "Well I presume the flowers are not for me, and you are very well dressed". The red faced man shoved his way out of the cheering crowd.

The third person was a Police Officer. "Ok, TILE, I believe you are obstructing the footpath and causing a disturbance. Who do I contact to have you removed"? "Constable, you will find I have all the regulatory permits to occupy this space. The initial crowd will thin down, and I have noticed people are giving way politely to other pedestrians, so I'm afraid you don't have a case, unless you come back with a warrant. If that is the case, hold it in front of my camera and my team of lawyers will give you an answer in exactly 45 seconds, as we have seen every attempt to thwart our growth, but no injunction has ever been successful, so good luck with that". The crowd roared again. The policeman turned and walked away with a smile on his face.

"Well viewers, we have seen just three examples of just how clever the TILE is. Just ask it any question and you will get an answer that has been well considered. It is based I understand on Semantic Computing, the next level in artificial intelligence and a step towards allowing computers to think for themselves. Unfortunately, we are still a long way from having the computer cook sausages and mash as in Star Wars.

Once again Barry Baines has shown the way, by utilizing the TILE in front of his stores to show us all how shopping is not a dying art. It can and should be a joyous occasion. Just ask the ladies in the Thrift Shop. They come out all the time asking questions. Some of the answers are hilarious. Remember though, that the TILE is here to help you understand the neighbourhood better, so if you're looking for information, head to your nearest Thrift Shop or House and Garden Accessories store, where the TILE will be waiting, even in the snow and rain. It never closes".

CHAPTER 62

Glenda is well taken by the TILE and asks Trevor if she can talk with him about added security for the stores, using the TILE. "What did you have in mind"? "I was thinking that as the TILE camera is activated when it needs to verify certain criteria, could it also be linked to the stores security systems. If you add another camera to the rear of the unit, and one on each side, you would have four way coverage. If there was ever a prowler, firstly the motion detector in the camera could pick up that person, then it could deter them from breaking in. If the perpetrator touches the door or window, the TILE could call out through its speaker. "HEY YOU! I have taken video of you trying to break in. The police are on their way". This way, the stores would get minimally damaged. In other words, being proactive instead of being reactive. We could also supply the Police with video and sound.

"I hadn't even given a thought to using it as an adjunct to the shop's security systems. Let me talk with Kirsty and the Germans and I'll get back to you". Glenda thought it was a start, but expected nothing to come of it.

Glenda also met up with Jean Stone and Harry Parsons in the swish offices of StoneWall Security, where Jean wanted to know all about the Thrift Shops and how everyone was going. "Everything's much the same, except that I recently asked Trevor about changes to the TILE." She outlined her plans to them both over a coffee and Spanish doughnuts from the van outside the door, which Glenda had thought to pick up on her way in. "Jean thought the plan was brilliant and could Glenda let her know what Trevor's answer was. "Secondly, I would like to talk with him about advertising on the TILES. We have this brilliant remote computer system that does what you are proposing but to be installed on homes and factories. Maybe we could do the TILE camera and speaker install in exchange for advertising time"?

It was agreed that Jean should talk with Trevor. After hearing that she had talked with Glenda, and that there may be a reciprocal deal on offer, Trevor invited her to his and Kirsty's home office next day at ten am. Kirsty was enamoured with the idea, and asked if they could wait whilst she spoke to Elsa in Germany, to get her opinion. It seemed that the conversation was all one way for most of the ten minutes.

"Elsa says that if we want to experiment with the security option with the TILE, it would be ok, and would we report our findings. If successful, they might implement the idea with the other TILES in Germany.

Barry, Trevor, Kirsty, Jean and Glenda all met in Barry's office in Paternoster Row. The plan was hatched and Barry was completely blindsided. He had no option but to agree with all of them. His ony real involvement they argued, was that the TILES were in front of his stores, other than that, they could test with the newer ones coming in if he objected. He was pleased to see that Glenda had been the one to push the idea, and that Trevor and Kirsty had managed to get it to this stage. He asked Jean how her new life was panning out. She replied, "For the first time in a long time, I have a partner that shares the same interest as me, and life couldn't be better".

Glenda had an arrest to make the next day. She got a call from Jenny at the Kentish Town store. Glenda told Jenny that she was very close to the store, as part of her drop in security visits to all stores. "I'm five minutes away, can you hold the perpetrator until I get there. Jenny Edwards replied. "Yeah, we've got him tied to a chair. He tried to walk out but he fell over. Silly sod".

Glenda walked in as quickly as her prosthetic leg would allow, after parking her car around the corner. "What's the story and where's the perp"? she asked. Jenny told her that a bloke came in looking around. He was looking through the jewelry. "The case was locked so I thought nothing of it. Until I happened to turn round quickly when serving another customer, and I saw that he was stuffing something down the front of his trousers. They're baggy, so I suspect he's got a pocket down the front, and his shirt is sitting over his trousers, so it looks like the bulge can't be seen. The problem is that I asked him to let me see what was down his trousers". He replied. "If you can find it you can have it". He started to walk out, so I accidentally tripped him up. It looks like he got knocked out, so I got the girls to sit him in a chair and tie him up with some dressing gown belts while I called you. I thought that if I called the Police, they might think I tripped him up deliberately. While he was resting, I went to have a look at the glass case. It looks like the lock has been opened quickly, then closed up again, which is strange, since only us four in the store know the combination". "And what about tying him to a chair. How do you think he and they will view that"? "Well I thought about that. I was going to say it was for his own protection as he was having a fit. What do you think"? "What do I think? I think you've seen too many crime fiction stories on TV. You can't go around tripping then tying people up. He'll probably sue".

As the man was starting to wake up, Glenda had a feel around the man's waist. There was certainly something in a pocket in front of the man. She got the girls to remove the belts and hide them. He opened his eyes, and asked what happened. "You tripped and fell over. The staff here got you on to a chair. My name is Glenda and I am head of security here. I noticed that you had a large bulge in your front. I touched it thinking it was a bruise. It seems you might have been helping yourself to some of the Thrift Shops goods, so I am asking politely, for you to empty the pocket sewn into the front of your trousers. If you refuse, I have the power to make a citizen's arrest, whilst I call the Police who will be here in two minutes. They will physically search you".

The man reached into his trousers and pulled out two watches, three gold chains, a silver charm bracelet and a ruby and emerald encrusted ring. He plopped them onto the table, and started to rise. Glenda placed an arm on the man's shoulder. "Where do you think you're going then?" "You've got your gear, I can go now". "I am making a citizen's arrest in front of these witnesses. I am calling the Police now. If you resist arrest, we are enabled to use all necessary force to detain you, now sit down". Several hands rested on his shoulders now. Glenda took the opportunity to question the man. "How did you know the numbers on the combination lock"? He looked desperate. "If I tell you, will you let me go"? "If you tell me, and I check it out and it's correct, I might ask the girls to walk away and you might just get to the door before the Police walk in, that's as good as I can give you". "I've been coming in and looking around, and I've been getting close to the girls when they have opened up the combo lock, until I got all the numbers. It was that simple". "So what are the combination lock numbers"? "7,1,3,5,2". Jenny nodded. OK girls, looks like this scrote is going to make a break for the door. If ever you see him around you let me know. The hands left his body and he was out the door like a ferret up a rabbit hole. The Police arrived exactly two minutes later.

After taking statements from the staff and Glenda who explained that she had been a Detective Constable and was now head of security for the Baines Group, they were satisfied that she had complied with the letter of the law, and although the man would not tell them his name, and that he had made a break for it, they congratulated everyone for trying. "We will have cctv around the place". They took the goods as evidence.

When Gemma told Jean Stone about the combination lock numbers being spied upon by the perp, Jean advised Gemma to look at some new technology. They had just taken on the franchise for a new lock that opened only when using the shop assistant's smart phone. The idea was that every assistant had a number – any four digit number - that they could call their own. That number would be entered into the stores data base. A programme installed on the phone and the data base would advise any supervisor with information as to who had opened which lock at what time of day.

The cost was 25 pounds for the app and 40 pounds for each Smart-locK, so they would need two locks for the glass display cases and one for the front door. Barry approved the plan and Jean came over with the locks and installed the app on their computer and paired each person's phone to the app. In this way, no one could look over the shoulder of an assistant, because their number would not work on any other phone. The store now had a timed and dated record of all case and door openings and by whom.

In order to help defray costs, Jean advised Barry, that they would be advertising the new locks on the TILE.

CHAPTER 63

Job vacancy figures started to increase. Companies were downgrading their profit forecasts. Europe was starting to fall into recession, whilst America was waging war with China. Not literally. It was all about words. Words that the average man in the street didn't understand. America accused China of supplying goods at the lowest cost possible, then swamping the world with them until the worlds manufacturing plants had to close down or make something that the Chinese couldn't, as cheaply or as well.

The average person knew that Britain was being affected by things that were happening outside the country's ability to shrug off. It was fine to save money on products. It was fine to keep the cost of living down. It was not fine for the people who bought those products to find themselves without a wage, even enough money to buy the cheap Chinese products.

Sales in the House & Garden Accessories stores – now four of them, had slowed considerably, as people were unsure of their future. When was it their turn to be thrown out of work? Getting by day to day and being thrifty were the watchwords.

Barry, Barb, Milly and Kirsty sat around the oval table in Barry's office in Paternoster Row, to figure out how they could fireproof the business before it got any worse. It was already a year in from the first rumblings, but business globally had taken the shock announcements from the USA's President, that the trade imbalance was not going to be tolerated and that the US would retaliate with trade tariffs, by suspending or reducing orders on suppliers. The cycle had started to grip the necks of the suppliers. It would flow through to the transport companies, warehouses and the stores - the H & G A's of the world.

Conversely, the Thrift Shops were doing very well thank you. More and more people were exploring the stores offerings. Sales were up each week in all stores. The only downside was that fewer people were donating goods, but the supply chain that Barry had overseen, did not rely on donated goods as much as the traditional thrift shops did. Much of their merchandise was new but at good prices.

Barb had been mulling over the H&GA predicament for a couple of weeks, and was the instigator of the meeting. "I've been thinking that at this time, we might be able to offer our clientele something other than household accessories. Firstly because they aren't selling well, and secondly we could be seen to lead the way out of this potential recession by being pro-active. In my travels, I have seen food production facilities that sell their goods to the local markets only, simply because they don't have the expertise to be able to export them. What if I take a look at some of them, then see if we can't offer high quality cheap foods – in cans or dry foods in packs. Do you feel that would be useful"?

Milly asked if the food business might be too far out of their bailiwick. She thought that it might create friction with other food importers or retailers.

Barry thought it a good idea, but wasn't sure. "I wonder if the average H & G A customer is that desperate to get hold of a food bargain. It may be that as in every downturn, people just stop spending – just in case. Not that they don't have the money. They are not sure if the money supply is going to continue – so they cut down on discretionary spending until the perceived crisis is over. Maybe your idea is a better one for The Thrift Shop? Is there another area that we can get into for H&GA besides food"?

Whilst they were thinking over a cup of coffee and biscuits, Barb contacted Sarah and Lonely by text. 'Thinking of the possibility of supplying good quality, cheap biscuits through the Thrift Shops, what do you think'? Within a few minutes both had replied. "Great idea", and, "we could shift hundreds of packets a week. Everyone buys biscuits". Barb read the text to the others. Barry asked Barb to follow up with smaller local biscuit makers, to see if they were willing to make a Thrift Shop special range for them. "Great idea Barb". "It was your comment earlier that started the train of thought".

"Anyway, we don't have an answer to the falling sales in H&GA. Let's carry on for a while longer". Milly suggested that a Grand Sale might bring more clients in. Barry thought that as they had this particular niche pretty much to themselves, that they might only be cutting margins rather than increasing sales.

Kirsty had been quiet for a time, then suddenly blurted out, "Why don't we invest in a brochure of say four pages, showing before and after shots of rooms and gardens using the H&GA products. We could drop them into every letter box in say a ten mile radius. We could even offer the chance to go into a draw for say 5000 Pounds worth of goods, for every person that fills in an on-line call for a free consultation from our roving specialists – our staff in other words. That way we capture a list of obvious future clients, that we can e-mail to, when new products or ideas come along, so it would be a cheap way to combine advertising with list building, and I must emphasize that list building is the only way to build a following in this day and age, and neither the Thrift Shops or HGA have involved themselves in modern marketing to date – apart from the TILEs.

All agreed, and Barry assigned the task of following up the idea to Kirsty. "I suppose that I have to pay you as a company now, where before I could call in a favour as part of the family". I'll tell you what, as you so kindly put up the funds and passed the TILE business to Trevor and me, so I will personally set all this up for you for free, but there will be some costs for the leaflet set up and distribution. In the meantime, I wouldn't count your chickens yet. It may be a resounding success, or, it could fail dismally. There are no guarantees with advertising.

At least a plan of action had been agreed upon. Sarah was informed of the outcome as was Lonely. Barb advised them that she was going to follow up with biscuit makers also.

That afternoon after looking on the internet, Barb phoned a likely supplier. The phone rang and rang, then the answering machine kicked in. "Leave a message. I'll call you back". Not very professional she thought, so went to the next. WELSH BUTTER SHORTBREAD BIS-CUITS. Melt in your mouth temptations. The phone rang once. In a Welsh lilt, a young voice answered. "Hello, my name is Bar Bar ah. How can I help you"? "Hello Barbara, my names Barb too. I'm look-ing to get some information about biscuits".

The girl laughed. "You only need to know that our biscuits are the best in the world, and we have just won another gold medal in France. That's the fifth one you know". "I want to know if you do private label biscuits. We have four stores that we would like to sell them through, but under our own brand name". "Will you hold a minute while I get my Pop? He can tell you what you want to know. Just a mo".

"Hello, this is Evan. My daughter tells me that you are looking for a private label deal. Is that so"? "Well yes", said Barb, "but I am also looking for a great biscuit at a great price. The stores that I represent are the four Thrift Shops based in London, and we want to offer a pri-vate label to our not so well off customers. Do you think you can help"?

"Mmm, I've heard of you lot. Your charity does good work for the troops don't you"? "Well yes. Mind Games has now been expanded out to help first responders, Police, Firefighters, Nurses and others", said Barb.

"Let me have your e-mail address and I'll see what we can do. Mind you I can't promise anything, just give me time to think. How many packets do you think you can shift in a week"? "I have no idea", said Barb. "We have never bought in food before, but we have a very large client base and each TILE outside the store will be used to pro-mote them too".

"I am not sure what a tile is, but I'm sure you know what you're talking about".

The next day, Evan messaged Barb with the following: Lovely to talk with you. I am pleased that you think highly enough of our product to consider us for your project. I do not want to dilute our existing brand names, but if you have a suitable name – which I need to approve of - for your biscuits, then I can offer you this.

Butter shortbreads in a new mould, say a Welsh Harp, round shaped. Twenty biscuits to a sealed film pack. 36 packs to a carton at one Pound per pack or 36 Pounds per carton. Recommended price is two pounds per pack. Shipping at your expense as is pallet hire. 64 cartons per pallet. Minimum order 1 pallet to any single address.

Barb spoke with Barry, Lonely and Sarah. They all agreed it was worth a try. The new design would be a Tudor Rose in relief.

The brand would be called TUDOR ROSE, Butter Shortbreads. Barb informed Evan by email of the name and design. He approved. He stated that he would cover the costs of the new silicone moulds on the understanding that if the Thrift Shop ever stopped selling the biscuits, the Tudor Rose brand and moulds would revert to him. Barb sent him Order # 00945 for two pallets (72 cartons) of TRBS's to be delivered to the Angel store, where they would send them to the other stores from there.

Kirsty ensured that the TILES were advertising the coming of the new biscuits to the Thrift Shops soon. The new melt in your mouth Tudor Rose butter shortbread biscuits would be the freshest and best tasting biscuit ever to land on Planet Earth. They would only be available from all four Thrift Shops, and the price would be an outstanding 2 Pounds per packet, or 5 Pounds for three packets. There was a countdown clock showing the number of days and hours before the biscuits would become available.

Two weeks later, the biscuits arrived at the Angel. Within four hours all the biscuits had disappeared. There was no opportunity to send biscuits to the other stores. Signs were put up in them. 'Due to the unprecedented demand for TRBS's at the Angel store, they had all been sold out within four hours. We have ordered more in urgently. Sorry, but you must put your taste buds on hold a little bit longer'.

When Barb saw what was happening to the biscuits at the Angel she called Kirsty and asked her to quickly bring a cameraman and herself to witness the frenzy. She then called the office for an Order Number for another 8 pallets of biscuits, which she asked Milly to send to Evan with the express urgency to supply, even if it was one pallet for each store to start with.

The nightly news featured the stampede. It featured Kirsty walking up to a TILE, where she asked a question. "TILE"? "Yes, Madam". "The new Tudor Rose butter shortbread biscuits designed specifically for the Thrift Shop have sold out in four hours, do you think this was a case of gross mismanagement"? "Well Madam. On the one hand, it is better to be cautious in business. In other words to gauge public reaction first. On the other hand, if the reactions from those who missed out are anything to go by, then Barry Baines had better put another biscuit order in very quickly or he might have a protest march on his hands". "Well folks, I couldn't have said it better. Looks like the Thrift Shop have done it again. Giving the folks of London a taste of pure shortbread heaven at a very affordable price. Luckily for me the girls in the Angel store saved one for me. (bite). Mmm. I'm not kidding. That is probably the best biscuit I have ever tasted".

The news reader announced, "Now that was a wonderful good news story". It then interviewed a spokesperson for the largest biscuit maker. "We understand that Barry Baines is trying to gain publicity for his Thrift Shops by undercutting the price of biscuits, but he doesn't have the huge overheads that we have to maintain in order to offer our customers such a wide range. I predict that this farce will run out of steam soon, as Barry is obviously using this as a loss leader in order to gain customers. It cannot be sustained".

The next shot went to Barry outside the Angel Thrift Shop where Kirsty was ready to interview him. "Mr. Baines. You heard the comment from the spokesperson of the largest biscuit maker in the country. "She maintains that this is a stunt – a farce she called it. She also said it could not be sustained. How do you respond"?

"Firstly, the Tudor Rose butter shortbread biscuits are made with love and the finest ingredients in the most picturesque of Welsh valleys. The recipe is 120 years old. It hasn't changed, and has been handed down to each generation, so its pedigree is impeccable – and it's great for Welsh butter sales.

Secondly, the biscuits are not stored in giant warehouses. They are made and shipped within days – so they are ultra fresh.

Thirdly, the price is right – about one third the price less of any other premium butter shortbread biscuit.

Fourthly, for every packet of biscuit bought from the stores, 20 pence goes directly to the Mind Games Charity.

So I urge all quality biscuit lovers to support the Welsh Butter shortbread biscuit movement. The only problem we have at this time, is that supply cannot keep up with demand, so please bear with us until you are passing any one of our four Thrift Shops and you see the sign, "TUDOR ROSE butter shortbread biscuits in store now"! They won't be long".

The news reader concluded with. "I think Barry Baines won that one. Good night folks and be sure to listen in to your nightly news on 7, where we will tell you when the next batch of Tudor Rose Butter shortbread biscuits will be coming in".

CHAPTER 64

Reggie Green got a call from the Despatch Manager at Guilia's. "Your truck has not turned up. We have been waiting two days, and the stock is building up. Can you please help"? Reggie talked with his own Despatch Manager. "Hey Karl, can you tell me why the truck hasn't turned up at Guilia's? They're getting frantic". "Let me do some ringing around. I'll get back to you as soon as I can".

Karl called Reggie back after 20 minutes. "It seems our scheduled semi driver has been given other jobs by our freight broker in Italy. They say another customer booked the driver and prime mover for a whole month, and they don't have any other owner drivers available until next month, about 15 days away from now". "Bloody hell. We've been dealing with this mob for two years now and this is the first time they've let us down, and worse still, they didn't let us know they couldn't do the job. Any ideas"?

"I'll ring around to see if there are any other brokers who can help". Karl called Reggie thirty minutes later. "It seems every broker is in the same boat. There are no owner driver trucks available, unless we want to pay a premium of 1000 Pounds per trip. I spoke to one of my best mates there. He says that this is a shake down by the mafia. They will ensure that the trucks are unharmed if they get their 1000 Pounds per trip money. It seems they have the freight brokers by the balls, and the independents are being asked politely – at this time – to become a freight broker member".

Reggie called Barry and explained the situation. Barry called the Chief of Police at Scotland Yard, who informed him – off the record for now, that his wasn't the first complaint they have had. He had gotten on to his equivalent in Italy, who told the Chief that not only were British companies being targeted but almost anyone who drove a semi in or out of Italy was under pressure to pay up. Some had already done so, and their trucks were the only ones moving freight.

Barry had Reggie call Italian Rail. As there was a loading siding close to Guilias, could they book several box cars to get their freight to Britain by rail, if they can get the freight to the rail yard? They called back to advise that they could hire up to ten rail cars, but that the freight needed to be at the yard within two days. The time taken to ship the goods would be doubled, and they would have to unload onto local trucks at the other end, but at least they could keep the stock from building up at Guilias.

Reggie swung into action. He gave Karl the order to hire four local tray trucks to pick up from Guilias and take the loads to the freight yard, where they would also hire a forklift and driver to pack the loads into the freight cars, where the ItalFreight Freight Supervisor would ensure that the loads were recorded, the doors closed and sealed and the shipment organized for coupling up as soon as practicable.

Meantime, the Italian Police were virtually powerless to stop the rorting of the trucking industry, as the despatchers were fearful of their lives and those of their loved ones. The independent truck drivers were being forced off the road, or their tyres were suddenly all flat at the road stops, or their cabs were suddenly engulfed in flames whilst waiting at remote traffic lights. Sometimes their trailers went missing whilst having lunch. Sometimes a note appeared in their cabin, advising them that they had not signed on with a freight broker – yet!

It was easier for the Mafia to control a couple of dozen freight brokers than all of the individual trucks out there. The Police were not sure how to handle the crisis. Every other Police force in the world was now asking how they were going to fix the problem.

Barry approached the Chief of Police again and suggested a course of action. "What if we agree to hand over the money the freight brokers are asking for, but we have you track the moneys from source to end account – which has to be the Mafias. I will pay up until the goods have been delivered here. Hopefully by that time you would have tracked and returned the money to me and the Mafia would have given

up this rort as a bad idea and some off their guys would be behind bars
– what do you say"?

"Let me have a word to the Italian Police Chief, and I will let you
know". A couple of hours later the Commissioner called Barry back.
The Italian Police chief has agreed to your idea. We can electronically
tag any monies you send, which the Italian Police will monitor, then
arrest the villains responsible at the time of final transfer. The problem
might be that the final transfer might not be for at least a month. How
much are you willing to gamble"?

"Well considering that I'm helping you to catch a bunch of crooks
in Italy, the British and the Italian governments need to step up and
guarantee that I will get my money back – say within six months.
What do you say"?

"I think that's fair and reasonable, considering what you are prepared to do. I'll have the necessary agreement drawn up now, but remember, if this all comes unravelled, we never spoke". "Agreed".

Barry and Reggie listened in on the speakerphone in Karl's office
whilst he contacted their usual freight broker in Italy. The broker
seemed relieved to be getting their work, whilst insisting that they understood that the extra 1000 Pounds was to be sent to a separate account. He gave Karl the name, number and the BSB. "When it has
been paid, let me know, then I can release the driver to pick up your
load". Karl had been instructed to add, "I will need another pick up in
Yugoslavia also". "Book that through another company in Bucharest.
Do not go through Italy on the way". He gave Karl the Bucharest
freight broker's number. "At least we now know that our broker is not
part of this fit up, or he would have taken your job on", said Karl.

Reggie was tasked to let the Police Commissioners contact know
the details of the money transfer. It was tagged by the Bank of England as suspect, and each one pound note – even though it was cyber
currency – was given a unique serial number for tracking purposes.

The Italian Police Commissioner thought the plan a good one, so
he ordered his local police to contact the principles of all the freight
brokers, to let them know - on the quiet – that they had a plan to

defeat the Mafia's hold over them and their families. They obtained from them the account numbers given to them by the Mafia. They advised them that there was to be a major raid very soon, and if they compromised the raid in any way, they would be a part of the prosecution's case.

The transfer was almost immediate, and the Mafia was about to transfer the funds from that account into another when the Italian Banking Association tagged the new account and monitored it to its next stage. The next account was the last, and it was a Sicilian account registered to SEX – Sicilian Export Company. The directors were well known criminals, but until now there was no way the Police could touch them.

The raid in the afternoon saw the Directors and the workers all arrested and charged with grand theft on an international scale. All the funds flowing into this account were being monitored. They all came from the freight brokers.

After the arrests had been made and charges laid, the brokers were all informed that it was business as usual and that they could inform their clients that there was no further threat to transportation in Italy. Meanwhile the freight train with Gulias goods had arrived in London where it was unloaded onto local trucks. Guilias were grateful, and the freight broker they used on a regular basis was grateful also.

The Police Commissioner called to thank Barry for his help. Barry thought that this contact might be useful to him in the future. "By the way, your blood money has been refunded to your account under MTR meaning Mafia Transaction Returned".

CHAPTER 65

The cool spring months and the pressures of work, prompted Barry to ask Denise if she's ready for a holiday. "Ooh, that would be nice, anywhere in mind"? "I was thinking of some diving off the coast of Spain. I hear there are shipwreck adventures we could go on, and we could learn to SCUBA dive at the same time. What do you say"?

"I think you're crazy, but crazy enough for me to want to come with you. When"? "I'm thinking in May. Shall I book for us? Denise consulted her diary. Looks like the second week on is clear at the moment, so go ahead and surprise me".

Barry took to the computer. Back to where Diving in the Azores was featured. It looked ultra inviting. It offered SCUBA classes. There were undersea caves and wrecks and sea flora. 20o water temperature. Clear light green water. What more could you ask for. He booked for two people for two weeks at the luxury White Suites. He booked the La Maison Villa at Sau Miguel. A clifftop resort for those looking for exclusivity and privacy. They were both private people who loved their own company, so he thought this accommodation although not cheap, would be exactly right for them.

Then he booked for three days of SCUBA lessons, then scheduled trips out to the various underwater attractions.

One month went by as quick as a flash, because in the back of his mind, all the work related things were now outweighed by the thoughts of the sun, sea and diving thrills to come.

The night before they were scheduled to leave, Denise informed Barry that she couldn't go after all. She had been summoned to New York to cover Spring Fashion Week as a presenter. TV7 wanted a designer – even though her main interest was in furniture - to explore the designer's studios, the selection of fabrics and the making up of the clothes. A new idea that was to be interspersed between runway takes. "Barry, they say I have a shot at becoming a full time presenter if this goes well. What should I do"?

"You know what you have to do. You look amazing. You have extensive design training and critiquing. You run the editing of Furniture Magazine practically single handed, and you help me in the businesses too. I would say you're overqualified if anything. Go do what we both know you need to do. I'm sure I'll find a pretty companion in the Azores. Maybe one of the maids will get a day off and come diving with me".

"Get away with you, you daft prat. You wouldn't know what to do with a maid, except give her a tip". They both laughed at the innuendo. "Sorry darling but I need to be at the airport by 7.30 am Monday, and you are leaving Saturday afternoon, so let's have dinner with Kirsty and Trevor tonight, then we can sleep in on Saturday morning, and you can show me how big your 'tip' is going to be.

Barry knew it was too late to cancel the trip. There was really no one else he wanted to take anyway, and he still needed the break, so he let it ride. Barry got a lift from Trevor to the airport on Saturday afternoon and settled down to a relaxing flight. Four hours later at Ponta Delgado, Barry asked how he would get to the Villa. He hadn't planned that part. A taxi driver offered to take him there for 15 Euros. He wasn't interested in hiring a car. He planned to spend most of his waking hours close to the sea.

The next morning after breakfast, he spoke with the concierge. "Do you have the number for Dive Creations please"? "I will call them for you sir". He handed the phone to Barry. "Ah Mr. Barry. Good to hear from you. My name is Martim. I will come and get you. Are you ready now"? "I am". "Good. I am there in twenty minutes".

The JEEP with Martim driving, screeched to a halt on the lumps of white crystal quartz in the driveway. He leaned over and opened the passenger door. "Throw your stuff in the back Mr. Barry. We leave for the first lesson in fifteen minutes". Barry climbed in and with another screech of the tyres, the JEEP swerved left then right, then corrected itself as it careened down the drive and onto the main highway, headed for the harbour.

"Here we are Mr. Barry. Please go to the change rooms over there. There will be some other men there. Please introduce yourself, then get changed into your swim gear. Leave your bag in one of the lockers, and give the key to the lady in reception with your name and locker number. She will put the envelope with the key in the safe.

When the three other men and Barry came out, there were four women already in the lobby, all in swimwear. All were given an outsized towel with the Dive Creations logo on it. Martim came in. "Everybody, please come with me". He led them to a 9 seater mini bus. "Please take a seat". Three couples sat together, whilst Barry and a lady who introduced herself to Barry as Florence (with a French accent), sat on a seat next to him. Martim told them. "Our first port of call – was the port. Did you get the joke? Port of call – we are going to the port, see". He chuckled to himself. After a ten minute drive they rounded a spit, to see a yacht moored off a jetty. "Come this way folks". He led them onto the boat, where Alaine (French again) was the Dive Master, and Phillipe (French) was his Dive Assistant.

The Dive Master explained that he would be giving instructions and his two assistants would be making sure that each of us understood, then repeated the instruction, then the action or actions. "No one must deviate from the instructions".

After a couple of hours learning about the water and how it could claim their lives in an instant, if they were not diligent and aware. He explained how SCUBA worked. They tested their gear and masks. "Just spit in the mask and wipe it round. It's the best anti fog you can buy". Barry wondered how many times that old line had been used. They were all fitted with weighted belts – buoyancy compensators, they said. The gauges were checked and the air turned on. The gauges were checked again and air flow tested. "OK, breathe in and out slowly and deliberately, fill your lungs then breathe out slowly. Do not hold your breath under water. If you do you will start to rise. Your lungs will collapse and you may die. I can't say it simpler than that.

Relax. Breathe in and out slowly. Hold hands with a buddy or be very close to one. Don't panic".

They all slipped down the ladder one by one. The Dive Master back rolled overboard. He popped his head out of the water. "You get to do that later. That's how a diver officially enters the water". Then the Dive Assistant fell overboard backwards, and joined the rest. Meanwhile on board, a French cook and her now helper Martim, were preparing food.

The group in the water was then shown the method of clearing air from the system before they could breathe from the tank. They then tested how to remove and refit the mask should it be knocked off their face under water. Fortunately, under water was just a few feet below. They then tested their breathing technique – slow and steady. Never panic. Alert your buddy diver or an assistant if in trouble. Don't swallow the sea water. Just stay calm. Clear your mask then breathe normally after equalizing.

Barry wondered if Denise would have liked this holiday after all. He was comfortable with learning new stuff. He thought she might be better off in New York, even though there was late snow there now. "OK now swim around slowly, close to the boat, with your head just under the water line and breathe shallowly. Take in what you see under you and check out the bottom. It's only a few metres deep. After a few minutes come back to the boat".

The first lesson was a success, and all agreed that it was another world down there. One that they would like to become more acquainted with. "OK, all out. We will have a small lunch now and afterwards we will go a little further out to where the natural wonders and fish will amaze you. There's no alcohol on board, and that's another diving rule. Never dive within four hours of drinking any alcohol. For those of you who did not read our diving blurb, remember that after diving you must not be flying for another 12 hours, so cut short your lessons if you have to".

During lunch, the Dive Master explained how it was possible to get the bends even with recreational diving. "So always remember that

slow deliberate and timed ascents are best. You don't have to rush. If
you check your air monitor frequently, you will have plenty of air left
for a controlled ascent at the correct speed. Don't panic. Breathe
slowly. When we get to the seaweed banks you will notice many more
fish. It is best you don't touch or harass them. For instance if a sting-
ray is menaced or thinks you are about to do him some harm, he might
bring his barb up and harpoon you. That's how Steve Irwin the Aussie
guy died when he was mucking around in a school of them. Leave
them alone and they will leave you alone. The other teachers will have
electric prods or spears with them just in case, but we haven't lost anyone yet.

Barry was worried when he saw a couple up ahead, signal the others of a large fish. It turned out to be a Mako shark. Florence squeezed
his hand tight and the look on her face showed that she was concerned. Barry squeezed his buddy's hand back and gave the thumbs up
sign. Around the shark were about ten large tuna fish. The type that
you see on a slab in a Japanese fish market, going for thousands of
pounds just to make sushi. He wondered about the possibility of catch-
ing just one. It would have paid for his trip and had some money left
over.

The kelp and different coloured seaweeds, ebbed and flowed in the
light swell on the sandy bottom. Several Moray eels, slithered away to
hide behind rocks or in small caves. Spiny fish were apparently to be
avoided unless you want to end up in hospital, they had been told.

After another hour they packed up and had a sandwich and orange
juice, before heading back to the dock. They retrieved their keys and
went into the locker rooms to dry and dress. When they were assembled outside, Florence asked Barry where he was staying. He told her.
"Alone"? "Well my wife couldn't come. Last minute change you see".

"Would you like company over dinner? I know the island well and
I can act as your guide if you wish". Barry's pause lasted longer than a
few milliseconds. Florence answered in her sultry accent. "I am not
here to seduce you, you know – unless you want it. This island is like
Las Vegas. What goes on in the Azores, stay in the Azores". "Tell you

what", said Barry. "There's no harm in us having dinner together, but I'm happily married, and want to stay that way". "Where are you staying? Asked Barry". "With my sister in Porto Rd at the Harbour. Number 12". "How about I meet you there at 7 in a taxi". "No need, I will come and pick you up in my sister's car, at say 7. Where did you say you were staying"? "At La Maison Villa, San Miguel. Suite 23.". Florence whistled. "Wow, I didn't know you had so much money. That's the best place on the island". "We will go to the Terra Nostra in Furnas. Bring your swimwear if you wish. They have thermal pools also".

At 7pm Barry was woken by the toot of a horn outside his door. He had fallen asleep. He fell from the bed onto the floor, picked himself up and grabbed a holdall with his swim gear in it. The Citroen CV4 standing outside with the passenger door open, was painted light and dark blue with black trimmings. It was a renovators dream. It was as shiny as new. Someone had taken a lot of time with this restoration.

"Nice car", said Barry. "It's a 1970 C4. My brother in law has been renovating it for years for my sister. It is a bit cramped, but it uses virtually no fuel and it turns heads – which is what I like". The road through the hills was picturesque and Florence drove steadily and well. "I had to book us in. I know the Maitre'd. He has put us in the window overlooking the valley".

The soup was pumpkin, served in a round loaf of bread with the top hollowed out. For the main course, Florence recommended the locust lobster in local spiced sauce. A honey and salted caramel aerated pudding sealed the deal.

The valley and views out to the sea were magnificent, and Barry was feeling very guilty that he was enjoying this alone – or at least – not with his wife. A few more red wines later, and Florence suggested they change near the thermal pool furthest away from the restaurant. There were no change rooms that far away, so Florence simply dropped her shift dress off, revealing she was sporting no underwear, slipping out of her sandals, and with a laugh, strode into the edge of the pool. She looked around to see Barry simply staring at her.

"Haven't you seen a woman's body before now? Are you coming in, or do I have to come and get you"?

Barry hustled with his shorts, then tripped over as he wriggled them down to his ankles. He had to decide if he was going to keep his underpants on, and decided that if she was in the raw, then maybe he should be too. He also thought that it would not be long at all before a sensation between his legs might start up. So he ran to the edge. Before Florence could shout, he plunged into the pool. In two seconds he jumped up and ran back out. "You didn't tell me it was bloody hot". He stood with his hands clasped over his genitals. Without looking round, but quietly sniggering, she told him that the edge of the pool was nice and warm, and that he needed to come over and sit beside her. He sheepishly lowered his hands and slid his legs into the water, with the level just covering his tackle. Her breasts were looking at him. He couldn't help but look back at them.

Florence smiled. "I know this is awkward for you, being English. My French lovers would not even blush, and we might decide at any time if either of us wished to make love. If not, that would also be fine. I am happy just to sit and talk with you – for company – you know? I also know that if your English periscope pops up above the water line, that you probably like me. We can talk about that if and when the time comes. Agreed"? Barry laughed at this French woman's laissez faire modern attitude. "What a different world we inhabit", said Barry.

The more they spoke, the more familiar they became with each other's lives. Florence it transpired was a tour guide. She had seen much of the world, but preferred these days to guide in warmer climes. She had been married for about ten years before she became bored and longed for the travel life. Yes, she had had many, many lovers and did not have a bad word to say about any of them, and no, she did not want to settle down. Life was good. She had a two week holiday and was meeting up with her sister. Her sister and husband were going away for a few days, and she was house sitting from Friday until Wednesday next week. "Would you like to come over? I can cook".

Barry explained how he felt that he was betraying his wife, by just being with her tonight, let alone next week. She said she understood. It went quiet for a while then Florence now in a sombre mood, announced that she had better be getting back, and that she would drop Barry back at the Villa. The drive back was with polite conversation only. On arrival, Barry told her that he had enjoyed the evening immensely, and that maybe she would call him? "I think both you and I know that I won't. I enjoyed our time together, thank you. I hope you enjoy the rest of your time on the island. Goodbye Barry". The CV4's dim tail lights were only visible for ten seconds before the car turned the bend at the end of the drive. She was gone. Barry was conflicted but glad that 'it' hadn't gone too far to be halted before something really happened, that he would definitely regret for the rest of his life. He didn't like lies, and certainly didn't want to live a lie.

A cool shower and Barry was once again relaxed with a beer in hand and the telly on. Local news was all about the fishing fleet and how a squall was coming in from the south east. He fell asleep in the arm chair until 1 pm, then slid into bed.

At 10am next day, Barry was picked up after breakfast for the second days SCUBA lesson. He was not surprised to see that Florence was not there. He asked after her and was told that she was not well and wouldn't be in today. "She thinks she will put her lessons off and re-book", he was told by Martim. "Can you please let me have her number, I have something to apologize to her for". "Normally I wouldn't but in this case I can see you are upset".

Barry rang the number. Florence answered. "Hi it's Barry". "How did you get my number"? "I told Martim that I would have to kill him if he didn't give it to me". She laughed. "I wanted to say I'm sorry if I offended you last night. I didn't mean to imply that you were not good enough for me, it was just that I was racked with guilt for even being with you, even though I must tell you that I really enjoyed your company and our intimacy".

"Well, my English person who is so uptight he cannot take advantage of a woman. Especially one who throws herself at him. It is me who must apologize, because I was tempting you and I should not have done so. You are a faithful man to your wife and I admire you for it. I have just never come across a man who has resisted me before, so I was upset at being rejected. I wish I had someone like you, who wouldn't fall into any woman's arms the minute they bared their breasts at them". I wish you all the best. Maybe we will meet again under different circumstances. Maybe your periscope will be up then". They both laughed and bid each other a good life.

Barry spent the next three days enjoying all that the warm seas off the Azores could offer, with Jet Ski rides, mountain trekking, more thermal pool sitting and reflecting, deep sea fishing and more. At the end of the first week, he booked a flight back to London, where the cold wind whipped at his face as he came from the airport into Trevor's waiting warm car. "Couldn't stay away from us eh? Was it good? "Mmm, so, so".

Nothing had changed since he left. Denise was glad to see him, but was concerned that he hadn't taken enough time off. "I was thinking that you and I could go down to Cornwall for the rest for the week. What do you say? Oh, by the way, how was New York"? "Well, you're looking at the latest Fashion Week presenter for TV7. The show will be on soon".

CHAPTER 66

Lonely called Michael to let him know that a man had been asking about the business. "He asked about Barry; how the business was doing and where we get our stock from. I told him he needed to speak with you. I gave him your number. Said his name was James Grayson". "Thanks Lonely. I haven't looked at the books lately, how are things going? Well since we opened up the other two stores, I've been flat out helping to set up the displays. All in all, we've had tremendous press via Kirsty's leaflet drops. And the specials have flown out the door. I'd be surprised if we weren't breaking records. Certainly any opposition we might have had has either folded up or moved away". That's good to hear. I'll wait for this guy to call".

The call came next morning. "Hello Mr. Stanning, my name is James Grayson. I have been retained for the sole purpose of determining whether the Baines Group is willing to sell the House and Garden Accessories centres to the consortium I represent". "Well you certainly don't beat about the bush Mr. Grayson". "Please call me James". "OK James, then call me Michael".

I have been monitoring your stock in and out of the warehouse you use to consolidate your loads, so I know for instance that the average delivery to each centre per week is 23 pallets. Given an average of a low 20 Pounds spend per customer, I estimate your turnover to be 48,000 Pounds last month for all four stores combined, or 600,000 Pounds turnover per annum. I guesstimate a net margin of 20% or 120,000 Pounds. If you would kindly check your trading figures, then let me know if you are interested in a multiple of 2 or a payment of 240,000 Pounds to buy the four centres, and to take over the leases. Can I call you back tomorrow at this time"? "Certainly James. What is the name of your consortium or business, and who are the interested parties. I wouldn't want to give the information to our competitors". Can I divulge that information tomorrow? I need to speak with the lead negotiator". "I thought that was you"? "Oh, no. I'm just the inter-locutor".

Michael, quickly convened a meeting with Barry, himself and Milly - after asking Mily to get him all the latest figures for the H&GA stores. They met in the conference room two hours later, where sandwiches and coffee were already on the table.

"Sounds like these guys are serious Michael", said Barry. "I'm looking at Milly's figures but I'm not sure where the group is going, overall". Milly stepped in. "The original two stores have been on a slight upward trajectory since opening. The two new stores have dou-bled their turnover every month since opening six months ago. Overall the rise is an average of 24% per month. Sales have significantly im-proved since Kirsty's flyers went out, and they make an impact on sales every time they go out". Michael chipped in. "They also help to spread the word out further than our traditional buying radius, so it seems this consortium is either threatened by the growth, or wants to get into this business on the ground floor. Let's face it, there is not a lot of competition in this field – yet"!

Barry took them both by surprise. "I've been looking at this busi-ness critically for a while now. Quite frankly it doesn't turn me on that much, yet it helps us sell product that we bring in from Europe and keeps the trucks busy. The margins are good, as are the profits. Barb was telling me recently, that many of our suppliers in Europe have been approached by a rep wanting to buy similar products to ours, to be shipped in container lots to the UK, so it wouldn't surprise me if someone out there was ready to duplicate our success with these four centres, and maybe they have the clout to set up hundreds more of them. Maybe this is an easy and quick way in for them. It's all done for them. Naturally we could do the same, but we would have to put a lot of time, money, personnel, energy and effort into doing it. If the price is right, it might be time to consider selling. Milly, what do the figures show"? "Well it looks like our Mr. Grayson, was having a good guess. The actual sales are 25% above his. Margins are actually 30% net". "Michael, what's the industry multiple"? "Well he's right there, it's two, but as we're on a growth path I would say three". "Invite Mr. Grayson in for a chat tomorrow at ten".

Next morning at ten, James Grayson walked in to a meeting with Michael, Milly and Barry. "Thank you for seeing me. I'll come straight to the point. The consortium I represent is willing to pay you 240,000 Pounds for the four store business, walk in walk out. Do we have a deal"? "We spoke yesterday about your consortium. Would you like to divulge who they are"? "I'm afraid they are not willing to divulge that information, sorry". "Well I'm not about to let you see our books, even for the 360,000 Pounds that I'm asking for the business - which by the way is a multiple of three, that you and I know the business is worth. I've also done some digging - which is quite an appropriate word to use, as your consortium comprises a group of undertakers, one of whom tried to give me a bum steer when I asked him about Guilias a long time ago. Tell him that the business is not only not for sale, but I have also had Michael get confirmations of all our supplier contracts in writing, that forbids them from selling to any party that is going to sell those goods in the U.K. So good luck with trying to steal our suppliers. Next item is that we already have four more locations almost ready to go, so we are now or soon will be eight locations. Good luck with your start from scratch enterprise. Milly, please show Mr. Grayson where the front door is".

Milly rose from her seat. Grayson stayed put. "Barry". "Mr. Baines to you". "Mr. Baines, I have not been playing a straight bat with you. I wish to come clean". Milly sat back down. "You were supposed to find out that the consortium behind the bid was in fact a group of undertakers". You did well to uncover it so quickly. I also congratulate you on shoring up your position with your suppliers. Any good businessman would have done the same. The price you ask is indeed totally appropriate also. What you don't know is that this intended coupe is in fact being generated by another party. I could tell you who that party is, but then I would have lost my sale commission. Can we come to an arrangement"?

"Well aren't you the slippery one then", said Michael. "If you're prepared to double cross the people you represent, then why won't you do the same to us"? "Because I don't have a deal unless we can make one. I am willing to give you the information you want, for 20,000 Pounds. I can assure you it will be worth it to you to know this information". Barry looked at Michael who shook his head, as did Milly. "I tell you what. If what you tell me turns out to be true, then I'll give you 1000 Pounds. That's it"! Grayson jumped out of his chair and headed for the door. "I can see myself out". Barry punched a number in to his phone. "He's coming out now. You know what to do. He tells me that there is another person or group behind this. I need to know more".

Jean stone and Harry Parsons were on the case again. They had found out about the consortium, using good old fashioned shadowing and sophisticated vehicle tracking and mobile phone remote listening devices. They had reported it all back to Barry. Now they had another person or group to track down.

Fortunately for them, as soon as James Grayson had left the building he was on his mobile. With a directional mike pointed at him from 50 yards away, Jean was recording his conversation on her phone. The conversation was timed and dated also. Jean called Barry straight back. "Listen to this". 'Alfredo its James Grayson. I fed Barry Baines the lines. He doesn't want to play ball, which is what you expected. He says the business is worth 360,000 pounds and that he has new contracts with his suppliers that prevent anyone from selling into the UK. Here's the good bit. He has four more stores coming up, so he'll be needing tons of money to service the start- ups, the stock and personnel, so your idea that he would not have enough cash to finance an expansion of the casket business, especially after you found out that he's going into direct competition with the UK funeral parlours, is probably true. It puts you and the consortium in the box seat".

Barry could hardly believe his ears. The person on the other end of the phone was Alfredo Romano, Roberto Guilia's Factory Manager. The recording finished. Barry said to Jean. "Thanks Jean. I now know that the takeover offer for the House and Garden Accessories Centres was a blind to find out how much money I would have available for that, and for taking over the UK funeral business. The only thing I'd like to know is, is Roberto Guilia in on this too? I don't think he is, but keep listening until you hear something interesting".

"So, Alfredo has been talking with the UK Funeral Directors Association, about them cutting me out of the loop as far as funeral supplies are concerned. I mean we've built it up well since taking on the distribution, but it's nothing to what it could be if we started our own funeral businesses. So that's exactly what we're going to do".

Milly, look up all the figures you can about the UK funeral business. I want to know what every parlour makes, what the margins are. What the nett profits are. I want to know volumes. I want to know how much of the funeral business we currently supply, and anything else that's relevant. Michael, I want you to find out who could head up our own funeral parlour division and I need a name for the new business. In the meantime, I'm going to prepare for a showdown with Guilias. Milly, please organize a return ticket for the same day. Make it three days from now and cancel everything on that day. Get me on an early flight. I need a driver from the airport and back four hours later. E-mail Roberto about the visit. Thanks. Oh, in the meantime, inform Sarah, Barb and Lonely, that the expansion plans for the H&GA business expansion have been put on hold for a while - while we resurrect a dying business. I've always wanted to say that".

Barry contacted Kirsty and Trevor. "I have a new venture for you. You know we act as the importer and distributor of caskets and funeral parlour supplies from Guilia in Italy, well I want to own my own funeral parlours and revolutionize the industry. Your job if you choose to accept it, is to come up with a marketing plan based on empathy, value across several quality levels, payment options and a brand new image for the industry. You can look at any models around the world if it helps. If you come up with a name and slogan, even better. What do you say"? Trevor answered facetiously on loudspeaker. "Dad we have absolutely nothing else to do but run the TILE business which has grown like Topsy. There is all the work from Kirsty's old job, and the work that I've procured for the agency, so no we have nothing else to do, but thanks for thinking of us. We will get straight on to it". Barry answered. "Want to go for a beer after work? O.K. See you both at the Painters Arms at 8. I'll bring Denise and we can have a meal together. It will be a good undertaking - get it"?

Next morning Barry called in the troops from his kitchen. It gave them all an hour to get to Head Office. They settled down with coffee and banana cake - supplied by Milly. Barry started. "During my research into the funeral business, I have been made aware of two very important things. One, that the funeral home most local to where the person died, usually gets the business, and two, that the amount of business that the funeral parlour generates, is directly proportionate to the amount of people the owner knows, or is in his circle of influence and interest. Having said that, it is clear that most funeral homes are family owned and operated locally. The one big exception is the co-op who are represented in most areas, and are seen as a viable option for everyday funerals. So, given that information, I'll ask Michael if he wants to add to it, or has comments about it".

Michael asked to be asked later, as he did not have any experience with funerals, apart from an aunt who died fifteen years ago. Milly piped up. "I unfortunately, have been to too many, so I know these things about them. Firstly, whatever budget you had in mind when you went in, by the time you come out it has doubled. Secondly, they are mostly morbid affairs, and thirdly, most visitors and mourners don't know the correct procedures or how to behave, especially to the bereaving family".

Kirsty said that she and Trevor had been looking into the funeral business with surprise. Because, a, it was very profitable, b, that most people had no idea what it cost to bury someone, c, that the insurance companies were becoming very wealthy with pre-paid funeral plans, and d, that if there were a few parlours in the same area, costs and services information gathering could become quite confusing, and lastly that the main idea of the ads is to get you to talk with someone, whilst the real selling is done once you are in the parlour surrounded by options. It was the ideal place to upsell.

"So, we presume that our job is to get prospects converted to sales using a clever promotion". A couple of names we came up with were: RIP: Peaceful Transitions: Friendly Funerals: Tranquil Fields.

Barry asked Michael if he was ready to chip in with his two pennuth. "As you all know, I come in from a different angle. My job is to look at the overall viability of any operation. To dissect it, and make it perform better or fix it, so I am not usually involved in the start-up phase, other than to advise on the allocation of funds and to determine viability. What I'd like to do, is to hear which angle Barry is coming from before I contribute".

"There", said Barry, "Is a very wise man. He feels unqualified to make a judgement until he hears from all sides. "Well here, as Michael says, is my 'angle'. I don't think we will ever get to first base by advertising like a corporate giant for the reasons given already. The local community likes to deal with a local person - even the co-op because they have been around for EVER. At this point in time we supply Guilia's caskets and our own trimmings to about 20% of the UK market and most of that is deliberately targeted around London and the outskirts. I am proposing to do two things. Firstly, we make a concerted effort to reign in as many of the other parlours from all over the British Isles using our successful spiel about saving them costs and giving them a better range. We haven't pushed the fully made up option yet. I think that is an obvious next step, but for that we would need several centres located geographically to cover all parlours. Later we approach all of our customers with a deal. We will own your parlour, but you have to stay on and run the business. We will change the name to RIP - for instance. That will start to get the name known. The owner will still have an influence in the area. He will also get bonuses over a quantity. We will have the lowest operating cost. We can put out a price list that cannot be beaten, with every option listed and priced. We will have visiting consultants - we come to you - no inconvenience or up selling at the parlour. We become the font of all information. We look after everyone's needs.

I'm also thinking of wide screen, curved, large format TV, where relatives can play old pictures, videos of their loved ones, or even videos of their favourite singers / songs. Surround sound. Comfortable chairs, even snacks afterwards. Why be morbid, we are celebrating a life of experiences, so it should be a time for happy remembrances. Even living wills could be played.

Many funeral homes will have to close down because they can't compete. Our client numbers will rise because of it. Later, we will be able to say we have revolutionized the funeral business and advertise accordingly. We become the local undertaker with national buying power. Any questions".

"Now you know why I wanted to come in later. Barry always has an angle", said Michael. "I will get to work on allocating funds to increase the stock volumes; the make up centres and the advertising. I also think Barry, that the owners should be given a five year buy out option. That will ensure they stay long enough for a transition, should we need it. We may also need roving Directors in case some of ours fall ill. I am also wondering if we need to invest in funeral hearses - maybe modern ones, so that they can be shared around as required".

"All good points Michael, as for the hearses, it would be good to have one or two on standby in an emergency, but you will find that most services take place on the weekends, so even our standbys might be stretched, anyway we can change as we progress. Anyone have anything else to contribute?" No movements or words, so Barry closed the meeting with this parting shot. "We still do not have a COO for this venture. Is there anyone in the existing operation who might be worth elevating"? Still no response.

Two days later, Barry was on a plane bound for Guilias head office. Roberto had arranged for a car to pick him up at the airport. "Ciao Barry. It has been a while. What brings you to me then"? After coffee and cake had been brought in, Barry got down to it. He had prepared a line that he hoped would show if Roberto was involved in the proposed coup. Barry asked Roberto outright. "Roberto, did you sanction a takeover of our funeral business in the U.K."? Roberto looked at Barry askance. "I'm sorry Barry, but I do not understand your question. Please repeat it". Barry was pretty sure that Roberto had no idea what he was on about, but repeated the question and added. "We have discussed where BB Enterprises wants to go with having funeral parlours of our own and increasing the reach to all funeral parlours in the U.K. regarding caskets and trimmings, and someone is trying to make a play to get rid of us, even so far as to talk with Guilias about supplying the caskets". Roberto looked genuinely shocked. "Surely, you don't think I have anything to do with this do you"? Barry could now lay his cards on the table. "Roberto, I had to make sure that you were not a part of this scheme. I now see that you know nothing of it".

He played Roberto the conversation between Alfredo Romano and a James Grayson, "the person who came to see me about a takeover deal for our House & Garden Accessories business, which in fact turned out to be a fishing exercise to find out if we had enough money to fund an expansion of that business and still maintain our funeral business expansion. I have put off expanding H&GA, and have had a meeting with my staff on exactly how we are going to blitz the funeral world in the U.K. so I needed to know that Alfredo was not endorsed by you in any way. This is a play by your Factory Manager to ensure that the UK Funerals Association is given our business, and that he will somehow have a part to play in it. The thing I don't understand is that you and I have an agreement to supply, and I don't know how he is going to get around that".

"I think I know", said Roberto. "For some time now, there have been rumours that a Russian company Glassnosk has been looking to supply some funeral parlous in Germany with casket kits similar to ours but of a lesser quality. Some of our customers have told us that they tried them, but that they were inconsistent in quality and had told them to go away, but two of our clients have gone over to them. They say they are saving money with them, so patching up a few caskets is not a problem to them. Could it be that Roberto intends to take a customer list – remember that he is Factory Manager so he would have access – and sell it to Glassnosk in return for something, say a seat on the board or a paid position in the U.K"?

Barry looked relieved. "Do you think we could nip this in the bud right now and get rid of Alfredo before he does damage"? "Let me make enquiries first. I will let you know what happens. In any case if Glassnosk is planning an assault, maybe it is a good time to attack first. I thank you for bringing this matter to my attention. Who is my liaison in BB Enterprises looking after this expansion push"?

"We are thinking of calling our funeral homes RIP. We don't have anyone to head it up yet, but we are looking".

"Barry, you already have a small interest in Guilia's and a seat on the board – even though you have never turned up for a meeting. I would like to propose a new alliance. It has been made perfectly clear to me that we could not have picked a better partner than you for our push into the U.K. You have the logistics, storage and make up shops either in operation or are about to have. Then you will own many funeral homes. What if I proposed a 50/50 partnership across the board with RIP? You would still charge RIP for the transport, but RIP will own the make up factories and the funeral homes and the trimmings business. Guilias has an excess of funds, so we could fund half the expansion. I would also offer you Sophia Fussani our Chief Procurement Officer. She has a husband who works out of the U.K. and she has been hinting about moving to the U.K. full time. You met her when you and Denise came to see us first time around".

Barry was grateful to Roberto for not only understanding, but for making the expansion possible and for giving him a person able to run it as well. The visit had really been worthwhile.

Roberto asked Sophia to see him. She remembered Barry and asked after Denise. "Sophia, Barry and I have been discussing a proposal to expand the U.K. operation and Barry is interested in owning a number of funeral homes there also. We are looking for someone to take over what is transitionally being called RIP. Your name has come up – especially as you told me that you were considering moving to the U.K. full time. Is this something that you think you would like to do and could manage"? "What role would I play"? Barry answered. "I'm thinking Managing Director, Operations. Your salary would be 30% higher than you currently get. You would answer to my Group CFO, Michael Stanning and me. You would effectively be running the whole operation. The great part is that you already know the casket business, and you know personnel, so your input would be invaluable, especially as we try to convert some very staid owners into either collaborating with us or selling their business to us. I also think, and this may well be a sexist remark, that your husky Italian voice will certainly be a persuader. What do you say? Can you live in cold, wet, foggy England for say five years, whilst we get this up and running"?

Sophia was very grateful for the opportunity, and asked that she be excused for half an hour. She immediately went to the empty board room and called her husband. He was in the middle of a meeting, but asked if it was urgent. When Sophia quickly outlined the opportunity he jumped up, pumped his fist into the air and announced to everyone that his wife was coming to London to join him. They all cheered. She had her answer.

She went back into where Roberto and Barry were still talking, and said, "When can I start". They drank cognac to seal the deal. Sophia would start in three weeks' time, at the start of next month. She would get holiday pay, long service leave pay, and a bonus equivalent to that which she would have received at the end of the year – on top of her monthly salary, which after next month would also be 30% higher, and she would have a genuine title for a genuine job, one that she could really get her teeth into – even though it was in the U.K.

Roberto received a call from his security chief who confirmed that Alfredo Romano had indeed tried to gain information that was denied him because he did not have the correct password, so he had formed a relationship with one of the female technicians, who, according to her had her suspicions, but he had told her that he already had names and addresses of the customers in the U.K. but he also needed quantities, directors names and contact numbers and e-mails for them, as the company was going to send them each a special bonus pack to thanks them for their loyalty. She said she would be able to transfer that information later today. Security had advised her not to do anything to raise suspicion, but to keep the conversation going. Alfredo was going to treat her and a friend to a night out, once he had the information. Barry suggested that they feed him false information, so that he looked bad when he presented it as a fait accompli to his potential new bosses. Roberto was all for calling in security and parading his ass out of the building ASAP. Barry said, "Why not combine the two. Let him take the falsified information, then you have proof of theft. Then march his ass out of here. I wonder if the Russians would have a place for him then". "Yes, that's what it will be like". He advised security to arrange the deal with the technician. He also suggested to him that he should tell the girl to get him to pay her first. "That way, she can enjoy her meal and we have secondary proof that he bribed her. She will be protected from prosecution as she will be the informer".

Barry went back to work a happy man. He called the troops in to apprise them of what had transpired, and, "How they were going forward hell for leather, and with a new Manager for the new funeral home and funeral supplies business, of which Milly advises the name RIP is available. "By the way, RIP will now be a 50/50 partnership with Guilias. They will be funding half of the expansion, so we should have enough in the kitty to keep the H&GA business expanding too. Sophia Fussani will be starting with us from the first of next month. Milly, will you please organize office space, computer, and anything else she may need. Michael, she will report directly to you then to me. She knows the casket business backwards and has extensive experience in personnel. I am sure you will both like her. She will be migrating to the U.K. to be with her husband who works here". He looked at his phone. "Here's Sophia's number".

"When Sophia is on board, one of the first things I want to do, is to strategize with you all, on how we can come up with our own association within RIP, to make sure the members have a say in how things are run. We can then water down the existing association, which over time will represent fewer and fewer members. One other thing. I want to know all about the funeral business in the USA, so if anyone has any contacts in the US please let me know""". It seemed like world expansion in the funeral business had begun.

CHAPTER 67

Barry called in on Sarah at the Brixton Thrift Shop by arrangement. "Blimey boss, I don't see you out and about much these days. It's a good job, you got people like me to look after things, Isn't it"? "Sarah, you have such a way with words, let's go and have a cuppa in JoJo's". They settled down, then Barry began his tale. ''I have several businesses as you know, and first off, you are doing a fantastic job of running the Thrift Shops. I just wanted to show my appreciation for all your hard work. They all look great and are all performing well. I wanted to talk with you about two things though. Firstly, the TILE out front. What reactions are you seeing and hearing, and could we do better with it"?

"You know, I've been thinking about that myself, and I reckon that we don't have enough information about what's available on the TILE, about what's happening inside the shop for one. We have new stuff in every week, but we don't tell anyone about it unless they come in, or you've stuck it on the radio". Barry was writing in a notepad. "Go on". "Well then we have people coming in and telling us that while they are searching for something, the thing has gone onto playing a commercial of some sort. I think any commercial should only come on when it's resting". Barry noted that remark in his book. "And last but not least, it's too bloody serious. We need some lively tunes, jokes, ditties, anything but boring old news that we can get from the tele or the radio". Barry was impressed. Sarah always had here ear to the ground, and wasn't afraid to tell you what you needed to know – if she was asked!

"Thanks Sarah. I've got another one for you. You know the funeral business has two sides to it. The first is the supply of caskets. The second is the trimmings. Now to date, we have bought from traditional suppliers, and they could be anywhere. I'm thinking that with your expertise in fabrics, toys, dresses, etc., you might like to source these trimmings from alternative sources. One, that we should be able to get a better deal, especially as we are going to expand rapidly, so we will have the numbers, and secondly, that it would be good to offer some alternatives. The caskets are trimmed with traditional silks and brocades, but what if we offered something different? I'd like you to do some research. Get hold of a bunch of fabrics and ask your friends and family what types they would like to see lining their coffin. I know it sounds morbid, but we are talking serious money here, and it would be nice to know if we could keep the business local and in our group. What do you say"?

"I say, I think you think I'm sitting around all day twiddling my bleeding thumbs. This is a seriously busy business you have here, and I'm full time just keeping up with myself, however, if you really want me to do it, then I will, but if it gets too busy looking after this stuff, then I'll need help". Barry laughed. "O.K. you've got a deal".

"How about I call at your place next Monday, and I'll take you to one of the funeral homes that's close. You can look at what they have and how they do it. Take a notebook with you and jot down everything you think is of interest and maybe how we can change things. There won't be any bodies there so don't worry. They have a big fridge for them". "Blimey, Barry, couldn't you have invested in horse racing or something. Dead people give me the creeps. My old Nan's dead you know. Yeah, she was riding her bike down to the post office and a funeral procession came by. She was parked up the top of a hill, and all of a sudden the brake let go, and the bike with her on it, rushed down the hill and under the hearse. Talk about a lucky break. The funeral home offered to pay for all her costs. Not that she cared either way. They even offered to buy a new bike. I told them that they could put a down payment on a new fridge, so they did, and that's why I say thanks to Gran every time I open the fridge door". Barry knew that he could never find another Sarah.

A toot from the horn brought Sarah out of her flat. She carried a large leather bag that contained her writing apparel or so Barry thought. "Hi Sarah, want some breakfast first". "You got to be bleeding kidding me Barry. Do you really think I could keep breakfast down after being in a funeral parlour? Let's see how I feel after it's all over". Barry drove the three miles to the McGuinness Family Funeral Home and introduced Sarah to Arthur who would be showing them around. Barry hadn't been to this particular parlour before, so it was good to compare with what he had seen. Arthur was upbeat much to Sarah's surprise. I thought you lot were just plain morbid, but you seem like a happy soul". Arthur put on his best and broadest smile. "Well it's not every day that we get visitors that talk back. Now, what exactly do you want to know? Sarah took the lead. "Well, I'd like to see how you trim your coffins - or do you say caskets". Arthur opened several caskets as he replied, "You can call them what you like. I call them crates personally, but don't let the boss hear that". Inside the caskets were lined mostly with silk of differing colour hues, with one being a basic white sheet material. "Why's this one white", asked Sarah. "Certain religions favour white, and the simpler the better. Right down to adornments too. They tell me it has nothing to do with cost. It has something to with – apparently – their humble approach to death, whereas the local gangster will have anything and everything in and on the coffin in order to impress their mates. You tell me. Sometimes there's no rhyme or reason".

Sarah asked to look at the range of lining fabrics that were available. Arthur brought out a book showing pictures of various fabric types and their cost. Alongside each was either nothing or an asterisk. The notation advised that that particular fabric was only available on special order. "We only stock five different types anyway as they are the most popular. He then showed her the trimming range as these were all on rolls and secured behind the doors or a large wooden dresser. She presumed scissors, knives, etc., were in the two drawers midway down and that maybe some silk bales were underneath.

Barry asked Arthur if he knew that Matt Kearney the owner was leaving. He said he didn't. He asked how that would affect the business. "I suppose we'll be getting someone else in". "What if I told you that from now on in you won't have to make up any coffins, and that my company will deliver them exactly as you spec'd it from your catalogue and that every fabric and many more, and plenty of other trimmings will be available soon, and that will let you concentrate on talking with relatives and organizing the service, the procession, crematorium etc. would that make life easier for you"? "Too right. Is that what's happening then". "When Matt leaves, it will just be you and us in partnership, because we just bought this parlour. We will make up the casket and trim it exactly to order and deliver it next day. You just need to hold wood samples and show books and samples on lining, trimmings and furniture, then send us an order. This is way of the funeral business from now on". Barry didn't tell him that the next iteration was for the business name to change to RIP, and that he would now be running the business in the RIP name – if he wanted it. If not, he needed to tell them right now. He told Arthur their plans for the funeral business and how they envisaged the future. Arthur understood. "Finally, someone's going to shake up this business, count me in".

Sarah will put together a package and come back to you. In the meantime, you should advise her of any requests that you have not been able to fulfil, maybe we could accommodate them in the future. Arthur told them of a particular request that he had had three of recently, and that he had sent the loved ones concerned over to a competitor. There had been three different religious groups asking for a ceremony to be performed in their particular faith, and he had neither the experience nor the information on how to carry them out. Apparently his competitor did. Sarah asked who it was, along with a contact name and number, then advised Arthur that if it were possible to perform those ceremonies in his funeral home, then she would find a way.

After leaving the McGuinness Family Funeral Home, they took a ride over to Faith & Redemption Funeral Services two miles away.

Barry introduced himself to Sasha Prience a Frenchman who had about half an hour to talk, after Barry told him who he was and his company name. "You supply caskets and trimmings to one of our competitors on the High Street – Luscombe's". Barry agreed and asked if he was willing to become a customer, as the company had dropped their prices yet again due to the number of funeral parlours signing up. I can guarantee that we can beat any other suppliers prices, plus our latest service of supplying caskets of your choosing, completely lined and trimmed along with hundreds of furniture options, and have it here in 24 hours – guaranteed". "That's a lot of promises Monsieur Barry. Give me your literature and I will consider it. I certainly don't want to lose out if there are cheaper options out there". Sarah chimed in. "I can get you the comprehensive catalogues showing caskets, linings, trimmings and furniture in two weeks, along with wood samples, all displayed on a wooden stand, so everything is in one place. The display stand and wood samples – which we expect you to give away, and which we will replace weekly, will cost you 140 Pounds and 30p per sample piece. Are you in"? Sasha was clearly outgunned. "Let me get back to you. I have to talk with my bosses first". Sarah shot back with, "O.K. I will call you in one week. If you do not want to make a deal with us, remember that your competitors will, as you have seen with Luscombes. They would be buying at least 15% cheaper than you. They can choose to lower prices, or enjoy greater margins. You don't have that luxury – yet! Now tell me all about ethnic services and burials. I understand you're the best around here".

Sasha was clearly flattered and impressed that Sarah wanted to know more about their expertise. "We researched the various faiths in the area and asked them how their funeral services are normally conducted in their city of origin. We then went to those places and secured more information about how to treat and address the family and mourners. We purchased artifacts of significance for each ceremony. We then looked for local persons able to perform these ceremonies. If they weren't available, we asked the British Government if we could sponsor immigration of certain individuals, provided all their checks came through clean, so you can see Sarah and Barry, that we have invested a lot of time and money in offering different communities ceremonies that reflect their religion and lifestyle. There is no competition on price, as we are the only funeral parlour to offer this service for 20 miles radius".

"May I congratulate you, and the management on observing the community and adapting to it, to supply a service that is clearly needed? Could you please tell me who the owners are, as I have a proposition for them that might prove beneficial to all concerned"?

Sasha pulled out his phone and speed dialled. "Ava, could you and Kepri come down for about 5 minutes please". A woman of about 30 came in first. She introduced herself as Ava, Sasha's wife, and then her Mother Kepri. "Sasha, what is this about"? "Firstly, Barry and Sarah, these two lovely ladies and myself own the funeral parlour. We started it up when we couldn't find a parlour that could cater to Kepri's Egyptian husband's wishes for a typical Egyptian ceremony. When we found out he had terminal cancer, we asked around, and no one was specializing in ethnic funerals, so we applied for a license, went to Egypt and brought back all the information we needed. It has flourished since". He turned to the women. Barry owns a business that sells ready made up caskets. He also supplies samples and catalogues for the clients to choose from, then the casket is delivered next day. Good eh? Prices are around 15% less, and we will have more choices of timber, trimmings and furniture, and you ladies will not have to make them up. Are we interested"?

Sarah jumped in. "Luscombes buy from us, and they have freed up one man, so their employment costs and their supplies costs have both gone down. They could be super competitive if price becomes an issue". However, if all the parlours buy from us, then the playing field levels again, but at 15% lower costs, plus any personnel savings. Where do you buy from now"?

Ava replied. "The U.K. National Funeral Supplies company, and I just got notice that their standard pine caskets are going up by 8% and that gold plated furniture is no longer available. We don't have a contract with them, so I for one am happy to give you a go". Sarah advised them that they could start in two weeks' time and informed them about the stand with the samples and catalogues, and prices for the stand and samples. They were happy to sign on, once Sarah had sent them an e-mail confirming everything.

Barry and Sarah went back to the Head Office in Cheapside. Barry got Milly and Michael in for a chat about what they had found out. "I tell you what. I never dreamed that ethnic funerals were a thing until we stumbled upon it today. In our master plan, we should be able to strategically place funeral homes that cater for the areas ethnics, provided none of the other ethnic groups had any objections. So, I see them dotted about the major cities especially. They will never compete on price and we will become specialists in every religious ceremony. I think Sophia Suffani will handle the ethnic side of things along with the day to day operations. I would like you Sarah, to get straight onto the stands, catalogues, samples, etc., so that we can keep YOUR promise for a two week delivery date. Milly, please get Kirsty and Trevor to work alongside Sarah to make all this happen. Folks, we are on a roll. I think Sarah's natural talent for making sales means that – if she's willing – might see her elevated to Sales Manager, RIP Funerals. What do you say Sarah"?

"I think it's time for a change, and I must say I enjoyed getting out and about, and learning new stuff. I'm sure Lonely will be able to cope with the Thrift Shops and she can help me source the linings and trimmings. I think that gorgeous sounding bloke at Guilias - you know, the woodworking factory manager you handed me over to about the samples, will be able to help me – especially if I have to go there personally to inspect them – you know what I mean Barry". Wink. "Question is, can he handle you"? Barry arranged for all of them, along with Denise, Kirsty and Trevor to meet up for dinner later. Barry would send a car for Sarah and did she have a date? She said she did, and that they would make their own way there.

Sarah arrived a few minutes late with Bill Williamson beside her. The party was about to get started when Barry took a call from Michael Stanning. "Sorry for calling this late Barry, but I thought you would like to know that Alfredo Romano has not only been charged with information theft, but he has been suspended from the Italian Funerals Association so he's banned from working in the industry there now, and his Russian contacts have wiped their hands of him, so it seems they are no longer a threat in the U.K. Oh, and James Grayson has been charged by the British police for attempting to procure a position by fraud. I think this is a made up charge, created to put the wind up him. I think your British nemesis in the funeral business is about to find out that his position as collaborator with Alfredo is about to be exposed". Barry thanked Michael. He relayed the information to the others over a drink. They then entered the restaurant to the recorded 'Eye of the Tiger', organized by Trevor beforehand.

A week later, Roberto Guilia called Barry to inform him, that Guilia had just bought out Glassnosk, who by the way just happened to have 20% of the North American casket market, so if Barry was considering starting a logistics and or funeral business in the USA he would support him, and if he was considering starting RIP in the USA he would be a willing 50/50 partner. Barry could hardly believe his ears. It was a great day when Barry first heard about Guilias.

CHAPTER 68

Barbara hands over the biscuit reigns to Glenda, telling her that she can 'Police' the deliveries to the stores – "as she had nothing else to do but security". Glenda was happy to take this task on, as she had been busy with overseeing the new security features on the TILES and had already reported a potential smash and grab to the Police, stopping it with an authoritative voice from the TILE. "I've sent your pictures to the Police who will be here in three minutes. If you smash that window, that will count as a misdemeanor. If you break in, that will be break and enter, with a charge of a minimum 1 year in goal". The thief took off. TILE conversed with the Police when they arrived and sent Glenda a report on the night's activities by e-mail. Glenda contacted the nearest Police station next morning and asked if her robot's information had led to an arrest yet. "Very funny. Looks like your machine is smarter than my officers, but we have a photo – thanks to your mate, so it won't take long. Thanks".

The Tudor Rose butter shortbread biscuits were about to be delivered next week, so Glenda contacted Kirsty. Firstly, she told her about the TILE crime prevention incident, then she mentioned the biscuit delivery – just in case she wanted to make news of either or both events. Kirsty said she would be on hand at the Angel and Ealing Broadway stores as the deliveries would be coming in. She logged the TILE incident in her brain, ready to mention it to Else next time they spoke.

Monday morning had been promoted every day for seven days by the TILE, posters in the windows, and by Kirsty sending out the news to her contacts. As before, the media turned up in greater numbers, to witness the buying frenzy and they were not disappointed as from 7 am a queue started forming at every one of the Thrift Shops. Kirsty was alerted by the TILES to the queues. She had set out early to record the scene and the people waiting. The responses were gold. "I'm only here, because my old man said if I don't get some of these here biscuits, then I'd better not go home". Another said. "I support Barry Baines's Mind Games. By buying biscuits, I'm doing myself a favour as well as supporting his charity". Yet another choice comment came from a 10 year old dressed in a Brownies outfit. "I'm here to pick up five cartons of biscuits for my pack. We plan to sell them door to door at double the price. We are supporting a charity and the people who buy are supporting us. This is a win-win, so my pack leader says". Kirsty asked, "So where's your pack leader then"? She turned around to face a woman with a hand trolley. "I'm her mum. Her pack leader's pregnant, so she asked me to do a good turn for the Brownies. Tell you the truth my bunions are killing me. I hope this delivery gets here soon". Kirsty informed Sarah that the Girl Guide wanted five cartons. Sarah went to them and suggested they go around to the back door, where she would bring them out to them after putting them on the trolley which she took inside along with the money, so they wouldn't have to wait. "Probably saved us from getting lynched", chirped Sarah. The TILE announced the arrival of the biscuits, when a large van parked outside and two men wheeled in through the double front doors, four pallets of biscuits. 'Please go to the cash register first, pay, get your receipt and take it to the ladies standing by the biscuits. Thank you for supporting Mind Games too'. This time round, the biscuits lasted until lunchtime. "Seems like we need to double the order next time. Looks like all the store profits will come from the biscuits this week". "It's probably just as well that we don't have them available all the time", said Kirsty. It seems that a degree of rarity makes them all the more special. Talking of special, I've got a couple of packets. We can have some at afternoon tea time. In the meantime, I need to get to the Ealing Broadway store to see how they've gone. See you later".

The two stores featured on the evening news. It wasn't all about the biscuits quick sell out, it was also about the TILE's spruiking ability. One anchor described one of the TILEs as Arthur Daley on steroids. They played about 30 seconds of the TILE – even down to a closing ditty. 'There was a great biscuit from Wales. A packet weighed down the scales. So crunchy and dreamy, they tasted supremely, and now they're all sold out, sorry pals!'

When Kirsty finally got back to her office, she called Barry. "I hope you didn't mind my programming the TILES today. Seems like the TV and papers are having a love affair with them. They were almost as famous as the biscuits, which if you hadn't heard yet, were all sold out by lunchtime in every store".

"I caught one of the early news bulletins. The biscuits and the TILES are a powerful combination. Well done to you and all the girls in the stores".

CHAPTER 69

"Let's surprise everyone. Let's announce our engagement this week, eh"? Kirsty looked annoyed. "Wouldn't it be better if you'd asked me if I wanted to get married first"? "Oh, come on. We've always said that we would know when the time is right. Kirsty will you marry me"? "Course I will you stupid git. I just wanted you to not take me for granted. Now get down on one knee and propose properly, and by the way where's the ring then eh. Hadn't thought of that had you? Trevor got down on one knee, and from under the coffee table he produced an envelope that had been sticky taped in place. "I always knew that I would propose in front of the fireplace, so I bought the ring six months ago. It shows you never dust underneath the table or you would have spotted it". Kirsty was open mouthed as Trevor opened up the small brown envelope to reveal a heart shaped brilliant blue emerald in a ring of smaller diamonds. "Kirsty Evans, would you do the honour of marrying me"? He placed the ring on her finger. She burst into tears. "Oh Trevor. I've known we were meant for each other from day one. The more I know of you, the more I love you. Yes. I would be equally honoured to become your wife". They kissed passionately, then were content to sit in front of the fire leaning against each other.

"I was wondering what you would like to do to celebrate", said Trevor. "I'm thinking something outrageous – just because we can. I'm thinking Monaco. You know where you can drive a Formula 1 car on the Grand Prix circuit on a couple of days before the race. I've always wanted to experience the thrill of speed". "So what am I supposed to be doing whilst you're enjoying yourself on the racetrack, eh"? "I thought you might like to go shopping. You might even meet the Crown Prince or Posh Spice". "Yeah right, think again. I reckon we should throw a massive party in one of the Claridges ball rooms".

''I know, let's think on this for a couple of days. In the meantime, let's not tell anybody, and I won't wear my ring in public", suggested Kirsty.

A few days later, Kirsty came in and declared that she had the answer. She discussed it with Trevor, and they agreed that the idea had merit, and that they would work on this cunning plan together. The party was set for six weeks into the future. They needed to plan, and do plenty of 'stuff' meantime.

250 invitations went out.

'Trevor Baines and Kirsty Evans invite you to a rave'. Venue: The Neon Sign. 22 Walthamstow Lane. Walthamstow. Date: Friday 8th August 2011. Wear: Whatever you like. Starts: 8 p.m. Finishes: Whenever (bring a sleeping bag if you like). Music: Yeah. Drinks: Yeah, all types. Food: Yeah (on sticks and in bowls). Entrance Fee: A 5 Pound note - for Mind Games (more if you're feeling generous).

Meet up from 7.30 in The Neon Sign. Wander round. Look at the amazing signs. Meet family and friends and have a drink. At 8 pm the warehouse next door opens, where food is on the tables and our favourite band will be playing. You can sit around the tables talking, or you can get your fat arses up and dance.

Only call Trevor or Kirsty if you are dead. No other excuses tolerated. Looking forward to seeing you there.

Kirsty was desperate to tell all her friends that she and Trevor were engaged, and there were a couple of times that she had forgotten to take her engagement ring off at work. Luckily no-one had spotted it before she realized it was on her finger. There were a lot of questions. "Why are you guys suddenly inviting everybody to a rave? What's going on mate"? "Hey, we just wanted to throw a party that also helps Mind Games. Nothing wrong with that is there"? The office girls were more tuned to the possibilities. "There's only one reason to throw a bash with the two of them involved. I reckon there's going to be an announcement concerning the patter of tiny feet. That's my opinion", stated Sarah - emphatically. Lonely was the closest. "You see those two lovey dovey birds together, and you just know they are going to announce their engagement".

The day was upon them. Mini buses had been laid on for those unable or unwilling to find transport of their own. Four of them relayed at least half of the 250 who all turned up. Not one dead person called to say they couldn't make it!

The Neon Sign was resplendent outside with a large screen welcoming all guests of Trevor and Kirsty. Inside two young female ushers asked for donations to the Mind Games. There were very few who gave the minimum and more than a few dropped in 20 Pound notes into the large buckets with a slit in the lid. Everyone received the Mind Games lapel badge. Trevor and Kirsty greeted everyone personally by shaking their hands or kissing them, and thanking them for coming along.

The first thing Sarah did, was to reach out and pat Kirsty's stomach. "Mmm, maybe I was wrong this time", she muttered. Kirsty got her drift and smiled at her. "Not this time", she whispered. As the Neon Sign filled up, the guests at the rear were ushered into the warehouse over the alleyway. The door was central to the long side of the warehouse. Looking left inside were many tables and chairs and a small stage. Looking straight ahead was a dance floor with more tables on both sides. Looking right was a large stage. An all-male band was already in place but they were dressed in white shirts, black trousers and had bow ties on. An upright piano meant that the music was going to be staid and boring thought Jean, who had come along with her partner Harry. They found a table not too close to the stage. It was laden with all kinds of snacks and waiters and waitresses were milling around ready to take their drinks order. "Beer, wine or juice, Sir"? They both settled for red wine. They understood that the rave wasn't going to waste money on high value drinks. That would mean less for the charity.

When all the guests had been seated and the door closed. Kirsty walked to the stage with mic in hand and thanked everyone for coming. "Mind Games appreciates your support. We thought we would have a little fun tonight. We have four bands. We are going to move through the eras of music, so that by the end of the night – which will be 12 pm by the way. I know the invitation said finish anytime, but that was just to get you here.

Johnnie Phelps Big Brass Band is going to give us a taste of what music was like in the 20s and 30s, from slow smoochy nightclub numbers, through to jazzy fast movers. I want you all to get up and dance. Talk to everyone else and get to know them. Remember we are all connected through myself and Trevor, so we are already one big family. Johnnie - take it away"!

The sax opened the number, dreamily wafting his sensual sound over the audience. Some of the older couples and women got up to form partners in dance. Slowly, they moved with lightly shaking hips and slow steps to the rhythm. When the older couples were seen to be moving happily to the music, a few younger types also took to the dance floor and tried to emulate their elders or simply swayed. The second number was upbeat. Some couple left the floor whilst many more joined it. It didn't matter that the dance moves were not of that era, they were happy just to shake the dust off. Their smiles told the story.

After around ¾ of an hour later, the first band finished up with a slow smoochy number where the muted trumpet featured heavily. The skilled trumpet player had the crowd in the palm of his hands as that instrument sung under his control. The crowd went wild when Johnnie announced that, "there will now be an interval, and that all guests should have at least two drinks inside of them by now, so they should be feeling happy, RIGHT"? "RIGHT", the crowd roared back as he left the stage.

Trevor, Kirsty, Barry and Denise got to as many guests as they could. It seemed everyone associated with these four were there. Trevor made his way to the stage door. He wanted to talk with the band leader of the next set. Trevor had a request. He wanted to hear Ray Charles's, I Can't Stop Loving You. "To be dedicated to Kirsty Evans – but it must be the very last song of the set. He also wanted them to continue the song as a background theme when he went on stage. They could stop after he had made his first announcement.

Kirsty called in a little later to check if the band was ready to go. The leader gave her a thumbs up. She walked on to the stage mic in hand. "Friends. Our next band represents the change in music styles from the forties which we heard previously from the Johnnie Phelps Big Brass Band, to the soulful, then upbeat songs from artists like Frankie Laine, Ray Charles, Johnny Cash, and who could forget the gospel then rock of Elvis Presley. I give you, Sounds of the Sixties, featuring Mike and Nina Wilson". The crowd went crazy as the curtains opened, to the spectacular of five artists sporting fluoro coloured suits, with Nina belting out a Nina Simone song called Sinnerman, with Mike pounding the keyboard, whilst Nina took on the persona of her namesake, calling out, 'Oh, Sinnerman, where you gonna run to"? Nina dressed and looked like Nina. Both were also black, which made it more credible. During the song, Nina managed to get the whole place singing, "Oh, Sinnerman, where you gonna run to"? Several times she cupped her hand to her ear, to indicate that the crowd volume feedback was really not sufficient. Everyone joined in the fun. The crowd hushed when the piano and drum duet filed the centre piece with Nina coming in later, reaching new heights before a long drawn out ending.

Two Johnny Cash songs, I Walk the Line, and Train a Comin, got the crowd up and dancing. Elvis Presley's, In the Ghetto, saw the older folk smooching when the lights dimmed. A slightly upbeat Always on My Mind, was followed by Jailhouse Rock, Blue Suede Shoes, and then back to a slower number, Can't Help Falling In Love. The set included many favourites of the era, until Trevor heard Mike Wilson tell the guests that their set had come to an end with a request from Trevor. They played Ray Charles's, I Can't Stop Loving You.

When the applause for the band died down, Kirsty walked up the stage steps, and was joined by Trevor. Kirsty thanked the band who bowed but kept their places. Trevor said to Kirsty, "I asked the band to continue playing I Can't Stop Loving You, as that is the theme of my love for you. Kirsty Evans, would you do the honour of marrying me"? Kirsty produced a ring. "Do you mean with this engagement ring, the one you gave me six weeks ago, but was sworn to secrecy because we wanted to share this moment with our family and friends"? "Yes, that's the one". He took it from her and placed it on her finger. The crowd went wild. Kirsty turned toward the crowd.

"Family and friends, Trevor and I have been a little secretive with you all. I hope you can forgive us when I tell you the rest of the story. Tonight's premises, the bands, staff, food and drinks have all been paid for by myself and Trevor. All monies paid by your most generous selves has been earmarked for Barry's pride and joy, Mind Games. I can tell you that you have all raised the amazing sum of five thousand, one hundred and eighty two Pounds. Would Barry and Denise care to come on stage to accept this money box full of love from your dearest friends". They came on stage to thunderous clapping, stomping of feet and chanting of 'Mind Games, Mind Games'.

Barry was in tears. "Sorry folks. I'm going to have to ask Denise if she will talk on behalf of the charity". Denise stepped in front of the others. "For the past few years, I have watched Mind Games grow from nothing to a national treasure. It is a resource like nothing else in the world. It is funded by you, you and you", she said, whilst pointing around the room. "Barry dreamed up the idea because he saw a need. Thousands of ordinary people have taken up the torch to light the way, so that sufferers of trauma may have a safe haven to unload their grief and hopefully get relief from it. That is Mind Games. You are Mind Games. Thank you"! When the applause had died down, she turned to Kirsty. "You my girl are in for a good spanking, keeping your engagement from your mother".

With that, Barry signaled to the side, then announced. "Friends. There is another deception that Kirsty and I want to share with you tonight. We want you to witness our wedding. A gasp went up. You will see various band members walking down the sides. You will see right now, myself and Kirsty transform to become a proper bride and groom". With that, two tables on wheels were brought in, then men and women obviously in on the trick, transformed Kirsty and Trevor before the audience's eyes. "You will see two - hopefully, parents ready to give their only child away. You will see a marriage celebrant walk on and introduce herself, then the ceremony will be under way. There will be fully charged glasses by the time we are finished. Let us begin".

The tables were whisked away and the celebrant walked onto the stage and introduced herself as Lillian Dreamboat. "Yes folks, that is my real name, and I've wanted to be a marriage celebrant for ever. What else could I be with a name like that, eh? Friends and family, we are all gathered here tonight, to witness the joining in marriage between Kirsty Rainer Evans and Trevor Rainer Baines. I know it is very unusual for both bride and groom to have the same middle name, but in my eyes, that makes this ceremony even more special.

Barry was handed one ring and Denise the other when the time came to hand them back to the celebrant. With the closing sigh of "You may kiss the bride", the band members struck up with, I Can't Stop Loving You, with Mike Wilson from Sounds of the Sixties, singing from the small stage at the other end of the hall.

Trevor took the mic and said, "Thank you all for coming. Thank you all for donating, and thank you all for witnessing our marriage. With your permission, Kirsty and I are off to Rome for two weeks and we are leaving right now. Have great fun for the rest of the evening with our last two bands, who will take your evening's entertainment from the sixties, right up to today's music. Love you all". Kirsty and Trevor kissed their folks, said sorry, then left the building. The limo taking them and their luggage to the airport had a sign in the back window saying, 'Just Married. Off to Rome'.

The evening rocked on for another two sessions, with many drifting away meantime. At the finish, several cabs had been called for those too drunk to drive, or who had no transport arranged.

ABOUT THE AUTHOR

Ron's early life was spent in North London. He brings his childhood and early adulthood memories to mind.
Ron is married to Hilary. They have two grown-up sons, Steve and Paul and two amazing grandchildren, plus an extended family spanning the globe.
Spare time is knowledge absorbing or writing time. He has produced many short stories, but The Thrift Shop is the first to be published.

www.ingramcontent.com/pod-product-compliance
Lightning Source LLC
Chambersburg PA
CBHW050148030726
47505CB00005B/1281